The Essential E. W. Swanton

THE ESSENTIAL
E. W. SWANTON

The 1980s Observed

EDITED BY GEORGE PLUMPTRE

WILLOW BOOKS

HARPER COLLINS

Willow Books
William Collins Sons & Co., Ltd
London · Glasgow · Sydney
Auckland · Toronto · Johannesburg

First published 1990
© E. W. Swanton 1990

A CIP CATALOGUE RECORD FOR THIS BOOK IS AVAILABLE FROM THE BRITISH LIBRARY

ISBN 0 00 218354 4

Designed by Judith Gordon
Set in Bembo by Phoenix Photosetting, Chatham
Printed and bound in Great Britain by
Mackays of Chatham PLC, Chatham, Kent

CONTENTS

AUTHOR'S NOTE

For the contents of this second anthology of my writing, following *As I Said at the Time*, I am chiefly beholden to the Editor of *The Daily Telegraph*, Mr Max Hastings, and the owner of *The Cricketer*, Mr B. G. Brocklehurst, whose permissions cover the major part of the book. I have also to thank the Editors of *Wisden*, *The Spectator* and *The Field* for work appearing in those publications; and Pavilion Books and Stanley Paul respectively for leave to use my Introductions to Ian Peebles's *Batter's Castle* and Teresa McLean's *The Men in White Coats*.

As to *Wisden*, the usual obeisance is due. Now coming up to its 127th edition it is the prop and stay of every cricket scribbler. So too now is the *Who's Who of Cricketers*, the comprehensive work of Philip Bailey, Philip Thorn and Peter Wynne-Thomas.

When one asked oneself whether there was a sufficient quantity and variety of writing to restrict the book to the 1980s the bulk of possible entries came as something of a surprise. It is one of the consolations of my old age that I can continue what I have always enjoyed doing. Whether the result justifies this book is for readers to decide. In any case I must thank George Plumptre for his shrewd and conscientious editorship. This is the sixth work in which our names have been coupled since I recruited him as an Assistant Editor of the 1980 edition of *Barclays World of Cricket* shortly after his coming down from Cambridge.

We have included some eighty diary entries of differing lengths, thinking that they may help to illustrate the quite diverse scope of my activities in the 1980s. In addition to my wife Ann, who has kindly allowed me to read much of this diary material for her approval, I must thank my secretary, Mrs Doreen Waite, for her patience and understanding. Lucky the octogenarian who is still enjoying a happy married life, good health and the company of his friends!

E. W. Swanton
Sandwich
January 1990

EDITOR'S INTRODUCTION

E. W. Swanton joined the Amalgamated Press in 1924. He has been writing about cricket ever since. Despite giving up full-time journalism when he retired from the post of cricket correspondent of *The Daily Telegraph* in 1975, he has continued to write regular articles, in particular for that newspaper and *The Cricketer*, of which he was editorial director and is now president. Far from slowing down during the last few years his output has increased, especially during 1989 when he was asked by *The Daily Telegraph* to contribute regular articles on major cricket topics, including a Monday commentary during each of the six Test matches between England and Australia. No small undertaking for a man past his eighty-second birthday.

It might appear misleading to call a book *The Essential E. W. Swanton* when it covers only one decade out of a career of seven. But if not all-embracing in the years it covers, the book is 'essential' in that it contains this most senior of cricket writers' view of cricket during the last decade. And what a decade it has been: turbulent, at times sensational, with peaks such as the 1981 home Tests against Australia and troughs such as the 1987–8 tour to Pakistan. There have been profound changes both at home and internationally, while events off the field have often been as significant as the game itself. Some, such as the bicentenary of MCC in 1987, have been occasions for celebration. Others, such as the ICC vote on South Africa in January 1989 and the subsequent recruitment of an English side to tour that country, have caused grave concern. Great players have retired while many others, whose playing careers ended years previously, have died. In their place new faces – and among them a few stars – have emerged.

Apart from description and analysis E. W. Swanton's writing reveals three fundamental qualities: his experience, his affection for cricket, and his abiding appetite for it. There is no doubt that during the years immediately after he relinquished his full-time post on *The Daily Telegraph* he enjoyed something of a break from the demanding routine of a corre-spondent's job. He concentrated his energies elsewhere, for instance becoming a full committee member of MCC during the same year and playing a leading role in the establishment of the Indoor School at Lord's, opened in 1977. In a different field he became a churchwarden of his parish church in Sandwich. Shortly afterwards, with the appearance of Kerry Packer in 1977, there was a great deal about cricket and the road that it appeared to be taking which profoundly disturbed him and which he would probably admit he preferred not to be associated with.

Any falling away in his interest and enthusiasm which this brought about was purely temporary. Making allowances – although precious few – for advancing years, it was not long before the modern game was commanding his full attention again and, equally important, his views were constantly being sought. One strength of his comment has been its objectivity. Situations and personalities have been judged on their own merits – or lack of them – and not with a tendency to comparison with 'the good old days' which might have tempted someone with such a lifetime of cricket behind him.

Of course, there have been plenty of occasions for nostalgic memories of the past and throughout the decade the author has enjoyed opportunities to remember personalities and events. Many of these have taken the form of obituary pieces written for either *The Daily Telegraph* or *The Cricketer*. These gave him the chance to recall men who were the heroes of his youth or his own contemporaries. In other cases an anniversary has prompted a story, 1987, for instance, being the centenary of Frank Woolley's birth. As a result, although the book's contents may have all appeared within one decade their subject matter is far more wide-ranging.

There is no doubt, however, that the meat of the book is to be found in the writing about the contemporary cricket scene. Few, if any, of the decade's major problems and dilemmas escape discussion. Intimidation by fast bowlers and the demise of spinners; the onerous task of the umpire and the decline in his relations with players; the pros and cons of four-day county cricket; the surfeit of one-day and Test cricket – and the effect upon players; the question of covered wickets; the failure to find a long-serving England captain, either for Tests at home or tours abroad; South Africa: on all these matters the author has strong views and convictions, tempered by the perspective of his experience. Behind it all is a set of simple but cherished ideals: good manners, orthodox technique and sportsmanship, cricket as a game that is strong in all its varied departments and enjoyable for both players and spectators.

The bulk of the contents originally appeared in *The Daily Telegraph* and *The Cricketer*. One sign of the professional in E. W. Swanton is the degree to which he knows his audience. The often light-hearted and colloquial style of his regular monthly 'Watching Brief' for *The Cricketer*, where he discusses a subject – or subjects – of his choice, is quite different from the sonorous tones of his commentaries in *The Daily Telegraph*. While these pieces are invariably stamped with authority, it is perhaps in the 'Watching Brief' articles that the breadth of his cricket knowledge is demonstrated.

For both publications he also wrote regular book reviews, many of which have been included here. These reveal the high standards he expects from his fellow writers as well as his capacity for congratulation.

Amongst these articles are scattered pieces from a variety of sources: two book introductions; two long and important articles for *Wisden*; *The Field* and *The Spectator*; the journal of the Cricket Society; benefit brochures and anniversary brochures. Together they demonstrate that the author has almost invariably been happy to write something when asked.

But if cricket dominates the book it does not have a complete monopoly. There are pieces on rugby football, a reminder that the author was rugby correspondent of *The Daily Telegraph* some years ago. He has also expanded notes and entries in his diaries into some eighty short pieces which, written retrospectively, give a flavour of his life – cricketing and otherwise – from year to year. They reveal, as do regular pieces on West Indian cricket in successive springtime issues of *The Cricketer*, that he annually spends a few weeks in February on holiday in Barbados; they show his passion for golf, his involvement in the church and his strong religious beliefs; and they also reveal his work for Kent cricket, as well as some of the more humorous episodes that he has been involved in. They are, in a sense, the leaven.

As he hints in his preface, E. W. Swanton is a happy and active octogenarian. He is also amazingly productive, as the contents of this book – and the larger selection of writings not included – testify. This productivity may have prompted occasional alarm and protest from his wife but it has been greatly enjoyed by enthusiasts for the game. The consensus of opinion is that the author has mellowed in recent years and there is a feeling of benignity about the book's contents which confirms this. Where he has been critical he has abided by the principle he spelt out himself in the introduction to *Barclays World of Cricket* – of fairness.

George Plumptre
Rowling
January 1990

1980

NEW LAWS
FOR A NEW DECADE

Virtues of the Fifth
MCC Code

Cricket has been described as a beautiful but complicated game. So it is, and its complexities can only be reflected in the Laws governing it. But in the 1980 MCC Code, which comes into operation this season, the chief object of the revision is greater clarity, and I believe that the verdict of umpires and captains, who are those chiefly concerned, will be that this has been achieved. It has been a difficult exercise, undertaken on his retirement from the Secretaryship of MCC with characteristic thoroughness by S. C. Griffith (now the President) in collaboration with T. E. Smith, formerly secretary of the Association of Cricket Umpires.

In 1980 we have only the fifth date to add to 1788 when MCC, formed the previous year, announced its first Code, followed by new ones in 1835, 1884 and 1947: quite a milestone! Junior cricket is mentioned for the first time, the pitch being laid down as 21 yards – a welcome reminder to schoolmasters and coaches of the folly of making small boys bowl the full length.

An entirely new Law 'Timed Out' – to eliminate time-wasting – is introduced, allowing a batsman 2 minutes between the fall of a wicket and his appearance on the field. On appeal the bowler's umpire, if he is satisfied the delay is wilful, shall declare the batsman out. Hitherto the non-appearance of a batsman was penalized by the loss of the match, the side being deemed as 'refusing to play' – and so, of course, was rarely if ever invoked.

Just a little of the onus has been removed from umpires in that they are no longer required to declare the light unfit unless and until they are appealed to by the batsmen – one appeal being allowed per session. But an idea of their modern responsibilities can be gauged by the fact that the last Law in the book, No. 42, 'Unfair Play', is much the longest, occupying almost seven pages. What would they have thought of that in 1884!

Legislation against fast, short bowling has given Mr Griffith and his advisers their greatest headache, just as its implementation is sure to give cricket authorities one of their biggest worries in the 1980s. The words 'systematic' and 'persistent' have been omitted, it being realized that a single ball is capable of being intimidatory. So, certainly, is a fast, high full-pitch or 'beamer', mentioned in the Laws for the first time and now penalized in the same way as the fast short-pitched ball. The procedure is as before in case of infringement: two warnings followed by removal from the attack for the rest of the innings.

The umpire has a strong Law behind him in this and other instances of Unfair Play. The difficulty has always lain in the extreme reluctance of umpires (which is natural enough, generally speaking) to apply the Law and so brand a cricketer as a cheat. The sad truth is that, reflecting the morals of the age, cheats and blackmailers now exist – including a few at the summit, where their example is to be seen by millions.

So far as bouncers are concerned, in English cricket this year a maximum of one per over is to be allowed, on an experimental basis, as was first suggested by G. O. Allen and L. E. G. Ames in *The Cricketer* last summer. This is obviously a step in the right direction, though I happen to believe that the ultimate solution may have to be, despite the manifest difficulties, a line drawn across the pitch beyond which the ball must land.

However, for the present the Law-makers, with the advice of the ICC, are prepared to give umpires – *and captains*, mark you – yet another chance.

THE DAILY TELEGRAPH
9 APRIL 1980

─────────── *An Astor Memory* ───────────

Michael Astor's Memorial Service at St James's, Piccadilly. Attendance a cross section of several worlds: the literary, artistic, political, sporting and

Society with a capital S, including, as ever, so many who other than at memorial services never darken the doors of a church. Michael was a delightful man, sensitive, fastidious, aesthetic – the complete opposite of his mother, the famous Nancy, who as MP for the much-bombed Plymouth used when in her sixties to cheer the spirits of her constituents during blitzes by doing hand-springs and somersaults. Playing golf with Walter Robins years ago at Burnham Beeches, I had one characteristic sight of her. The little old lady skipped through us almost on the run, oblivious of her companion. It was a sort of hockey-golf: unforgettable.

DIARY
9 APRIL 1980

Contrasting Reflections from Barbados

How many followers of the game have ever heard of Softball Cricket as an organized, scientific off-shoot of the real thing? Not many more, I suspect, in this country anyway, than those who read an article in *The Cricketer* of February 1979 by Trevor Bailey, who mentioned – and commended – it as part of his picture of Barbadian cricket prompted by a visit to the island with a party of old players under the direction of Fred Rumsey.

On my annual visit to Barbados I took the chance of acquainting myself with Softball Cricket. The ball used is a tennis ball which, if necessary, can be injected with water to add weight. The pitch is normally 18 yards, and at that range the ball reached the batsman extremely fast. His reactions needed to match its speed, and there was small hope of survival unless the basic principles were obeyed.

The bat, which is of regulation size with a flat back, cut out of a single length of wood, has to be swung straight. No pads or gloves are even thought of, for hits on hands or body by a soft ball may sting but are readily absorbed. Thus no one fails to get into line and, in fact, to bat – though they have learned only by watching the leading players – according to the textbooks. I was greatly impressed by the style and quality of both the batting and the bowling and only wished I could have had the chance of seeing one of the league matches which take place, some on the beaches, some on odd scraps of turf, all over the island on Sundays.

A league? Yes, indeed. The Barbados National Softball Cricket Association, I discovered, was founded just twenty years ago by a young man named Winston Connell. He started with 18 teams and now has 120, located in divisions in all the eleven parishes into which Barbados is divided. The Barbados Government is actively sympathetic to the idea since it gives exercise and enjoyment to all without cost.

As Trevor Bailey remarked, what is to prevent Softball Cricket being introduced on a wide scale into English primary schools where cricket seldom exists and certainly doesn't flourish? The average playground is certainly truer and probably no more constricted than the beaches and fields of Barbados. And what about *our* beaches? One of my earliest memories is of playing cricket with a tennis ball on the firm sands of Birchington and Felpham.

My introduction to this new face of cricket could scarcely have come at a more timely moment for, at the end of what has surely been a disastrous winter for the game, news had come of the utter débâcle of the West Indies tour of New Zealand. We had absorbed John Woodcock's sombre summing-up of the visit to Australia headed 'England Just Extras in a TV Show' wherein he had quoted *The Australian* verdict on the season as 'an abysmal attempt to turn cricket into a sort of three-ring circus. The three national teams have been weaving from state to state in an artificial atmosphere of brass-band ballyhoo which has resulted in little memorable cricket, a great deal of loutish behaviour – and the swamping of the Sheffield Shield as an important part of the Australian cricket calendar. . . . The game must not be killed off by the lack of a long-term policy and the demands of importunate promoters.'

The English press have been reviled in Australia only less venomously than the poor England captain. But here was their own national paper hitting the nail on the head with a sledgehammer. All this, and then New Zealand, with Holding kicking the stumps over, Croft barging into the umpire, and the West Indies barring themselves in their dressing room 10 minutes after the game should have restarted after tea. If the umpires had gone out at the proper time and the batsmen, following them, had then appealed, New Zealand must have been awarded the match according to Law 17 of the old 1947 Code under which the series took place. (According to the 1980 Code, new Law 22, the West Indies would have forfeited the match automatically without the need for an appeal.)

To have been in the West Indies when all this palaver was going on was to see for oneself the chagrin of the responsible section of the community at the sickening way in which, in a few weeks, by thoroughly feeble leadership and management, the West Indies party threw away all their hard-won Australian laurels. I have every reason to know that the West Indies, having packed and removed their bags from the ground the evening before the rest day, were resolved to abandon the tour and fly home forthwith. Luckily the orders they received over the telephone from the West Indies Board were couched in strong enough language to put a stop to that.

The series was continued to its bitter end, whereupon the manager, W. E. Rodriguez, whom one recalls as a highly temperamental Trinidadian spin-bowler of the 1960s, far from making any gesture of regret, let alone apology, brought New Zealand indignation finally to the brim by refusing to talk, saying 'a press conference would be an insult to me, and a waste of my time'. Insult to him, indeed!

But, again, let the comment come from a critic intimately involved. After the Trinidad Umpires' Association had come out with a statement highly condemnatory of the West Indies team, Tony Cozier, *The Cricketer* correspondent and the leading West Indies cricket writer and broadcaster, who had covered the Australian tour though not the New Zealand finale, came out in the *Sunday Sun* of Barbados with the strongest possible censure. After making due allowance for staleness and the assumed low quality of the umpiring, he shuddered to think what West Indies reaction would be if on their tour next winter England were to demand the replacement of an umpire, or if an England bowler deliberately ran into one. When the players no longer accept decisions, whatever the provocation, 'anarchy reigns and sport is impossible'. With the 'new professionalism' that the players talk so much about comes a greater responsibility for 'setting examples for adoring youngsters to follow'. The team had won glory in Australia: how tragic 'that its great hour should have been so sullied'.

'Player-power' – how sickening it is! And what a relief one found it enjoying the cheerful friendliness of those young cricketers on the beach!

THE CRICKETER
MAY 1980

───── *The Two Sides of John Beck* ─────

Played in a foursome that included John Beck in what turned out to be the last game he ever played – he died, aged eighty, ten days later. John and his wife Baba (still going strong at eighty-eight) had a unique triumph. In 1938 at St Andrew's he captained the first Great Britain and Ireland team to beat USA in the Walker Cup, while the same day she was winning the Irish Women's Championship. After the war Baba likewise captained Great Britain and Ireland's Curtis Cup side, which was honourably defeated, at what used to be called the Merion Cricket, Golf and Country Club, Philadelphia.

John was highly convivial company, eminently clubable, but proverbially peppery at times on the golf course if an opponent offended his sense of etiquette. If some unwary fellow, when it was John's turn to putt, said to his partner, 'Shall we see that one in?' or 'You've got two for the hole – let's see one', John would at once pick up his ball and, if questioned, say, 'You've conceded.' Golf is played in the mind and he was strictly right. Like Charles Lamb's Mrs Battle, John was all for 'the rigour of the game'.

Two handsome oak wing panels, for the names of future captains of Royal St George's, flanking those of the club's first hundred years, remind us of John. They were presented by some American members among whom he was a great favourite.

DIARY
12 JUNE 1980

───── *The Don in Full Spate* ─────

Fifty years ago today Don Bradman made 309 not out on the first day of the Headingley Test, and came in as fresh as could be. An accumulation unrepeated, of course, in Test cricket – unrepeatable. I can see burly Dick Tyldesley now, not built for speed, turning at mid-on, chasing firm pushes past the bowler as they maintained their momentum down the slope to the football stand, never gaining on the ball. Don celebrated that night – with a pot of tea in his room at the Queen's Hotel; a teetotaller then, not now.

DIARY
11 JULY 1980

--------------- *An Eton Coach* ---------------

At Lord's for the Eton and Harrow. Refreshment on and around their coach with Charles (Eton and Middlesex) and Vivienne Robins, whose son was playing for his old school. How amused at the scene would have been Charles's Highgate father!

DIARY
12 JULY 1980

Who Did What in Tests

There is something about cricket which draws from so many of its devotees an irresistible urge to research, and, once embarked, a dauntless diligence in their labours. What other game can boast either a library of 8294 items or a man such as E. W. Padwick to collect all 8294 into a bibliography?

Christopher Martin-Jenkins, whose broadcasting earns the respect of the cricket world if only because, unlike so many of his frenzied sporting contemporaries, he does not sprinkle superlatives around like confetti, has tackled a job not, I think, hitherto attempted in his complete *Who's Who of Test Cricketers*, published today by Orbis at £10. There are some 1600 of them all told, and although in the nature of things most of the information is second-hand, the author has missed seeing scarcely any of those who have graced the Test scene during his seven crowded years as BBC cricket correspondent. Moreover, he acknowledges much help from Michael Melford, whose experience goes back a further quarter-century and more, and also from the Editor of *The Cricket Society Journal* and a well-respected authority, J. D. Coldham.

'For reasons of space,' says Mr Martin-Jenkins, 'the pen-pictures are largely factual.' This could scarcely be otherwise. There are, however, certain judgements, mostly well founded, though few – with the possible exception of the subject – would quite subscribe to the view that Fred Trueman's 'fastest speed was as quick as anyone before or since'. A splendid bowler, yes. But as fast as Tyson? Larwood? Lindwall? Holding? Hall?

The first entry in the book, that of Bobby Abel, underlines how generous – or haphazard – Test status used to be. Among the achievements of this household name is listed his scoring of a hundred in the second of all matches against South Africa in 1889–90.

The two games on that tour of Major Warton's team, captained by C. A. (later Sir Aubrey) Smith, which were posthumously labelled Tests, were the only ones not played against odds of anything up to twenty-two opponents. Never mind, this manifest absurdity gives the author a good story. One of the two so-called Test cricketers in that side, who played no other first-class match either before or after, was the Hon. C. J. Coventry, who later took part in the Jameson Raid. 'He was reported dead – having been seen under a blanket "kicking like a shot hare" – and arrangements were made at his home in Worcestershire for a funeral service; but news came through shortly before the service began – with all the mourners in attendance – that he was alive. Dancing on the village green, top hats, frock coats and all, was hastily arranged.'

I tried out as a 'test case' of another sort one Lall Singh, with whom I chanced to sit at lunch during the first match of the first Indian team to tour England, in 1932, at Hove against Sussex. Asking the little, light blue-turbaned figure who was the best fielder in the Indian team, I had the smiling answer, 'I am the best.' The book says, 'Lall Singh was an extraordinarily quick mover in the field. It was said that he glided over the ground like a snake.' Colourful stuff in every sense!

I have only one niggle. Someone has been too clever by half in delving into parish registers for hitherto unpublished Christian names. It is a taxing enough job for the average reader to sort out the two branches of the great Lancashire Tyldesleys without dear Ernest being made unidentifiable as G. E. And who is the better for knowing that staunch old Russell (A.C.) of Essex, 'Jack' to all and sundry, who in 1921 made a hundred in each innings against Australia, was in reality Charles Albert George?

This minor detail notwithstanding, Mr Martin-Jenkins must be congratulated on the industry and balanced judgement which mark a book that should be a must for the reference section of any self-respecting cricket library.

THE DAILY TELEGRAPH
22 AUGUST 1980

What Hope for Spin?

We can surely all subscribe to the proposition that, if speed provides much of the excitement of the game at top level, then in spin lies its fascination. Variety is the spice of cricket and the secret of much of its charm. These thoughts, which only labour the obvious to men of my generation, though they may not be quite so apparent to the young, are induced, as may be imagined, by the current imbalance of the Test attacks of the leading countries. Whereas it used to be almost unheard of to provide a Test captain with fewer than two slow bowlers of repute – sometimes he had three – now the ration is one, and sometimes not even that.

Several factors, of course, have combined against the interests of the spinner, beginning perhaps with one of the more grotesque decisions of the old Advisory County Committee directly after the war, that the new ball could be claimed after 55 overs. When Don Bradman's 1948 Australians arrived here with Lindwall, Miller and Bill Johnston young, fast, and raring to go, they could scarcely believe their luck at getting a shining new one to fling down on an average, say, every 130 runs or so. To keep these three fresh Bradman used, as required, the slow-medium left-armer, Toshack, bowling with the utmost economy, and the minimum of movement, at the leg-and-middle. And very boring stuff it was.

There were two good-class spinners in the party in McCool and Ring, and an off-spinner in Ian Johnson. McCool, however, despite his successes in 1946–7, did not get a Test, Ring had one, and spin accounted for just eight of the eighty-nine English wickets that fell in the series.

It took three years for the 55-over folly to be diluted by a change to 65. Seven years later it became 75 and after five more (in 1961) to the present 85. Whereas before the war, when the new ball came only after 200 runs and fertilizers were not showered upon outfields to keep them green and lush, the number one spinner could reckon to get the ball into his fingers after perhaps an hour's cricket (occasionally, as with 'Tich' Freeman, after 10 minutes), as the years went by he became less important.

Another Advisory brain wave, the maximum 75-yard boundary – now discarded – was a further discouragement to spin. Perhaps,

though, in English cricket at least, the chief factor militating against
the spinner even before the advent of limited-over cricket in the
1960s was the mental approach of captains. More and more it came
to be a matter of keeping the out-cricket tight. The balance swung
increasingly from attack to defence. Short-of-a-length stuff just on
the quick side of medium became the order of the day – but I need
not underline the depressing story.

When the Gillette, the John Player League and the Benson and
Hedges, in turn, took firm root, this style of bowling was reckoned
even more emphatically to be the best medicine, and only those
spinners who had learned their craft when the County Championship was the one available prize were given the chance to hold their
own – where the prime objective was not to dismiss a batsman but
to pin him down.

The situation in Test and county cricket being what it is, it is
unimaginable to suppose that any law change might bring back
spin-bowling to its old position in the scheme of things. In Test
cricket especially, fast bowlers will rule the roost, as for that matter
they have almost always done whenever a country has been lucky
enough to have a pair of them working in harness, let alone three or
four.

The outright banning of the bouncer would change the situation,
obviously, but I suppose it will need a fatality or two to bring that
about. Meanwhile, the cricket authorities can scarcely aim higher
than to keep naked intimidation at arm's length – against batsmen
increasingly armoured – and in the West Indies and Australia at least
that will be problem enough.

What then is the prospect for at least a more reasonable balance in
bowling method in first-class – and, indeed, in all – cricket, since
styles and fashions at the top are generally reflected lower down? I
wish I could be more hopeful, but we must accept that in these days
of tight, restricted cricket few captains are prepared to allow a
spinner any latitude in finding a length – even if he may have gone
days or weeks without being given an over. Moreover, not many
captains understand any more the proper function of a spinner as an
attacking bowler – unless the ball is turning a great deal. More often
than not he is asked to bowl a few economical overs to keep the
quicker men fresh. Again, most of the best spinners have taken
years to develop and master their craft. Also, they must be kept in
regular practice, and here one comes up against the current

dogmatic attitude about the type of bowling considered suited to
the pitch. If it's 'one for the seamers', as it is so often thought to be,
no other type gets a look-in. The value of contrast for its own sake
has been largely forgotten.

Perhaps a growing realization that bowling of the faster type
undiluted is boring to watch – and to bat against and to field to – will
have some beneficial effect before it is too late. Meanwhile, I find
myself thinking that – especially in English county cricket – the best
immediate hope might be to encourage the younger element whose
places are secure as batsmen to attune their arms and their wits to
spin-bowling. All, or most, will in youth have been bowlers of
some sort or degree, and I can think of several who, as boys, could
spin the ball. They might well 'come again' if captains and coaches
were more flexible in outlook and really encouraged them to work
at it. I am talking of both sorts of orthodox spin, right-arm and left,
and wrist-spin, too.

Finally, one comes to the question of whether a change in the
Laws, aimed specifically to help spin-bowling, would be justified.
In the May *Cricketer* Ray Robinson was telling us that Australia are
going to support the proposal of Jeffrey Stollmeyer, president of
the West Indies Board, that the batsman could be out lbw to the ball
pitching outside leg stump. It is not too difficult to presume the
hand in this of Sir Donald Bradman, who was advocating this
extension in 1938. Now, as then, it would be limited to right-arm
bowlers operating over the wicket and left-armers bowling round.
The concession would not apply to anyone bowling either right-
arm round or left-arm over, who might get undeserved reward
simply by firing away at the wider follow-through marks from the
edge of the crease. The idea clearly is both to encourage spin
generally, and in particular to remove the advantage the law gives
to the bowler turning the ball in to the batsman over·the one who
aims to turn it away.

The big practical difficulty in extending lbw to the leg side has
always been the scarring of the pitch by the marks of the follow-
through. But anything advocated by Mr Stollmeyer with the
approval of Sir Donald obviously deserves the most sympathetic
hearing. If no more is immediately achieved, at least the international authorities are talking and thinking about spin-bowling.

THE CRICKETER
AUGUST 1980

A Golf Contrast

Royal and Ancient Autumn Meeting. A round with Pat Ward-Thomas, who has this in common with Bernard Darwin – both wrote about golf like angels, but as players were sometimes possessed with devils: angry beyond measure with themselves and so difficult to play either with or against. In an otherwise friendly and relaxed foursome Bernard's partner once heard him address the Almighty in tones of anguish: 'Oh, God, why do you make me play this game? You know I hate it so.' I was almost moved to anguish myself after getting into that tiny bunker in the middle of the 15th fairway in the Medal: several abortive blows – consequently 'no return'.

Following my earlier reference to John Beck, I ought to add that these well-known exceptions only underline the fact that the standard of etiquette and general deportment of the best golfers, both amateur and professional, has been, in my view, a model for all other games to follow.

DIARY
15 SEPTEMBER 1980

Present for Uncle Fred

At Barclays Bank CC Dinner 175 were present, 100 of whom bought copies, which I signed, of the second edition of our World of Cricket, *just launched and published thanks to the patronage of the Bank. Press-ganged? Possibly they were, but the book did wonderfully well – 664 pages for £18. At a Hatchards book-signing the presiding genius, Tommy Joy, beamed and said, 'Yours is our Uncle Fred book this Christmas. You know – what on earth can we give Uncle Fred?'*

We brought the book together in a Bank office in the city, with young – just down from Cambridge – George Plumptre as resident assistant editor and general dogsbody, John Woodcock as my associate editor, Hugh Montgomery-Massingberd as publishing editor – all 750,000 words passed his critical gaze en route to the printer – and, not least, Humphrey Stone as designer.

DIARY
3 OCTOBER 1980

J. H. Parks –
3000 Runs and 100 Wickets

James Horace Parks, of Sussex, elder brother of Harry, father of the rather more famous Jim and grandfather of R. J., who played in the latter part of last season for Hampshire, has died aged seventy-seven.

Jim Parks, Sen., was the personification of the highly competent, unspectacular professional cricketer of the inter-war years; a steady opening partner over many a season with John Langridge, and a bowler of just below medium pace with a hint of in-swing and, on any pitch which was in the slightest susceptible, a distinct straightening from leg to off.

At the age of thirty-four he was chosen for the Lord's Test against New Zealand to take in young Len Hutton, who made 0 and 1 on his baptism before fulfilling the beginnings of his promise with a hundred on his second appearance.

For Jim Parks there was no further cap in store, though he went on in that summer of 1937 to achieve what was never done before nor has been since, namely to make 3000 runs in the season and take 100 wickets.

With the Parkses, the Langridges, the Oakeses, 'Young George' Cox and a succession of fine cricketers to lead them, Sussex in the 1930s were a side to reckon with. Three times in succession they were runners-up to the champions, with Jim Parks always in the picture, always giving his all, and his round face generally wreathed in smiles.

THE DAILY TELEGRAPH
22 NOVEMBER 1980

Dictionary of Sports and Games

Two things stagger me just about equally regarding this book of 900 pages and, unless my arithmetic is far astray, around 2 million words. One is the prodigious weight of effort, the skill in research and the wealth of scholarship which has been put into it by the sole author, J. A. Cuddon. The other is the utter lack of any attempt at design and presentation such as would have made in some degree digestible a volume which runs on from one entry to the next without a heading of any sort, with no division between one game and another, with no photograph or any illustration other than a few technical line drawings, nor any index. As a final gesture of disregard for the conventions of typography, each of the three right-hand columns per page has a jagged or, as it is known in the trade, unjustified margin. This inelegant fashion would have been indication enough that the book was printed in USA.

The book covers an even wider field than the *Oxford Companion to Sports and Games*, published five years ago by OUP under the general editorship of John Arlott. This was well illustrated, with some hundred contributors listed. Mr Cuddon's book deserved a similar treatment, though, since it weighs about 6 lb, the text would have needed some abridgement. The author was at Brasenose College in the early 1950s, a contemporary there of K. M. Spence, whom he thanks for help and advice on rugby football, as he does many others, chiefly in connection with the more obscure sports and games. Sir Fitzroy Maclean, for instance, was a source of information on **buzkashi**, a game on horseback resembling polo, apparently played in Central Asia since Alexander the Great, and chiefly – though little now, no doubt – in Afghanistan.

Mr Cuddon was himself a sportsman, having played for Oxford, though without getting a Blue, at rugger, hockey and cricket. Naturally one searched for **cricket** and there it was, some 25 pages about it, the name of the game in bold type of the same size as the article and of the brief preceding entry: **cribbage** BILLIARDS.

As it happens the end of cricket is followed, without even a ¼-in break, with: **cripple** A BASEBALL pitch thrown when the count is 3–0 or 3–1. To have précied the evolution and subsequent history of cricket worldwide, noting the salient technical points, and bringing in chief personalities and events in chronological order, in the space Mr Cuddon has allowed himself, is a notable feat of compression. Other cricket references, scattered throughout the book, include a glossary of terms and short individual histories of the First-Class Counties with the names of a few of the outstanding players, an invidious choice inevitably. There is one irritating howler which should be put right, if nothing else is, in the paperback edition apparently to be expected: in the composition of the game's governing body, the Cricket Council, Mr Cuddon has gone completely haywire. It could not possibly have come from any of the several cricket writers, myself included, who are thanked as having been, through their work, 'important sources of fact and informed opinion'.

In a brilliant preface the author discusses the philosophy of sport, going back even beyond the Ancient Greeks, and characterizes no fewer than twelve categories of game, from Field Games to Street and Children's Games. A list of some major dates and events starts at 5200 BC – early form of bowls or bowling known in Egypt – and finishes with the World 12-metre Yachting Championships (held off Brighton, England) in 1979. Are you ignorant as regards skat, faro, or split the kipper? It's all there within these tough black covers, indigestibly incredible, incredibly indigestible.

THE CRICKETER
DECEMBER 1980

Centenary Without Tears

The second centenary of the summer at Lord's was celebrated in better weather than the major event, and, it need hardly be said, without the slightest suspicion of the hassle which saddened those present on the Saturday of the Test match against Australia. The Cross Arrows Club has been beholden since its inception in 1880 to the Gaby family, first to 'Old Dick', recruited by MCC in 1875 and as the Lawn Tennis professional an original member of the Cross Arrows, and secondly to R.T., also Dick, whose service overlapped his father's and who now, as the only life vice-president, has produced the concise and informative history of the club to coincide with its 100th season.

'Young Dick' was for many years ground and pavilion superintendent. Nor should one forget his brother Joe, who until his sudden death commanded the main pavilion door and was known and highly respected by every member. Such men as these epitomized the friendly spirit of Lord's which naturally has been reflected in the Cross Arrows Club, the backbone of which is the staff but to which members both of MCC and of Middlesex have always been admitted as members.

Until 1962 the Cross Arrows fixture-list, taking up every weekday in September, was fulfilled at the edges of the square on the main ground – the first time I played at Lord's was against the Cross Arrows, for whom a certain E. H. Hendren bowled me for a duck with a shooter. Now the games take place on the Nursery, which has an ample square and makes an ideal setting for a club match, the more so since the balcony outside the Indoor School bar forms an ideal vantage point.

There is scarcely a distinguished member of either the MCC or Middlesex staffs who has not turned out for the club, and many famous amateurs likewise. All is to be found in Mr Gaby's slim commemorative volume, reviewed in our August issue.

The star match in September was, naturally, the one specially designated to mark the centenary between the Cross Arrows and a combined XI of MCC and Middlesex, and a rousing affair it turned out to be. Despite the presence of Fred Titmus, their evergreen captain, John Emburey, Alan Moss and Bill Merry in the combined

side, Lt Col. J. R. Stephenson (the MCC Cricket Assistant Secretary
and as such by tradition the Cross Arrows captain) declared his
innings at 2.50 p.m. at 255 for 2. Bob Lanchbury took out his bat for
133. MCC/Middlesex went hard for the runs, notably Ian Gould
with 81 in 70 minutes. With one over to go the scores were level,
whereupon John Price bowled a maiden, moreover denying victory
by achieving a run-out off the last ball. A draw therefore it was – and,
mercifully, wholly uncontrived.

THE CRICKETER
DECEMBER 1980

1981

PRESIDENT OF KENT

Arthur Wellard:
No Mere Slogger

Arthur William Wellard, of Somerset, died peacefully in his sleep following a heart attack in the early hours of New Year's Eve, aged seventy-seven.

He was a cricketer after every schoolboy's heart, an ever cheerful all-rounder and, above all, a prodigious hitter of sixes. In a career of fifteen playing seasons, on either side of the war, he hit 500 of them, a much larger number than anyone before or since, though it must be remembered that in G. L. Jessop's day only hits out of the ground counted six. Twice on the Wells ground, admittedly a small one, Wellard struck five sixes in an over, a sequence unequalled until Gary Sobers smote all six balls beyond the Swansea boundary many years later.

Wellard, however, was no mere slogger. With enormous hands and using a bat little short of 3 lb weight, he had a sound defence and is one of the few all-rounders to have made as many as 12,515 runs and (as a fast-medium bowler who could also turn to off-spinners) taken 1614 wickets.

He played in only two Tests, and against Australia at Lord's in 1938, in a thrilling stand of 74 with young Denis Compton, helped save England from defeat, depositing a ball from McCabe into the Grandstand balcony in the process. He was chosen to go with MCC to India in 1940 and a better tourist it would be hard to imagine.

Wellard was born in Kent, but was reputedly told when applying for a job on the groundstaff that he had much better become a policeman, a story, writes R. L. Arrowsmith in *Barclays World of Cricket*, which 'will seem improbable only to those who have never tried to judge young cricketers'.

He qualified for Somerset, where he fitted the scene perfectly, a spiritual descendant if ever there was one to that immortal West Country hero, Sammy Woods.

THE DAILY TELEGRAPH
2 JANUARY 1981

Gilbert Ashton:
Last of a Famous Trinity

Gilbert Ashton, MC, who has died suddenly, aged eighty-four, at his home within sight of Abberley Hall, Worcester, of which he was for forty years headmaster, was one of the most revered figures from the heyday of amateur sport, and, games apart, in the community life of Worcestershire.

He was the oldest and last survivor of three Wykehamist brothers, all first-class cricketers and all-round sportsmen, of whom C.T. was killed in the Second World War and Sir Hubert died less than two years ago. They captained Cambridge at Lord's in successive years, 1921–3, all won Blues for soccer in addition, and Claude and Hubert likewise for hockey. All three brothers were Corinthian footballers, Claude, indeed, captaining England in a full International.

Gilbert went through the First World War, winning a Military Cross. He led the cricket XI of 1921, whose nine victories included five 'straight' wins against full county sides, as well as the overwhelming defeat of Oxford by an innings. This, by any reckoning, must be accounted the strongest University side of the century. Both Hubert, who made a hundred, and Claude were also members of it, and all three brothers later that summer took part in one of the most romantic of cricket matches when A. C. MacLaren's Amateur XI defeated Warwick Armstrong's hitherto unbeaten Australians.

The distinguished preparatory school thereafter was the centre of Gilbert's life, but he involved himself fully in public affairs (as Hubert did in a wider sphere as MP for Chelmsford, Government Minister, and a Church Commissioner).

Gilbert served for thirty-six years as a county magistrate,

commanded the Home Guard, was president of the British Legion, a Deputy Lieutenant, and over a long span successively chairman and president of Worcestershire County Cricket Club, for whom he played in his youth.

THE DAILY TELEGRAPH
10 FEBRUARY 1981

Brian Sellers:
Yorkshire Personified

Arthur Brian Sellers, who has died eleven days short of his seventy-fourth birthday, was second among Yorkshire captains only to Lord Hawke alike in the length of his reign and the number of Championships won. In his nine seasons, starting in 1933 and ending in 1947, Yorkshire won the title six times. He was second perhaps to his most famous predecessor in another sphere also, for as chairman of the cricket committee after his retirement until his resignation in 1972 he also wielded wide authority within the club, though never to the extent of Lord Hawke, who had been Yorkshire's benevolent dictator for nearly half a century.

Sellers rendered his most valuable services to Yorkshire on the field of play, coming in almost untried and succeeding by sheer determination and force of character in getting the best out of a side, most of whom were his seniors in age as all were in repute. His methods were direct, to say the least, but his men 'took it' because they recognized his essential fairness and his over-riding pride in Yorkshire cricket. Moreover, he was at least the equal of any of them (except Arthur Mitchell) as a fielder, and in insisting on the highest standards in this respect he certainly led by example.

Yorkshire's batting was so strong that they were seldom short of runs. Sellers himself was a valuable man at the crease, as may be seen from his career average of 23 for a total of 9273. Thrice he made 1000 runs in a season, and of his four hundreds one was against the Australians, another against the fast Nottinghamshire attack of Larwood and Voce.

Allowing the quality at his command it could be claimed for him in the late 1930s that there was no better captain in England.

He was a selector off and on from 1938 to 1955, and helped pick the MCC team to Australia in 1946, before joining the press party as a journalist. Late in the tour he voiced forthright criticism of Walter Hammond's captaincy which, justified though it may have been, was thought not to come well from one of those who had appointed him. Sellers was widely blamed, but unluckily so in that what developed into an angry controversy began with remarks made in private and not intended for publication.

His playing days finished, he brought his bluff outspokenness to a post-war generation of cricketers to whom his manner was less acceptable than to their forerunners, and in the troubles between the county and several of their most famous players Sellers was at the centre of the storm. When an action group within the club sought to bring down the committee in 1971 – and in fact defeated them at a meeting attended by more than a thousand members – after the sacking of Brian Close in favour of Geoffrey Boycott, their chief target was Brian Sellers.

Sellers was in some ways a paradoxical character, a strange blend of modesty and over-confidence. Tact was never his strong suit, but whatever his ups and downs no one ever questioned either his courage or his single-minded devotion to Yorkshire cricket.

THE DAILY TELEGRAPH
23 FEBRUARY 1981

Dexter Chooses
Thirty-seven of the Best

On a benign May morning at Fenner's in 1957 I saw young E. R. Dexter come in at number three for the University and by stroke-play of rare pedigree make a hundred before lunch against Lancashire. Before he was done he had demolished the second new ball just as easily as he had the first, and finally, after 4 hours' batting, reached 185.

It was an innings to remember, the first, for me, of a handful such: indeed, it so happens I can picture clearly more innings of substance and quality by E.R.D. than by any other batsman save Bradman and Woolley. Just why is, however, strictly immaterial to my subject – which is to comment upon his new book *From Bradman to Boycott, the Master Batsmen* (Queen Anne Press, £7.95).

Dexter first examines the basics of batsmanship and then sketches, sometimes necessarily at second-hand, the characteristics of thirty-seven famous players plus, as a gallant gesture, one of the stalwarts of women's cricket both before and after the war, Miss Molly Hide. The author is scarcely less interesting when he writes about a dozen or so whom he knew as men but never played with. Yet the book would have gained if it had been lengthened by the inclusion of a few disappointing omissions: Tom Graveney, for instance, and Ken Barrington, surely with Geoffrey Boycott the best English post-war professional batsmen.

This book, from such a source, will be specially acceptable to those who believe that, too many overseas players notwithstanding, the English game would be the stronger if less stress were put on gymnasium training for one-day cricket and more on instilling all that is involved in the beautiful, difficult art of batting.

Dexter remarks, in the course of his study of Sir Leonard Hutton, that 'natural aptitude always needs the complement of a great teacher'. Though there are many exceptions to this dictum, from Bradman downwards, few will disagree about the importance of sound teaching, particularly in English conditions which are so much more variable than those abroad.

Len Hutton, he says, had the advice of those legendary sages, George Hirst and Edgar Oldroyd. Peter May, universally agreed to be the best of all post-war English batsmen, and the author himself were admirably coached, at Charterhouse and Radley respectively, by George Geary and Ivor Gilliat, and both will testify to the value of their friendship at Cambridge with Cyril Coote, the wisest of guides to all sensible enough to seek his help. Colin Cowdrey, the remaining member of the great public school triumvirate, was coached at Tonbridge by C. H. Knott, but had to fend for himself at Oxford where they have never had anyone approaching a Coote. This may explain, at least in part, why over the last half-century twenty-nine Cantabs have played for England and only ten Oxonians.

Dexter's introduction comprises the talk he gave last year at a TCCB seminar for county and NCA coaches. This Epistle of

Edward is probably more profitably read than spoken, for it is a deposit of faith, so to speak, deserving slow digestion. Orthodox is best, he says, in a phrase, and sees 'no advantage in using other than the classical grip – although good players have clearly used so-called stronger grips. . . . Then, to achieve good timing, the bat end must be raised above the hands. . . . Only from this open and out position with a good back-lift is it possible to swing the bat truly, as opposed to pushing it.'

Incidentally, Dexter thinks that the present lbw Law (i.e., that of 1937), allowing the ball to pitch outside the off stump instead of only on the line of the stumps) 'has much to answer for in brutalizing and diminishing the variety of the game, and in reducing stroke-play and coarsening the batting art'.

The chosen subjects are divided into seven categories – Artists, Mechanics, Stonewallers, and so on. If this is not a wholly success-ful device – most of the thirty-seven men could properly be placed in two categories or more – there is much interesting observation on each.

The author is only a modified admirer of Boycott (for reasons he explains). Otherwise there is little that is not appreciative in his brief, illustrated appraisals of all the chosen heroes – Hobbs and Bradman to Vivian Richards and Greg Chappell.

THE DAILY TELEGRAPH
16 APRIL 1981

Aussies on the Links

Kent v Australians. No play because of rain, so captain Kim Hughes brought Allan Border and Geoff Lawson for a round at Royal St George's. Not noticeably big or strong, Kim hit it a mile, reminding us that in the Centenary Test at Lord's the year before he had driven Chris Old high into the top storey of the pavilion, the only time I ever saw it done. He gave me an Australian touring tie: a very kind gesture by a charming fellow – but how could I ever wear it?

DIARY
26 JUNE 1981

Presidential Week

'My' presidential Canterbury Week, in its 140th year, started on a Wednesday – almost without precedent. Equally so, it coincided with a royal wedding. We watched the Prince of Wales wed his marvellous bride on a television set installed in the President's Tent. Thus our Patron, the Duke of Kent, perforce postponed his visit until the Friday, arriving by helicopter at Simon Langton School up the road. It was decidedly damp, so the presentation of the teams had to be made on the Players' balcony. The Archbishop (also otherwise engaged on Wednesday!) was paying his first visit to the Week and he too met the players. Further, at the request of our assistant groundsman, Sam Fidler, to do something about the weather, Dr Runcie saw the sun come out, allowing a full afternoon's play, at the end of which Essex won a decisive victory.

Happily, in lovely weather we beat Hampshire equally comfortably in the second match. Among those present were the Bryan brothers, Jack and Godfrey, who had played against Hampshire in the Week sixty years ago. What with entertaining forty-odd guests to lunch each day and a few more for tea, hosting the old capped players' party on the Sunday, and attending the Old Stagers' performance of The School for Scandal – with Ann declaiming her lines as The Spirit of Kent following the annual Epilogue – it all added up to quite an eventful Week. And what a rewarding one! Tents and flags and bands and Ladies' Day hats and all give to Canterbury Week an atmosphere all its own.

DIARY
29 JULY 1981

Rector Approved

Ronald Roome, my fellow churchwarden, and I see the Rev. David Naumann, Vicar of Littlebourne and Rural Dean of Bridge, sent for our approval by the patron of the living of St Clement's, Sandwich, the Archdeacon of Canterbury. We approve and have never regretted it.

DIARY
20 AUGUST 1981

Harvest Songs of Praise

At the start of a four-month interregnum (during which the wardens are by law and custom responsible for running the parish and ordering the services) *we all appear, 300 strong, in a Harvest Supper edition of the BBC's* Songs of Praise, *presided over by our dear rector, Hugh Maddox, moving on at the request of the Bishop of Dover. All very thoroughly rehearsed and properly so, considering the audience was estimated at 8 million!*

DIARY
27 SEPTEMBER 1981

When W.G. and Fry
Graced the Game

In a letter to the Editor, written at the end of this summer's phenomenal series between England and Australia, I wondered whether anyone could recall W. G. Grace and C. B. Fry going in together in the former's last Test at Trent Bridge in 1899. Or, indeed, if anyone remembered G. L. Jessop's 104 at The Oval in 1902, to which Ian Botham's famous hundreds at Headingley and Old Trafford have been likened.

I quoted the recollection of a ninety-seven-year-old living in Buckinghamshire who thought she could still see W.G. and K. S. Ranjitsinhji going together to the wicket at Melbourne in 1897. She had allowed the two figures to coalesce, I suggested, since W.G.'s second and final visit 'down under' was in 1891–2 and Ranji's only tour was in 1897–8.

Well, not surprisingly, if Helen Campbell as a girl of about eight, watching from the Ladies' Stand with her father at the MCG, saw W.G., none of the readers whose memories were aroused has outstripped her. In seniority, though, she must give place to Miss Henrietta Densham, who was 101 last February and recalls how when she and W.G.'s daughter, Bessie, played together for Clifton High School, W.G. used to watch them. That was around 1898, shortly before he moved from Bristol to found the London County CC at Crystal Palace. A retired priest writing from Spilsby, Lincolnshire, was a regular visitor with his father to Trent Bridge and 'clearly recollects' W.G. and Fry together.

There was no more representative figure of the Golden Age of cricket than Charles Fry, but the game was only one of the outlets for his energy and talent. Though as a combined scholar and all-round sportsman his record is unsurpassed, the activity of which he was most proud was the setting-up and running of the training ship for merchant seamen, known as *The Mercury*, at Hamble.

Since W.G. did not die until 1915 there must be many not yet into their eighties with recollections of him – and, incidentally, I have yet to meet anyone who knew him and did not recall him with affection. 'I was a friend of W.G.,' writes one who lived two doors away in Lawrie Park Road, Sydenham. 'All the children loved him,' she says, as one of those who regularly accompanied him as he walked to the Crystal Palace. There she saw him play not cricket, but bowls.

Another reader tells of how his father, not long dead, aged ninety-five, recalled seeing all four heroes I mentioned – W.G. and Jessop for Gloucestershire, Fry and Ranji for Sussex – playing at Bristol in the same county match. *Wisden* confirms that in 1895 they did so, Jessop, aged twenty-one, making top score and, with his fast bowling, taking five cheap wickets.

An old friend writes that he met Jessop in the 1930s when he was secretary of Hendon Golf Club, and tells how his own love of cricket was inherited from his mother, who was the fast bowler in the first ladies' team in the 1890s. . . . 'I once asked my mother who taught her to bowl overarm,' he says. 'She replied rather tartly, "Why, Spofforth, of course."'

Finally, I come to a nonagenarian in a Hythe nursing home who, as a boy of twelve, was taken by his father to The Oval Test of 1902. In an enviable hand he writes that: 'I was less impressed by Jessop, for it was the sort of thing we more or less expected from our men in those days, who then played for their side instead of, as now, for money, than the tension of seeing, was it Hirst? come in to bat when England needed 4 (I think) to win. He, poor chap, walked from the pavilion in utter silence, more unnerving than anything, I should think.'

It was Rhodes, of course, who joined Hirst, and it was 15 they needed, and got, for the last wicket. Thereupon there was jubilation but no uproar – 'none of this insane chanting from the groups of spectators or the girls' school behaviour of the players embracing each other . . .'.

Many of all ages would echo this sharp comment even if they

would not quite subscribe to the jingoistic notes struck by some of these elderly readers. And what a distortion time has wrought on the recollection of one of the great innings of history! I hope Botham is luckier when his great deeds are recalled at similar range, in the year 2060.

THE DAILY TELEGRAPH
13 OCTOBER 1981

An Un-Waughlike Waugh

Thanksgiving service for Alec Waugh at Chelsea Old Church. Evelyn's vastly more amiable brother was one of the only men in his day to wear the garish red and yellow MCC blazer – an enthusiastic if not a formidable cricketer. Alec wrote fifty books (one a year), including Island in the Sun. *An incessant globe-trotter, his friends always knew they could find him at the Lord's Test match, where he annually held court.*

DIARY
22 OCTOBER 1981

Scrum in Perfect Balance

On a cold, crisp Tuesday in early December 1928 the right centre and wing of the Cambridge three-quarter line, Aarvold and Smeddle by name, in the first few minutes of the game scored three tries in Twickenham's north-east corner; and Oxford's supporters had horrific visions of yet another slaughter such as those of 1925 and 1926. Do old men forget? They are certainly unwise to trust their memories, and so I have confirmed with Sir Carl Aarvold that – in those less regimented days – they were both wearing the green and white hooped stockings of Durham School.

Such was my first memory of the University rugger match, the 100th edition of which is being celebrated on the Rugby Union ground next Tuesday. Bill Smeddle, hair gleaming smooth and heels flying, scored a fourth try in the second half, and the great Aarvold duly became (as he is still) the only Cambridge man to play in four winning sides against Oxford. But the darker Blues had fought back with utmost courage, and the following year they turned the tide.

To me, uncommitted (though with a partiality for Oxford which was always a struggle to subdue) and for all but forty years until 1964 a professional critic of the game, the great moments in the University Match stand out, in a long and varied sporting experience, almost as sharply as anything.

This one contest has had about it an heroic aura even when, as too often, the spoilers have had it over the attackers, or when, occasionally, a side has won too easily. Here were thirty men, brought to the utmost peak of fitness, and with a degree of skill that in some years made a Blue as hard to win as an international cap, straining every limb beyond endurance, yet, in this game of the hardest physical contact, strictly within the limits of chivalry.

Some, recalling ugly incidents of the early 1970s, may blink a bit at this. In 1960 one could still write of the 'high skill and impeccable sportsmanship' of the match, and so it seemed so long as Gwynne Walters, that prince of referees, was in annual charge. Since then in what games (other maybe than golf) have standards of conduct not declined? May this occasion bring out the best in all respects.

Great sides can be recalled by reference to the books: the 1934 Cambridge of Wilfred Wooller and Cliff Jones; Oxford in their two unbeaten years, 1946 and 1949, with their wealth of Rhodes Scholars and from 1947 to 1949 inspired by the genius of Clive Van Ryneveld; Oxford again in 1955, thanks to the dazzling half-back partnership of D. O. Brace and M. J. K. Smith.

It is safe to say that for many clear-cut reasons neither university will ever again come to Twickenham unbeaten, but in 1961 Cambridge under M. R. Wade had won all their fourteen matches before Oxford, led by the heroic John Willcox, went under only after a Homeric struggle. Cambridge, inspired by C. M. H. Gibson – for me the perfect mid-field player – were supreme in the early 1960s. In 1972–6 Cambridge achieved the unique feat of five wins in a row.

Yet it is the men and the moments that come so easily to life – match-saving tackles, for instance. Everyone alive who was present can see the Russian prince, Alex Obolensky, streaking across to hurl J. R. Rawlence into touch a yard short of the line, John Kendall-Carpenter, a front-row forward (!) likewise in the 77th minute ending a great run by J. V. Smith.

The biographies of the 700-odd Blues in the *Centenary History of the OURFC 1869–1969* by the late Ross McWhirter and Sir Andrew Noble – perhaps the finest record of any sporting club ever written – portray a company of high and diverse subsequent achievement, putting to ridicule those ludicrous yet too well remembered lines about 'flannelled fools at the wicket or muddied oafs at the goals'. Did Freud ever probe into the psyche of his contemporary, Kipling, I wonder?

John Forrest and 'Trilby' Freakes, Internationals both, were killed in the Second World War, as were seven of the 1937 Oxford XV. There were probably other Cambridge casualties but the counterpart to the Oxford book is yet to come.

I have sketched in some impressions of personal recollection, but the story of this historic fixture has been worthily and at times humorously told, decade by decade, in the 1981 Official Programme which I predict (having seen the proofs) will become a collector's piece: 80 pages for 50p, and between stiff covers at that.

Kenneth Spence, the Oxford captain of 1952, who has chaired the centenary match arrangements, traces those misty early years, and quotes the oldest survivors of the match, Reginald Honey, QC, aged ninety-five, a South African, and the legendary C. N. Lowe, now ninety. He pays respect to two of the greatest of the Edwardian era, K. G. McLeod of Cambridge and R. W. Poulton-Palmer of Oxford.

Lord Wakefield, most famous of all Cambridge and England captains, covers the 1920s, which saw the match transfer 'from homely Queen's Club to the Rugby Union's budding arena and its popularity accordingly transformed. Vivian Jenkins tells of the lush 1930s when Oxford's chosen paid £5 for a long weekend at the Grand at Eastbourne, meals and Palm Court orchestra thrown in, before they were transported to Twickenham in Rolls-Royces with dark blue streamers bedecking the bonnets. He declares – and who is better qualified to say? – that the finest full-back display he ever saw was that of his Oxford successor 'Tuppy' Owen-Smith.

Peter Robbins tells how Roy Allaway, the 1955 Oxford captain, informed his team in the coach to Cardiff that that great club were threatening to drop the fixture: result, Cardiff 6, Oxford 23 – a psychological equivalent perhaps of Larwood when about to bowl to Ponsford being shown a cutting wherein the latter told his readers that he, Harold, was not really fast: result, an explosion of speed and one broken left hand. The best crack belongs to Joe McPartlin, who describes his contemporary, Willcox, as 'a captain who makes the Ayatollah seem like a benevolent humanist'.

The 'gates' over the halcyon period 1946–64, we learn, averaged 50,000. A minimum of 35,000 are hoped for next Tuesday, by the way, at least half praying to see Cambridge score their forty-fourth victory and so for the first time in 100 years nosing ahead of Oxford, the present tally being 43 all and 13 draws.

THE DAILY TELEGRAPH
5 DECEMBER 1981

1982

THREATS
TO TEST CRICKET

To Twickenham En Prince

*An enjoyable start to the New Year to be invited to watch England play
Australia at Twickenham as guest of the Rugby Football Union ex-
president, my old friend and fellow Cranleighan, Stanley Couchman. Red
carpet treatment, excellent lunch and company. Was this one of those
over-cheerful fellows whose grilling of steaks on an upturned electric fire
(supper having somehow passed them by) had so annoyed the manager of
the Grand Spa at Clifton on a pre-war Easter tour and brought me, who
was supposedly in charge of the team, reluctantly from my bed at midnight?
It was, and how well his subsequent service with club, Surrey County and
on the RFU had fitted him for the honour. Equally so had the current
president, David Brooks of the Harlequins, earned his promotion. The
game has always been run – and, on the whole, well run – by the old
players.*

*England won 15–11 after an entertaining match – oh, such a different one
from that of my reporting time, thanks to the two major Law changes – no
direct touch-kicking outside the '25' and no need to play the ball with the
foot after a tackle.*

DIARY
2 JANUARY 1982

Premature Obit

*Lord Cornwallis, among many other achievements in life captain of Kent
and later President simultaneously of MCC and Kent, died this day. I
wrote most of his obituary notice in* The Daily Telegraph, *but it could not
appear under my name for this reason. Some months earlier I had answered
a request to telephone my advance piece, prefacing it with the time-
honoured words SET and HOLD. Alas, Manchester did not hold: my obit*

appeared in the first edition there, and there was the devil to pay with the family.

DIARY
4 JANUARY 1982

Time-wasting:
A Problem for Umpires

When the subject of time-wasting crops up, my mind often goes back to the New Year of 1955 at Melbourne, when a crowd of 65,000 booed England loud and long for bowling their overs too slowly. Yet, Len Hutton's team delivered 54 eight-ball overs in a 5-hour day, which works out at almost exactly 14½ overs per hour. The attack was well balanced as regards speed, as had been that of the Australians, who had bowled the equivalent of 18 overs per hour the day before. So it is no new thing that confronts us, though the evil gets worse and worse.

As to the India–England series, in all the words, both written and spoken over the air that I have read and heard on the matter, the responsibility of the umpires has not been mentioned. Yet it is perfectly clear. Paragraph 10 of Law 42, which deals wholly with unfair play and in the new Code of Laws is the longest of them all, devotes about a quarter of its space to the sanctions due to be taken by the umpires in the separate cases of time-wasting by captains, bowlers and batsmen.

In all these instances two cautions are to be administered, and after a third infringement the umpire concerned is enjoined to inform the governing authority, 'who shall take appropriate action against the cricketer concerned'. In the case of a bowler, the umpire is given the additional final duty, if two warnings have been ineffective. That duty is to bar the offender from bowling for the rest of the innings – the same sanction as should be applied to the persistent bowler of bouncers.

In India I have heard of no case even of a warning being applied to anyone, though the over rate has plumbed new depths. Yet, to be fair, what umpires of any country have intervened when for tactical purposes over rates have been deliberately slow?

Sooner or later, and the sooner the better, the International Cricket Conference will have to recognize that umpires, except in the most blatant cases and then probably under strong persuasion, make decisions of fact. They will judge in matters of inches and fractions of a second, but will not make a decision wherein they must judge intent, because maybe that involves a degree of moral judgement.

In plain terms, what is happening in India, as it has happened at various times in every Test-playing country, is just cheating – and every Test side has been guilty of it.

A solution? Many and varied have been the suggestions. I favour adding to the total at the end of every hour 3 runs for every over fewer than the prescribed minimum rate. That is an ugly answer, yes, but it is apparently no use relying on the written Law or on the tacit code of sportsmanship.

THE DAILY TELEGRAPH
6 JANUARY 1982

Yorkshire: The Pride and the Prejudice

Only those whose memories take them back to the halcyon years of the 1930s can recall a Yorkshire XI in which its massive following took *undiluted* pride. Here was a team as rich in character as it was abundant in skill: a team of conspicuous corporate spirit, led by a cricketer of only average merit but dominating personality called Brian Sellers.

Yorkshire have since then enjoyed spells of post-war success, notably under Norman Yardley, under Ronnie Burnet, a modest player brought in frankly as a disciplinarian, under Vic Wilson, and also under Brian Close. A stormy petrel himself, Close is also a man of indomitable spirit. His men followed him from feelings compounded about equally of respect for his physical bravery and fear of his verbal wrath.

Since the war, though, the internal feuding, with one player after another giving his version of events and his verdict on his contemporaries in print, has been a regular source of embarrassment and grief, both within Yorkshire and in the cricket world at large.

Yorkshiremen since Tests began have given service to England not excelled by any other county. Over the span of history – or at least since Lord Hawke took charge of 'a drunken rabble' in 1883 – their record in the County Championship is unapproached.

What then is the secret of these bitter inner conflicts, the most recent chapter of which is being enacted at the moment? Derrick Boothroyd's *Half a Century of Yorkshire Cricket* (Kennedy Bros, of Keighley, £3.95) evaluates the post-war breed with a shrewd, caustic eye. He says things about his fellow Yorkshiremen which, I suspect, he would not take from an outsider, certainly not this one. By and large he has the Truemans, the Closes, the Wardles and the rest well taped and, if his touch is less sure when it comes to swingeing cracks at successive committees, it must be said that their often autocratic attitude to players has fuelled some, at least, of the county's troubles.

But this book is far from being a saga of Yorkshire woes – we have read enough of that and to spare. The bulk of it is endearingly reminiscent and nostalgic, with two powerful concluding chapters. These look at the broad picture of modern cricket in a way which makes one regret that the author has not been a regular cricket writer rather than a feature columnist on the *Yorkshire Post*.

His father's utter devotion to cricket turned Boothroyd into a hero-worshipper, with Herbert Sutcliffe his particular idol and Maurice Leyland a worthy runner-up. Luckily, the idolator also had black hair, which in his early teens he plastered and parted *à la* Herbert, as he endeavoured to imitate the master's every mannerism and every stroke in the family net in the garden. He had been only eight when he wrote with infinite labour a 'passionately sincere and earnest' letter of congratulation addressed to Herbert in Melbourne after the greatest of his hundreds on the sticky wicket of January 1929. He gave it to his father to post, and many years later, on going through his papers at his death, was mortified to find it, unsent and inscribed: 'D's letter to Herbert Sutcliffe – very funny.'

There is a chapter of devoted acclaim to 'the greatest ever', Don Bradman, who on the first day's Test-watching of Boothroyd's life obliged at Headingley with 309 not out by close of play.

Boothroyd's outlook was by no means insular, and just as his father had told him with wonder of MacLaren and Fry, Barnes,

J. T. Tyldesley and other magical names of the Golden Age, so he remembered George Gunn, Woolley, Chapman, Hendren, Allen, Mead and 'G. E.' Tyldesley. Some slip here, surely. I expect one of those meddlesome smart Alecs has tinkered with the proof. Boothroyd means Ernest Tyldesley – who is but one of several great cricketers whom a few 'statisticians', with ideas above their station, have made unidentifiable by peering into parish registers and discovering Christian names unused in their lifetimes.

Of everyone's favourite, Schofield Haigh, 'Old Ebor' is quoted: 'The stranger to despair, the enemy of long-faced misanthropy and for eighteen years the sunshine of the Yorkshire XI.' No doubt all our memories are tinged a rosy pink, but the same could have been said of Leyland, or of Hirst – if not quite, perhaps, of Wilfred Rhodes, later a devoted friend, who, when young Boothroyd proferred an autograph book, told him gruffly to 'hop it'.

And so today. The author is no subscriber to the Boycott fan club; he believes much of cricket's administration is hopelessly out of date, and thinks (as I have always done) that the bald notice about 'no play being guaranteed, no money returned' is an affront and a stupidity.

But he reserves his deepest scorn for 'the unholy alliance between the Australian Cricket Board and Kerry Packer', and quotes Alec Bedser as saying that they'll be playing next with a ball with bells on. 'The vital need is for cricket to preserve its independence and not be swept along on the bandwagon of the commercialists.'

THE DAILY TELEGRAPH
6 JANUARY 1982

Thoughts from the West Indies

The Shell Shield is to the West Indies what the Sheffield Shield is to Australia and the Schweppes County Championship is to England. That is, the essential testing ground, where budding talent competes with the established stars in the traditional first-class – two-innings – match. There will be six weeks of the Shell Shield, and all the household names are expected to play before most of them fly to England for the new season.

The political reasons which prevented New Zealand from coming to the West Indies this spring are, indeed, a great sadness, but at the same time the embarrassment of a series of limited appeal contested by tired men has been avoided. Instead, the cricket world here [Barbados] – that is, most of the population – is enjoying the euphoria of a successful tour by their heroes in Australia and, in particular, the thrill of the culminating victory in Adelaide in what Clive Lloyd called the greatest Test he ever played in.

As distinct from happenings in the Antipodes last winter, the West Indies on their return home could congratulate themselves on a harmonious tour for which much credit must be accorded to their manager, Steve Camacho, of Guyana. He is a Test cricketer young enough to have played with the seniors among the present bunch yet with the personality to impose his authority in a restrained, commonsense way. No one with any knowledge of modern cricket management will underestimate the importance of finding men of the Camacho breed.

While the Pakistanis, not without some reason, were making a good deal of palaver over their itinerary and the umpiring, and while some of the Australian players were saying and doing things that antagonized every right-thinking sportsman, the West Indians adopted a low-key approach. Camacho left it to the end to remark that, unless the Australians changed the emphasis of their cricket, the one-day mania would destroy their source of supply.

No one has yet suggested that the limited-over game has ever produced a cricketer – nor, come to that, have I discovered any player with any relish for it as more than a necessary variant.

As the England tour of India has underlined, the over-emphasis in much of the media on the subjective view of the captains to the detriment of the critic's own detached and informed opinion is another current danger. Greg Chappell's strictures on the Melbourne pitch exemplified the folly of this trend. When a side's captain and finest batsman declares that no one can bat on it, what more welcome boost could the opposing attack possibly ask for?

The Combined Islands' victory in the 1980–1 Shell Shield led to their being divided for the tournament shortly due. This means fifteen Shell Shield games instead of ten and brings me to the perennial problem of West Indian cricket, that of cash. Unlike all the other Test countries, except possibly New Zealand, the West Indies can hope for no profit at all from series at home. The West

Indies Board expect around £80,000 from their Australian visit, which sounds perhaps a fair reward – until it is realized that England's tour of West Indies a year ago, thanks partly to the loss of the Guyana Test for political reasons resulted in a loss of £120,000.

It is manifestly wrong, surely, that WIBCO should be permanently on the breadline. Populations are small and ground capacities commensurate. Travel and hotels in the tourist season are expensive. Of all the difficult matters for the attention of the International Cricket Conference in July this is not the least. With its territories spread across more than 1000 miles of the Caribbean, the peculiar problems of the West Indies Board can, perhaps, be fully appreciated only by one who knows the Islands well. As president for seven years, Jeffrey Stollmeyer, of Trinidad, has held the Board intact with diplomatic skill – and despite the politicians.

Next in order for the presidency was Guyana, who, however, have recently lost by premature death their two senior administrators, Berkeley Gaskin and Glendon Gibbs, and who felt that they had no adequately experienced candidate. Accordingly, the presidency has reverted to Jamaica in the person of Allan Rae, who will be remembered as Stollmeyer's opening partner on the famous English tour of 1950.

Partly, maybe, in limited compensation, Guyana supply the new chairman of selectors in that admirable batsman, Basil Butcher, who will have with him Jackie Hendricks, of Jamaica, and the former chairman, manager and great cricketer, Clyde Walcott. 'I owe my position in life to cricket,' he says. 'I'll always serve it in any way I can.'

Will all old cricketers everywhere kindly note?

THE DAILY TELEGRAPH
10 FEBRUARY 1982

Test Cricket
Endangered

Think of the great cricketers of any previous age who have passed on, viewing the earthly happenings of this past winter from their celestial fields, and it needs little enough imagination to picture their feelings. Anger and hatred, we must believe, are for them forbidden passions, but if human emotions are still to be felt how deep must be their grief, how great the mystification as they behold what passes for the game they knew and loved!

The tempo of the play must be not the least of the surprises, the tactical go-slows and work-to-rules, the constant consultations, and not infrequently the obvious arguments and gestures of dissent: even a world-famous cricketer kicking another, and actually being allowed to remain on the field. How they must deplore the evident intention by fast bowlers to intimidate, unchecked either by captains or umpires! How the more theoretically minded must be puzzled by that unfamiliar gripping of the bat and the shortage of free swing which results – except when a prodigy or two like young Botham or young Richards lets fly! The fielding – ah, that's splendid, of course, better than that of all but a few of the old 'uns. That they can at least enjoy.

Let us hope that the media does not penetrate on high – the torrent of words, both written and spoken on the air, which, reflecting back over these last winter months, seems like one long ill-natured grumble, interspersed with explosions of utter indignation as in the despicable Lillee incident and in the happenings culminating in Boycott being returned home. The weightiest censures on the spot have tended to come from touring managements themselves: England in the wake of a Test defeat at Bombay complaining about the umpiring – and pleading they must not be thought to be 'wingeing'; Ijaz Butt, manager of the Pakistanis in Australia, declaring on leaving that his team were 'merely stooges' in an exclusively commercial operation; Steve Camacho of the West Indies, also there, deploring the surfeit of one-day cricket and its consequent devaluing of Tests.

There was substance, too, in most of the criticism. The Indian itinerary, for instance, was apparently as unnecessarily arduous as the umpiring was inadequate – though here it must be said that the TCCB send out their own expert months in advance of each tour to survey and agree the arrangements proposed. In Australia it is little wonder that the endless progression of one-day Internationals – fifteen of them in all, leading to a 'best-of-five' final which the West Indies were mercifully able to reduce to four by winning thrice – frayed the tempers of all closely concerned. The endless rushing about over that vast continent; the grossly unsocial hours that brought them back to their hotels tired and hungry at midnight with the prospect of yet another flight next morning; the exposure to every sort of publicity gimmick; rowdy and beer-sozzled crowds – it all adds up to a sport completely at variance with the game that has evolved through the centuries, a game of light and shade, of subtlety and vigour, of quiet skills and explosive power, of ingenuity and tactical invention, a game rewarding concentration and self-discipline.

Is that too starry-eyed a picture? Which of us does not recall to our cost Test and first-class matches containing such ingredients in mighty small measure? Yet at its best, granted a good pitch and captains with the right instincts, Test cricket as the ultimate expression of the game must still retain pride of place, if cricket itself is to survive in recognizable form. As for the one-day game, it has won its place in the scheme of things – in moderation. The best of it can be excellent fun just as, once the result becomes obvious, some of it is inexpressibly boring.

Let us consider now – and I fear it merely continues a dreary catalogue – the dangerously increased influence of the players in newspaper and radio coverage. In the press the independence of the critic is too often put at risk by an undue editorial insistence on 'quotes' from captain and manager, which at best must be subjective and at worst blatantly one-sided and only to be accepted with a large measure of salt. Other members of the touring party make their impressions known either in general or by name.

In India the work of the BBC's professionals on the spot, Don Mosey and Peter Baxter, was augmented by a regular procession of members of the team 'sitting in' beside the commentators, answering questions when asked and chipping in when one of the broadcasters seemed in need of a breather. Small blame to the latter if he does, with overs dragging along at a crawl and much of the batting likewise. In any case the players are being paid – and well paid – to talk about what's going on out in the middle. An Englishman is given out lbw, whereupon his friend at the microphone says the decision was 'no way' correct. What Indians listening in England, or for that matter on the World Service, must have thought of so one-sided a presentation one does not care to think. Thus is the function of the detached critic, straining for impartial objectivity, eroded.

One example may suffice. After the Madras Test Keith Fletcher, in his postmortem comments over the air, defended his no doubt reasonable decision to put India in, but added: 'If we had caught our catches we'd probably have had them out for 150 – perhaps 200.' In fact Gavaskar, dropped when eight, made 25; Vengsarkar, dropped at two, retired hurt for 71. India, their side with plenty of batting undisposed of, declared at lunch on the third day at 481 for 4. In a long catalogue of things better left unsaid this dictum by the captain must take a high place.

Yes, the players would be well advised to say less and do more – and, in certain cases, to behave better. 'Player-power' exists today, for better or for worse, demonstrated more forcefully and less acceptably in Australia and the West Indies than here at home. Some universally accepted and promptly administered disciplinary code is much overdue, and it needs a degree of optimism to visualize the International Cricket Conference upgrading itself to function executively (as it was never designed to do) and to exercise authority after the manner of FIFA and the supreme governing bodies of other great national games.

Yet, to end these sombre remarks – and no one dislikes the role of Jeremiah more than I do – on a more optimistic note, cannot the influence of the players be used as a force for good in certain important directions? For instance, I have yet to hear of a player – either the Australians or their visitors – who enjoys the one-day surfeit in Australia, or who considers either the playing programme or the travel conducive to the best cricket, whether present or to come. If the players were really to dig their toes in on this, it would be only in accord with the TCCB attitude, and probably that of the other overseas boards as well. Again, there is a healthy degree of trust as between the TCCB and the Cricketers' Association, to which all contracted to the First-Class Counties belong. I believe that the average county cricketer of today has an underlying respect for the age-old virtues of cricket and a consequent wish to preserve them.

THE CRICKETER
APRIL 1982

Robert Maxwell Off Cue

The Wisden *Dinner was chaired by Robert Maxwell, as owner of Queen Anne Press, who for three years (1982–4) published the* Almanack *for the proprietors, John Wisden and Co. In his speech he threw in the remark that the format (constant since 1864!) would need to be changed and brought up to date. He gave a grudging welcome to the cricket writers present, but said they produced little in the way of reviews. When we were introduced afterwards I at once asked him on what evidence he complained about reviews. 'If I told you that you were going to see a review of a column in tomorrow's* Telegraph, *would you call that satisfactory coverage?' Nettled, he moved on. Maxwell was on unfamiliar ground and the chairman of John Wisden forthwith decided to move him off it as soon as possible. He did not grace the following two dinners, after which the publishing contract was transferred to the McCorquodale Group.*

DIARY
15 APRIL 1982

The Quoting Habit

I can scarcely read a report or article nowadays without being thankful that my time as a travelling cricket writer ended when it did. Stories with political implications one had to do at times certainly, the long-running saga of Basil D'Oliveira being easily the most momentous and the most deplorable. Generally speaking, though, the game was the thing. Moreover, one travelled in greater comfort with a decent amount of elbow-room between matches, while as for sitting in press boxes until eleven at night describing blood-and-thunder stuff under arc lights – well, I ask you!

To a greater degree than formerly today's subject matter is prescribed. But what tends to give so many reports a dull uniformity, if I may very gently suggest it, is the ever more extensive reliance on quotes from captains and managers, they giving, not unnaturally, their own picture of events and future probabilities to newspapers in their own countries. In India a series of unprecedented tedium was not improved by the versions extracted from a captain who after a hot and tiring day in the field can have wanted only a drink or two and a shower.

The quoting habit has reached fresh lengths, but it is not new in games-writing. Did not Bernard Darwin, the king-pin of our craft, at a golf championship many years ago stump out of a press tent where a player after his round was about to be cross-questioned, saying, 'Damn it, it's what we say, not what he says, that matters'? Obviously the golf correspondent, who can see only a fraction of the action, is more dependent on information than his counterpart in cricket.

But, be that as it may, John Woodcock (whom God preserve) of *The Times* and at least some of his contemporaries would, as a general rule, echo Bernardo's dictum. No one can say that Woodcock does not speak his mind, and I was delighted to read the roasting which he gave – and to which our Editor added in the March *Cricketer* – to Lynton Taylor, the publicity man 'employed to market *all* forms of Australian cricket', as Christopher Martin-Jenkins pointed out.

Taylor, a chief performer in the Packer revolution, described Test cricket as 'archaic', and doubted whether it could be saved. He was good enough to add that he hoped so, but was not convinced. As it happened, within a week or so of this insufferable comment Australia and the West Indies, before crowds that filled Adelaide Oval each day, fought a thrilling duel which Clive Lloyd in Barbados not long afterwards told me was the best Test match he had ever played in. It is extraordinary how modern cricket can touch sublime heights one moment and plumb the depths the next – whether in one-day cricket or five.

Being engaged in the editorship of *Wisden*, Woodcock was lucky to miss India and to see some much better cricket later in Australia before the sudden eruption of the clandestine affair in South Africa had him hurrying off there. It happens that – for the first time, I believe, in the thirty years he has been writing on the game with such discernment and concern for its values – our views on a major matter do not run on a reasonably parallel course. I understand his South African sympathies, and those of many others, who stress the principle of the players' freedom of choice.

It is, of course, a perfectly tenable attitude, as surely is that of those of us who find it hard to forgive the players concerned for putting the future of Test cricket and therefore the livelihood of all their fellow county cricketers at risk – this after due warning from the TCCB of the likely effect of their actions. This time Fletcher was naturally and properly asked for his view and he said it all in four words. He was specially sorry that Graham Gooch would be lost to England, but, after all, 'they knew the score'.

My own over-riding sense is of thankfulness that our two young lions, Ian Botham and David Gower, did not succumb. Without them England's Test future over the next three years would look bleak indeed.

THE CRICKETER
MAY 1982

A Hill-Wood Tradition

The death last week of D. J. C. Hill-Wood, for the last twenty-two years chairman of Arsenal, came as a reminder of how it has become a tradition of many sporting families to serve in later life the games they played when young.

The affinity between cricket and soccer has always been particularly close. Consider, for instance, how these two games have been enhanced in terms of playing skill, leadership quality and administrative labour by such families as the Hill-Woods, the Doggarts, the Ashtons and, going back further, the Fosters and the Lytteltons.

In sheer brilliance on the field the Hill-Woods maybe were outshone by the other illustrious families mentioned here, but just as in soccer their administrative record is surely unrivalled so in cricket they hold a distinction to which (so far as I can ascertain) not even the Lytteltons can claim a parallel.

It is that of a father and four sons all playing for the same county. Samuel Hill-Wood (who became a baronet in 1921) appeared irregularly for Derbyshire for several years around the turn of the century. So, in their turn, did B.S., W.W., D.J.C. and C.K.H. Moreover, at least in an odd game or two, all five captained the side.

The second son, Willy (subsequently Sir Wilfred), was the most accomplished cricketer, member of the great Cambridge XI of 1922, but Charlie played three years for Oxford as a fast left-arm bowler who once saved the University Match by his batting, while Denis opened the Oxford innings at Lord's in 1928.

Willy, as the Eton captain, received a celebrated retort from George Hirst after his team's defeat at Winchester when he ventured on a postmortem with Hirst, then, in 1920, in his first summer as coach. 'Can't understand how we lost, George – what do you think went wrong?' 'What went wrong? Ye bowled too long and ye bowled too bad.' No one enjoyed telling the story better than Willy, as also does still an eye-witness, his great friend G. O. Allen, who, incidentally, in the first innings took 9 for 34.

The captain must have bowled better a fortnight later at Lord's since he contributed to Eton's victory over Harrow by taking six wickets and making the top score of 75 not out. In Hirst's eighteen years at Eton, where he was held in the greatest affection, Eton were never beaten by Harrow nor, again, by Winchester.

W. W.'s great moment was at Melbourne with A. C. MacLaren's MCC team to New Zealand and Australia. MCC had been hopelessly outplayed by Victoria until he and Geoffrey Wilson, captain of Yorkshire, batted out the whole of the last day undefeated at 282 for no wicket, both of course making hundreds. Willy subsequently served several terms on the MCC Committee. This staying in all day was a record in Australia, repeated two years later in a famous Test match, also at Melbourne, by Hobbs and Sutcliffe.

The four brothers played much club cricket together, and in a two-day match for I Zingari against Dorset Rangers once shared between them all twenty wickets.

The two whom I knew, Willy and Denis, radiated a peculiar brand of soothing benevolence that seemed unruffleable. Playing for MCC at Eton, I saw it tested once, though, Denis being the bowler and his son, Peter, struggling for his place in the side, the non-striker. The other batsman hit the ball almost straight back to father and called for a ridiculous single, putting him to the disagreeable necessity of running out his offspring by half the length of the pitch. 'I nearly chucked it at the stupid boy,' he said.

Peter, who has been acting-chairman of Arsenal during his father's illness, made the side all right and would have been a likely Blue if he had not gone straight into the City.

The impact of the Hill-Woods on football began when Samuel built up his own club, Glossop, at no small expense, to the point where just before the First World War they briefly reached the First Division of the Football League.

It was the memory of his days with Glossop, no doubt, that

prompted Hill-Wood to suggest many years later to Ivan Cobbold, head of the Suffolk brewing family, that he buy a football club. Thus it was that in the 1930s Ipswich Town began their ascent from the Southern League to their present eminence in the game.

As his son was to do, Sir Samuel chaired Arsenal for twenty-two years, until his death in 1949. These were the glorious days under the great manager, Herbert Chapman, whom Hill-Wood appointed.

Denis, who, after getting a Blue as a right-half and declining the headmaster's invitation to go back to Eton to teach, also played for the Corinthians and for Clapton. He was elected after the war to the Arsenal board and in 1960 he succeeded Sir Guy Bracewell-Smith in the chairmanship. At Highbury he was held in the highest respect, doing his utmost, as Robert Oxby wrote in his obituary notice, to preserve in an ever more pressurized world something of the old standards he had inherited of sportsmanship and good manners.

THE DAILY TELEGRAPH
12 MAY 1982

J. W. A. Stephenson:
The Great Enthusiast

There were few better amateur bowlers between the wars, and certainly no more enthusiastic cricketer ever, than Col J. W. A. Stephenson, DSO, who has died aged seventy-four.

As a regular soldier 'Steve' was available only when on leave for Essex, who in the 1930s with K. Farnes, H. D. Read, Maurice Nichols and Ray Smith, as well as Stephenson at their disposal, commanded the best new-ball attack in the country.

Stephenson's pace and method had much in common with those of Maurice Tate and Alec Bedser, and though he never could aspire consistently to such heights his life off the pitch on his day could be devastating.

In 1935 for Essex he took ten South African wickets for 110, thus playing the major part in one of only two defeats suffered by the tourists that summer. His great performance, however, was his

9 for 46 for Gentlemen against the powerful Players' batting at Lord's in 1936 when in the second innings he at once took the wicket of C. J. Barnett, the only one to have escaped him in the first. It was of that match that Sir Pelham Warner wrote, 'his fielding at short third man was akin to that of Constantine'.

It was said of him, probably with a touch of exaggeration, that at third man he once took a catch off his own bowling. He was an electric, effervescent cricketer if ever there was one, and he was generally rated unlucky not to have made the MCC side which toured Australia in 1936–7.

In three of the last four 'G. *v* P.' matches at Lord's before the war, he and Farnes took thirty-nine of the forty-seven Players' wickets that fell.

Col Stephenson commanded the 1/7 Battalion of the Middlesex Regiment from 1942 during the North African, Sicilian and Italian campaigns until 1945, earning the DSO in 1944.

Afterwards he turned with characteristic energy to publishing, and rose to become a director of Life International.

THE DAILY TELEGRAPH
25 MAY 1982

─────────── *The Pope at Canterbury* ───────────

An historic day – the coming of Pope John Paul II to Canterbury. We were lucky to be allotted good seats near the nave altar. Two pictures stick in the mind's eye: Pope and Archbishop in silent prayer at the scene of Thomas à Becket's martyrdom, and at the end the two together processing the full length of the cathedral, to sustained applause from the congregation all the way. The feeling generated was of hope and affection, over-riding four centuries of mutual indifference and worse. Unfortunately, the service, which was televized, over-ran its time and the worldwide audience missed the moving climax.

DIARY
29 MAY 1982

Garden Party

Buckingham Palace Garden Party. We are probably invited because of my membership of the MCC Committee. My impression is of the extremely broad cross section of British life represented. Lines are formed and equerries pick out a few in advance of two royal processions, one for the Queen, one for the Duke of Edinburgh. We are not selected. Music and a good tea, all highly agreeable.

DIARY
22 JULY 1982

Milestone at Lord's

Gubby Allen's eightieth birthday dinner in the Long Room, the one for Plum Warner on his eightieth being the only recorded precedent. Nostalgia unlimited. The Daily Mail led the publicity field with a double-page centre spread, showing a group of fourteen household names dinner-jacketed with the Grandstand in the background: appropriate text by Ian Wooldridge. Guest of the evening really quite chuffed.

DIARY
9 AUGUST 1982

Memories of Fender's Era

One seldom writes a reminiscent article on times past without getting a lively reaction, and that not only from those in the sere and yellow. Memories of Somerset recently seem to have caught on, though I had to accept a certain mild and well-deserved rebuke for omitting to mention the spectacular hitting of Guy Earle.

The senior living Surrey cricketer P. G. H. Fender reaches his ninetieth birthday on Sunday – which surely gives a touch of topicality to the fond Oval scene of my youth.

In 1921 my father made me, aged fourteen, a schoolboy member of Surrey (subscription half-a-guinea), thus opening up a new and exciting world which admitted me not only to the pavilion to watch county cricket, and, indeed, the Test match against Australia, but to apparently unlimited net practice during the Easter holidays.

We boys had in April the freedom of one of the county dressing rooms. We changed next door to magnificos like E. R. T. Holmes, of Malvern, a couple of years my senior, and another glorious hitter of the ball for Surrey later on, the Marlburian S. A. Block. We had two net innings each day under instruction, three even by making short work of our sandwiches and getting out there again before the official afternoon session started. Then, our own practice ended, we could wander across the field to watch the great ones at practice – Jack Hobbs, Andrew Sandham, Tom Shepherd and the rest – acquiring afterwards any names that were not in our autograph books already.

Kentish-born, I had long given my first loyalty to Frank Woolley and the ever glamorous Kent XI but, except when Kent and Surrey clashed at Blackheath and The Oval, I had room in my affections for Surrey, especially for the great Hobbs himself and also for a much less exalted member of the Surrey staff named Harry Baldwin.

Hobbs, with a ready word and smile to the youngsters as, with two or three bats under his arm, he strolled from the nets to the pavilion, was every boy's hero. But Baldwin (H.G.) bowled and coached in 'my' net, a small, dark, lively fellow, whose name I searched for among the Surrey scores, usually in vain. So strong was Surrey's batting that room could rarely be found for him, though as twelfth man he sometimes attracted notice by his brilliance in the outfield. Yet distinction came to him at last when he became one of the best umpires on the list and was elevated to the Test panel.

Surrey's bowling could never quite bring off the Championship on the adamantine pitches prepared by 'Bosser' Martin, a rather fierce, mustachioed figure, whose devotion to his Nottingham-marled square seemed scarcely to extend to the outfield, which I recall as being sometimes as rough as the middle was smooth.

Fender, however, with two quivering gear-changes in his run-up, made the utmost of his attack of Bill Hitch, who had real pace, as also had his equally stout-hearted successor, Alf Gover; of Alan Peach, afterwards mentor to the Bedser twins, who really swung the new ball; of Tom Rushby, the stock medium-pacer; and, not least, of his own guileful leg-breaks and googlies.

Six times Fender did the double of a thousand runs and a hundred wickets. Nearly 20,000 runs he scored, besides taking nearly 2000 wickets, and as a county captain did he ever have a superior, either before or since?

As his anniversary comes up with the three-day county game (and therefore, ultimately, Test cricket itself) under threat it is an apt moment to stress that Fender was a personality who always did his best to see that the public got its money's worth.

Northampton, not his beloved Oval, was the setting for a spectacular Fender performance that has not been equalled sixty-two years later – his hundred in the record time of 35 minutes. With Peach (200 not out) as partner, 171 runs were made in 42 minutes.

So one could continue almost ad infinitum to bring back the past, looking at it no doubt with the rose-tinted spectacles of riper years.

Let me conclude with the freshest memory of all. On 17 August 1926 I sneaked off from Fleet Street to The Oval, not, alas, in time to enjoy the famous stand between Hobbs and Sutcliffe on the sticky wicket. I saw Hobbs's off-bail tickled by Jack Gregory (172 for 1, last man 100) and watched Sutcliffe carrying on with successive partners until Mailey bowled him for 161 in the last over of the day. Another illicit visit the following afternoon gave me the final scenes of Wilfred Rhodes baffling the Australians with spin and flight, and of the youthful Percy Chapman leading his men through a wildly excited crowd, the Ashes – at long last – safely gathered in.

THE DAILY TELEGRAPH
20 AUGUST 1982

―――――――――― *Ties Will Be Worn* ――――――――――

Hoppers' Tie Club Dinner in the pavilion at Canterbury. Its origin is a sidelight of social history. There are today around 500 of us, all having been proposed for membership by someone who has played cricket for Kent. Qualification is Kent connection by either birth, marriage or residence. It happened thus: once upon a time (i.e., 1939) Kent CCC decided to have a tie, a red one with white horse insignia. A famous professional tried to buy one; was told they were not to be sold to pros. 'But it's to be a birthday present for my father.' No success. Orders were orders. Not exactly gruntled, the famous one informed his fellow pros. Result: 'We'll have our own —— tie.' Hence the blue tie with motifs of hops and barrels. If not worn on Mondays members, on being challenged, are required to purchase a ½ bin (or ½ pint) for members present, up to a maximum of ten. Officers of the club have titles – Binman, Picker, Measurer, etc. Leslie Ames is our Hop Controller and President, Derek Underwood his Assistant. How very English! How very Kentish!

DIARY
5 OCTOBER 1982

I Zingari –
Welcome Everywhere

I Zingari, founded in 1845, is by some way the oldest of the wandering clubs, the original prototype of those many nomadic bodies which own no premises of their own and are yet welcome on club and school and Services grounds the length and breadth of the United Kingdom, and even beyond.

In these egalitarian days it may seem an anachronism that a club so selective in its membership should still be tottering along, despite the surrender within the last decade or so of almost all the southern resident clubs to the stern regimentation of League cricket, which had for long been the order of the day in the North and Midlands.

Yet while the leagues have multiplied, bringing a keener and more competitive edge to the club game, there has proved still to be room also for well-organized wandering clubs of varying stature for whom a friendly match, strenuously contested, is an end in itself.

If IZ were not flourishing today its Governor and management, even with the generous support of Hambro's Bank, could hardly have envisaged bringing its chronicles, with all their quaint peculiarities, into the light of day. Nor could they have found two distinguished historians among its membership, R. L. Arrowsmith and B. J. W. Hill, to undertake the job of writing *The Story of I Zingari* (Stanley Paul, £12.95).

The ethos of the club was established at its very inauguration, which took place after dinner at a hotel in Bond Street, following a game at Harrow School. The present Governor (only the fifth in all), Lord Home of the Hirsel, in his foreword aptly describes its foundation 'in friendship, benevolence and vintage port'. When at this first meeting the question of a name was considered, one of the party, by then in a comatose state, 'suddenly murmured, "the Zingari, of course", and immediately resumed his vinous slumber'.

Next day the four founders informed a certain W. P. Bolland that he was the perpetual president (which he still is, though dead for a century or more) and twenty-one of their friends that they were Zingaros or gypsies, of which it is the Italian translation. Among the early members was William Ward, a figure to whom cricket is for ever in debt since when the Eyre Estate was prepared to allow Thomas Lord's ground to be substantially built on, Ward, a director of the Bank of England and MP for the City of London, stepped in and bought Lord's lease for £5000.

Thirty years after Waterloo and the opening of the present Lord's ground, I Zingari were in the van of the great mid-Victorian cricket expansion, of which the central figure was soon to be the young prodigy from Gloucestershire, W. G. Grace. Associated with the Canterbury Week since its foundation, I Zingari in the 1880s could give a hard game to the Australians at the Scarborough Festival. When the Hon. Ivo Bligh took to Australia the team that recovered the Ashes in 1882–3 he had with him three fellow Zingaros, A. G. Steel and the Studd brothers, G.B. and C.T. IZ Australia was founded in this decade.

When the Jubilee of IZ came round it was natural that it should be signalled by a first-class match at Lord's against the Gentlemen of England. This assembling of the cream of amateur talent at the dawn of the Golden Age – and when a Test match was still a rarity – attracted large crowds. The time when 'amateur' became almost a dirty word was worlds away.

The First World War naturally decimated the playing ranks, and when the average age of club cricketers (as I well recall) was distinctly older than today, IZ sides tended to be even fuller of non-benders than most.

Bob Arrowsmith records how in C. S. Crawley's first match for the club he acted as runner while a distinguished war-wounded colonel made a hundred, and when it came to fielding found himself in the deep at both ends.

It was in the 1920s that it was considered safe when batting to run to anyone wearing the IZ colours of black, red and gold. It certainly is not the case today, when the average age is probably under thirty and the standard in all three departments – and, equally, of sportsmanship – is faithfully maintained.

The authors of this nostalgic record, which wends its way to and fro from the sublime to the faintly ridiculous, have kept their story light and anecdotal.

In the 1980s IZ play just over thirty days' cricket, almost half of it, remarkable to relate, on country-house grounds. The membership (of all ages, 1200 strong plus 170-odd of IZ Australia) is drawn from a wider range of schools than of old.

The ancient rule applies, that a candidate is never informed that he is up for election, and hence there are no sore feelings if he is not approved. There is still keen competition to play both for IZ and against it; and it remains the only club whose match results are annually published in *Wisden*, as they have been for more than a century.

THE DAILY TELEGRAPH
19 OCTOBER 1982

The Public Comes First

PART ONE

It should come first, since without its continuing support and interest the first-class game must be doomed. Such public patronage is, naturally, the more difficult to foster and maintain in a time of recession. When a man who thinks of taking his son to a big match, say, two hours' journey away, works out the cost of fares, admission, and sustenance for the day at upwards of £40, he may take the plunge. But if when the two of them return home they are not satisfied that everything reasonable has been done for their entertainment and convenience the odds are there will be no next time. They will tend to stay put and watch the telly – and, to hold their attention indoors, the quality of the play and of the commentary, even so, must be acceptable likewise.

The question therefore arises: how conscious are those concerned – players, umpires, selectors, the TCCB and county committees – of the urgent need to keep public relations, as one might say, in good repair? At best I would suggest that, in the language of the school report, the general answer is 'Could do better'.

A special cause for irritation is the regular loss of playing time for bad light. Umpires are frequently guilty of pronouncing the light unfit when it is merely dull – and when they offer the option to the batsmen it is nearly always accepted – even when it might be thought tactically advantageous to the batting side to play on.

A classic case was England opting to go off on the Saturday evening of the Lord's Test against Pakistan with 3 runs needed to save following on. Result: anti-climax for the spectators and failure next morning. The loss of 50 minutes at the end of the Saturday of Canterbury Week probably shifted the balance of the game against Kent who, I grieve to say, were the batting side.

Most cricketers will agree, if they are pressed, that *indifferent* light is no great handicap, except in the case of real pace and a new batsman. I am not referring, of course, to the gloom before a storm. Umpires are often far too pernickety about both light and the fitness of the ground after rain – to the justifiable irritation of the paying customer. The pace of their walk, out and back, seldom suggests they really *want* the game to resume.

While I am about it, let me jump once more on an old hobby-horse of mine – the notice that greets every spectator at every gate and turnstile: 'Play not guaranteed. No money returned.' What could be less welcoming? There are difficulties, admittedly, in the event of no cricket being possible, in offering free admission next day to Test matches, because of upsetting advance bookings – though here some gesture of retribution should not be beyond the wit of the TCCB. But as regards County Championship matches the offer of a transfer to another day would not (sad to say) cause overcrowding difficulties, and the psychological gain of that ancient notice being amended would be considerable.

There is much more to be said on the topic of public relations, not least in regard to the attitude of players, and especially captains. (I cannot forget England's supine performance against India at The Oval in July.) I will hope therefore shortly to return to it.

The Public Comes First

PART TWO

Continuing my remarks on this all-important subject, let me first pose the question: how conscious are captains and the administrators behind them of the need to communicate positively and sympathetically with the paying customers, be they county members or those who come in through the turnstiles?

It goes much against the grain to criticize Bob Willis, since in respect of courage and determination he is an example to all. But if we turn our minds back to the last day of the Third Test against India at The Oval in July he gave surely a horribly insensitive comment on a day's cricket, which John Woodcock described as 'unacceptable', and for which some of his fellow writers had a ruder name.

The situation was that England, one up in the series, began their second innings on the penultimate evening 184 runs ahead with an hour's play left. Whereupon they jogged complacently for 250 minutes to 191 for 3, Willis's declaration leaving his opponents (lacking Gavaskar, their leading batsman) 376 to win and England a mere 160 minutes in which to bowl them out. India lost three wickets for 43, but then successfully dug in; Willis and Botham bowled only 4 overs apiece, and the game petered sadly out.

The England captain's summing-up of a game thus allowed to die was merely that this was a Test match, 'not a bun-fight'. Because of the damage to the image of cricket that this anti-climax created, did not the *Times* correspondent's criticism next morning hit the nail fairly on the head?

> Several times this season Willis has said that it is beyond his comprehension why so few people have come to watch these Test matches against India. Yet yesterday he was content to spare no thought for those who went to The Oval. This, no doubt, is what modern cricketers would call professionalism. More accurately, it shows a devastating ignorance of what wonderful surprises cricket holds, let alone when, as now, one side, tired after much fielding, is without its finest player.

After England's narrow victory at Headingley in the corresponding Test against Pakistan, Willis, in an otherwise reasonable statement, threw in the remark that some of his opponents had batted 'like buffoons'. What does this sort of thing achieve other than to inflame wounded pride in the opposition? The volume and frequency of Pakistani appealing in this series must have made umpiring a misery, as well as being counter-productive in terms alike of public support and umpiring performance.

Compare the attitude and behaviour of the top golfers to those of the leading exponents of other popular games. Whereas the performance of the latter, both in word and deed, is all too often the utter negation of sportsmanship as it has always been understood, the golfers – with even more of the cash, which is held to be responsible for such tensions elsewhere, at stake – come out almost invariably as civilized, likeable people, fit to be the heroes of aspiring youth.

The fact is that the R and A, the USGA and the other governing bodies of golf do everything they can to *enhance* the image of golf, and in this the top Americans undoubtedly lead the way. It may reasonably be argued that their Association has more readily amenable material to work on. A more significant point is, surely, that before the American golfer wins the Players' Card that allows him to play on the professional circuit he has to emerge successfully from a course in golf etiquette and public relations. Thereafter, any breaches attract appropriate penalties.

The mass of the cricket-loving public – excluding an alien element attracted by limited-over cricket – wants to see sporting standards preserved and the present playing generation revered, as were their predecessors, for the men they were. At a time when public support has never been more crucial, cricket authority at all levels must reinforce its efforts to preserve the standards enshrined in the age-old phrase. The TCCB might well take a leaf out of the USGA's book.

THE CRICKETER
NOVEMBER 1982

Opening Pairs
Still at a Premium

Whichever two batsmen walk out together to open the England innings at Perth this coming weekend it will come as a pleasant surprise to us in England if the partnership is successful. We wish them well, indeed, but not even established English pairings have in recent years built a steady foundation against Australian bowling.

If William Frindall is to be believed – and he is rarely caught out – only four of England's last thirty opening innings against Australia have raised 50, and only one of these four has gone on to three figures. Boycott has been involved in all thirty of these innings, mostly with Gooch, sometimes with Brearley and once with Larkins. No one will need reminding that none of these four is now with England in Australia. Yet, reluctant as he is to open and inordinately slow as his progress has been, Tavaré's record as number one since he first shouldered the job in India less than a year ago, is an advance on that of his immediate predecessors. In thirteen innings he and one of four different partners have raised partnerships of 155, 106, 103, 96, 82 and 62: surprising, perhaps, but true.

Nor are England alone in the lack of an established opening pair. Wood and Dyson have done reasonably well together without striking the sort of apprehension one felt at the names of Lawry and Simpson, or Barnes and Morris, still less Woodfull and Ponsford. When I was young there was something specially quelling in the sight of those two Bills walking slowly in together: Woodfull, 'The Unbowlable', and Ponsford of the broad and (for those days) heavy bat and sure footwork, each conscious of the job in hand – to make a sure foundation for the arrival of the conqueror, Bradman.

Yet how must our old enemies have felt when for seven rubbers out of eight – he was ill in 1921 – covering twenty years, they knew they would be confronted 'first up', as they say in Australia, by Hobbs, greatest of all professional batsmen, and one of those two indomitable Yorkshiremen, Rhodes and Sutcliffe.

Later, of course, came Hutton and Washbrook, since when there have been several successful partnerships of brief duration, notably those of Cowdrey with first Richardson and then Pullar, left-handers both.

Boycott and Amiss looked set fair to make history together when from 1974 to 1977 Boycott opted out of Test cricket. There has been a natural affinity between most of the great pairings, and it is not the least extraordinary thing about Boycott, who has scored more Test runs than anyone in history, that he has done so, both for Yorkshire and England, with so many partners.

Why is it that in Test and, for that matter, county cricket opening pairs today are at such a premium? It is true that the average playing life is briefer by a good deal, and hence the turn-round more frequent. Holmes and Sutcliffe, after all, held the stage together for nearly twenty years, Hobbs and first Hayward and then Sandham for rather longer.

I think that the greater accent on speed in bowling rather than spin has a good deal to do with it. With faster bowlers taking most of the wickets it follows that they are likely to strike earlier when the ball is new.

Seven of the thirteen batsmen in history with 40,000 runs to their credit have batted regularly at number one, and three of the remaining six often did so in county cricket. Nowadays I would hazard that the ideal batting place is number four.

Whatever the causes of the paucity, the discerning spectator is the loser. The closeness of understanding between two fine players was clear to see: their instinctive, often tacit judgement of a run; the unselfish subordination of one to the other – for in most of the great pairings one was the readier stroke-player, the other the less demonstrative half.

THE DAILY TELEGRAPH
9 NOVEMBER 1982

1983

MCC CHALLENGED
ON SOUTH AFRICA

Assorted Test Reflections

My intention this month was to devote my brief to comment on the First Test at Perth in the light of what one saw of it on television. But the fact is I found the 'highlights' as put across on the Packer channel sadly lacking in news-sense, in critical appreciation and balance.

In the first place what could be more fatuous, with minutes at a premium, than allowing Tony Greig to open the proceedings armed with gadgets purporting to show the degree of moisture left in the pitch, the humidity above ground and so on, grinning away as though on a 'commercial spot' – which, come to think of it, I suppose he was.

On the day of the crowd invasion minutes went by before it was disclosed that anything untoward had occurred. Then, despite the number of cameras nowadays deployed, we saw the minimum of the whole dreadful imbroglio – just a few seconds' worth before Alderman was shown in obvious pain on the ground, and Lillee (naturally) tangling with some of the drunken and mostly English mob. What a day for cricket!

It seemed that Channel 9 were concerned to play down the hateful affair, and it was left to the BBC on the last day to show something of the crude 'anti-Pom' pre-match television ads which, it was suggested by some on the spot, might well have helped create the atmosphere that sparked off the trouble.

Even more superfluous than Greig's tricks was another bit of preamble, the showing again of key incidents not of the day's play in question but of the day before that, by now, to English followers over the air, thirty-six hours old. Only after this were we allowed to see snippets from the current day, and we had the usual intermingling of fours and wickets and vain appeals, with many playbacks. I must count the number of balls bowled (excluding playbacks) in one of these half-hour programmes and see how many we get.

However the thing is done, though, a succession of incidents cannot give viewers a balanced picture of a day's cricket. What I am sure cricket-lovers would give much for is a straight summary of the play by a professional broadcaster such as Richie Benaud or Tony Lewis – in vision without gimmicks. No one can tell me that it isn't possible to give a fair verbal impression of six hours' play in, say, three minutes, because I've done far too many of them, to the apparent satisfaction of the BBC, with scorecard in one hand and stopwatch in the other.

Luckily, we had sound radio to rely on with Messrs Martin-Jenkins, Blofeld, Trueman, Carey and our old faithful, Alan McGilvray, on hand, with most of the regular cricket writers. I suppose my forebodings before this First Test were about on a par with most others of English sympathies – in other words, we would have gladly settled, in advance, for a draw. Though it came easily enough in the end, whether it would have been achieved if Alderman's injury had not reduced Australia to three bowlers was clearly doubtful.

Robin Marlar thinks, in the *Sunday Times*, that five of the England party could with advantages be replaced – without suggesting in the least that this was likely to happen. He also, by the way, accepts the Australian marketing boss's claim that his television ads and violence among the crowd were unconnected. Lynton Taylor claims, it seems, that the promotion activities increase the profits to the Australian Board by 40 per cent in an English tour year, 20 per cent in others. What I would like Mr Marlar to adjudge for us when Bob Willis's men, after the five-Test series, finally complete in mid-February their long progression of one-day games in the triangular series against Australia and New Zealand – it's ten if they don't reach the finals, twelve or thirteen if they do – is the cost, if any, to the spirit, the traditional decencies of the game, of the new high-pressure cricket. Meanwhile, I would correct him on one point – the ruling body changed their name some years ago from the Australian Board *of Control* to the Australian Cricket Board.

But some shrewd observation on the tour is also coming from Sir Leonard Hutton in the *Observer*. Turning his attention to

Christopher Tavaré – and, as he reminded us, he had plenty of leisure at Perth in which to do so – while paying due regard to his patience, he said that he counted at least twenty half-volleys 'which managed to reach mid-off in low gear', and concluded that the left arm must be weak. Sir Leonard urged English coaches to encourage their charges to hit the half-volley, and added that in his day, against the best Australian bowling, 'if you couldn't drive you couldn't get off the mark'.

THE CRICKETER
JANUARY 1983

Ray Robinson

There are a few lucky people whose names always conjure up emotions of affection – even in the tough and unemotional world of games writers – and this was emphatically true of Ray Robinson, who died last autumn aged seventy-six. He was everyone's friend, for he exuded benevolence and had the readiest, friendliest smile imaginable. His death was anything but unexpected, for he had been extremely frail for a long time, and after having an eye removed several years ago had almost lost the sight of the other.

Robbie went on writing about the game from financial necessity, even if one can scarcely imagine his not being present from choice. Yet the fact, as told by Phil Wilkins in his *Cricketer* notice, that as an old man Ray had to make the terribly exhausting trans-continental train journey across the Nullarbor Plain to report in Perth because he could not afford the air fare, does not say much for the way journalists long past retirement age are treated in Australia.

Though his freelance work appeared in most of the cricket capitals of the world, he was for many years chief writer on the game for the *Sun* of Sydney. Such he was when the press party of fourteen descended on Australia in company with the MCC team of 1946–7. But to most of us he was a friend already, having visited England with Don Bradman's 1938 side – if not, indeed, also with Billy Woodfull's of 1934. I was lucky enough to make eight tours of Australia with MCC teams, and there was scarcely a match at

which Ray was not present, watching every ball intently, sometimes through a small pair of field glasses, making notes incessantly
in handwriting so close-spaced that how he reconstructed its
content was a perpetual mystery.

He was the last to claim a deep technical knowledge of cricket and
far too honest and sensible to pretend otherwise. He perforce relied
where necessary on the opinions of old players, and of these Bill
O'Reilly stood foremost. Match after match, series after series,
they sat together, an amiable and by no means one-sided partnership, since Ray was able to contribute, for the benefit of Bill and, for
that matter, any other of his writing friends, the fruits of truly
remarkable powers of observation of men and small, undetected
but often significant happenings.

He wrote shrewdly but with never a shred of malice – which was
why he enjoyed the confidence and respect of the players to a degree
I have not known equalled by any other cricket writer. He will be
missed especially in England by readers of *The Daily Telegraph* and
The Cricketer, for he was Australian correspondent to both for
twenty years or more.

CRICKET SOCIETY JOURNAL
JANUARY 1983

Bryan Valentine

Bryan Herbert Valentine, who has died aged seventy-five, was a
splendid cricketer for Cambridge, Kent and England and, almost
from his emergence as a Repton schoolboy, a universally popular
figure. Though cricket was the love of his life, he was an all-round
sportsman who won the Public Schools Lawn Tennis Doubles for
Repton, partnering the subsequently famous Bunny Austin, as well as
gaining his Blue at soccer and cricket. He also became a scratch golfer.

Born at Blackheath, he played first for Kent as a schoolboy and,
although with his free, wristy style he needed a year or two to
tighten his defence in county cricket, by 1932 he was one of the
leading amateur batsmen.

Chosen for D. R. Jardine's MCC tour of India in 1933–4, he made 136 at Bombay in his first Test. Under A. P. F. Chapman, with Ashdown, Woolley, Ames and Valentine at the top of the order, and the captain and other stroke-makers to follow, Kent had as attractive a batting side as any in the country.

On Chapman's retirement Valentine shared the leadership for one summer with R.T., the middle of the three Bryan brothers, and in 1938–9 went with W. R. Hammond's MCC side to South Africa. There he made another Test hundred at Cape Town.

With the onset of war he had no further chance for England, so ending with a batting average for his seven Tests of 64. Badly wounded during the war, when he won the MC, he was still able to take on the captaincy of Kent from 1946 to 1948 and even had his supporters to lead England abroad. He would have done it well for he was always cheerful and everyone enjoyed playing under him. If it could be said of any man that he never had an enemy it could be said of Bryan.

Valentine made 18,306 runs (average 30), including thirty-five hundreds, and nine times made 1000 in a season. He was president of the Kent CCC in 1967.

THE DAILY TELEGRAPH
4 FEBRUARY 1983

——— *Sitting for John Ward* ———

To John Ward, RA, for one of two sittings for a pen and wash portrait which is to decorate or otherwise the jacket of As I Said at the Time, *due out under George Plumptre's editorship in the autumn. It is to be a wrap-around cover, showing a background of the St Lawrence pavilion and tents as in Canterbury Week. I wear a Band of Brothers tie (officially Kentish grey with black stripe) and a red (artificial) rose in the buttonhole of a blue jacket. The great painter is disarming and seemingly as relaxed as could be. We talk as he works, chiefly about cricket, to which he has a strong addiction. To commission him was a great coup, entirely due to George, who is a friend.*

Ward has done five portraits for MCC – of Gubby Allen in oils and of the last four Secretaries in the medium of pen and wash, which seems to suit his understated style. He is tutor, one might say, to the Prince of Wales.

When the Prince and Princess went to Venice in Britannia *two years ago Ward went too, and they spent all available time sketching on board.*

DIARY
5 FEBRUARY 1983

────────────── *Silver Wedding* ──────────────

Our Silver Wedding anniversary. I managed to smuggle down from London for a dinner party Ann's two sons, top accountant Billy Carbutt and stockbroker Eddie, with wives Sally and Sue, plus Billy's beautiful daughter, Emma, who with her law degree is up-and-coming with Warburg's, and youthful stockbroker son, George. My wife is allergic to surprises but she enjoyed this one.

DIARY
11 FEBRUARY 1983

Doubting the Benefits of Four-day Cricket

It is inevitable that in the economic climate of English cricket, and with the loss of the Ashes to be explained away, the advocates of four-day county cricket have been buckling their pads on and practising their strokes. There is an Enquiry Committee of the TCCB sitting now to examine (yet again!) 'the future structure' of county cricket, and the pros and cons of a four-day Championship will obviously be under discussion – but, I am sure, along with other possibilities. I gather their findings are not likely to be complete by the time of the TCCB spring meeting this month – which makes any drastic change in the format unlikely for 1984, though not impossible.

Personally, I greatly hope that the twenty-four match three-day programme will be given a go, as they say 'down under', for the next two summers, whatever changes, if any, are effected in the limited-over competitions. I like the logic of 'twenty-four', which is a fairer test of merit in that every county can play every other three times over two seasons. I like the prospect of every county cricketer getting more first-class innings in the season, and since more county matches must coincide with Tests, I welcome the extra opportunities that will be provided for up-and-coming cricketers deputizing for those away playing for their country.

Not least I like the fact that county members will be getting an extra six days' first-class cricket for their subscription, and that, in some counties at least, there may be the chance of showing the game to places which have unfortunately had to be bypassed since the introduction of the Benson and Hedges led to the drastic cutting-down of the Championship programme from twenty-eight matches to twenty-two. On the face of it the two extra matches must add to expenditure at a time when every county treasurer must be striving to keep costs down. Yet the present programme must be a spur to membership and also to sponsors at local level. Their patronage has never been so important.

As to four-day county cricket, Christopher Martin-Jenkins propounded in February's editorial in his usual fair-minded way several of the arguments for and against. Was it a better preparation for Test cricket? Would not bowlers need to attack more rather than contain? I would be more inclined to concede the second point than the first, though given positive leadership surely there is almost sufficient incentive for the bowler already. A better preparation for Tests? Does a maximum of thirty-two innings for batsmen to bat and bowlers to bowl, spread over four days, give more prospect of graduating to the highest class than a maximum of forty-eight innings, spread over three? I would say not, and would add with all the emphasis my shaky old pen can summon that what county captains and coaches need to bend their minds and energies to right away is the basic techniques of batting and bowling, and especially of batting.

There are not a few county cricketers who think that they 'know it all', and they can only be left to wallow in their own conceit. But is there not a more intelligent element prepared to be convinced that the orthodox way of playing is, for ordinary mortals, the best: that it is easier when batting to judge length and direction if the head is kept still; that the longer the blade of the bat is swung vertically down the line of the ball, whether playing forward or back, the better the chance of its being truly hit; that the pick-up of the bat and the follow-through are easier if the back of the top hand is facing mid-off rather than point? Etcetera, etcetera.

Note that I say 'easier', not that 'you must'. There is a degree to which great players are a law to themselves, and there is still room, thank Heaven, for glorious eccentrics like Derek Randall. Likewise an established player can scarcely be expected to turn his method inside out. Equally, a comparatively small adjustment, either in technique or mental attitude or both, can mean a lot. And I need scarcely add that I am prompted to write by the horrifying disregard of technique, both in batting and bowling, which we have had to endure, played, replayed, and as additional torture repeated in slow motion from every angle on our television screens this winter.

Though the England team mirrored to the point almost of distortion the current weaknesses of English cricket it was good to see how the quartet who had not been required in the Tests – Gould, Marks, Jackman and Jesty – all made important contributions in the one-day stuff.

So in the end almost everyone had a performance or two at least to show for oh, so many thousand miles of internal travel, so many packings and unpackings, so unnaturally peripatetic a tour *à la mode* 1982–3.

THE CRICKETER
MARCH 1983

OMT Celebrations

OMT Centenary. Rugger dinners are lively affairs, and not always respecters of persons. Should I accept their surprising invitation to propose the toast of the evening? Historically, they have been the leading Old Boys' club and in some years about the most successful side in London. It was an honour for me and to my old club that an OC should be asked. So I accepted and faced two or three hundred of all ages in the Porter Tun Room of Whitbread's in the City. Happily, they were kind to the old stiff on positively my last football engagement. In the Chair, T. F. Huskisson, a grand forward of the 1930s, and the penultimate of OMT's twelve Internationals.

DIARY
25 MARCH 1983

Fate of Hastings

The future of the Central Cricket Ground at Hastings is in some jeopardy. And it will come as a disagreeable shock to the world of cricket that the fate of this famous home of the game, as it has been for upwards of a century, is being decided by a ministerial inquiry now in progress. I understand that those opposing the proposal to turn the ground into a shopping precinct can voice their objections tomorrow.

When cricket ceased at Bramall Lane, Sheffield, Yorkshire were deprived of their earliest home, but loud though the lamentations were and grievous the loss, at least Sheffield United were utilizing the whole area for football. But to blot out history for a shopping precinct. . . .

H. E. H. Gabriel, the former president of the Forty Club, who played much club cricket on the Hastings ground, assures me there are alternative near-derelict sites conveniently available. I would not wish to venture into local politics further than to record his contention, but the thought that a field of such historic associations plumb in the middle of Hastings, overlooked by the castle and almost within sound of the sea, may disappear is hard to bear.

It was at the Hastings Festival that Sir Donald Bradman made the last but one of his hundreds in England, here that Denis Compton broke Tom Hayward's record of 3518 runs in a season. Maurice Tate used to say that Hastings was his favourite ground.

In one of the great local Derbies betweenSussex and Kent in 1929 'Duleep' made 115 in the first innings and 246 in the second. More recently, Ted Dexter also made a double-hundred there. Most memorable of all was the ultimate in G. L. Jessop's feats of hitting. For Gentlemen v Players of the South he made his first hundred in forty-two minutes and in all 191 in an hour and a half. There were thirty fours and only five sixes, because in 1907 the ball had to be hit out of the ground to earn six.

One such six landed in a garden in Devonshire Road, another through a window in Station Road, the owner of which was reluctant to return the ball. Yet another, according to the late Henry Grierson, as he was hurrying into the ground, landed among the hansom cabs not far from the town hall.

The ground was conveyed to the people of Hastings for use as a recreation and pleasure ground by the Cornwallis family for a consideration of £5000 in 1872. It is administered as a charitable trust and is used chiefly by the prosperous Hastings and St Leonard's Priory CC. Sussex nowadays play only one match a season at Hastings; current policy is to concentrate on Hove. But fashions and circumstances change, and if the developers win, Sussex and cricket will have lost this landmark for ever.

THE DAILY TELEGRAPH
12 APRIL 1983

───────────── *Grace by His Grace* ─────────────

The MCC Anniversary Dinner was dignified by the Archbishop of Canterbury, whose speech gave much pleasure. G. O. Allen was also pleased to approve his grace, which Robert Runcie accordingly wrote out for him. This was it:

> For food and drink and friendship
> We render thanks.
> Bless, O Lord, our table,
> Deepen our gratitude,
> Enlarge our Sympathies,
> Order our affections in generous and unselfish lives.
> Amen.

DIARY
4 MAY 1983

Thoughts on the Captaincy

When an England team returns empty-handed from Australia the captain's position is almost automatically in jeopardy. If he is a cricketer in the mould of a May or a Dexter he may well survive. Otherwise his tenure of office is strongly threatened. The present instance is unusual only in that Bob Willis has said, and repeated, that whereas he is keen to carry on he does not consider his vice-captain, David Gower, ready for the job.

On the face of it this is a naïve comment only to be interpreted in the light of the modern custom whereby the media urge the interviewee to blurt out his inmost thoughts. 'Honest Bob' obliged, intending, I am sure, only to be helpful and without any disparagement of young Gower. One cannot imagine, say, Arthur Gilligan making the same sort of comment on Percy Chapman after his 1924–5 tour, or, for that matter, Mike Denness about Tony Greig half a century later. Other times, other ways.

Willis has a point when he observes that our finest young batsman should be allowed time to consolidate his reputation as a world-class player without being distracted by the heavy burdens of leadership. Ideally, it is better if the captain is not one of the linchpins of the batting. Equally, the ideal captain is unlikely to be a fast bowler and number eleven batsman. Willis has shown an admirable example of wholehearted endeavour, but it was depressing to read of two or three hands, in moments of crisis, manipulating the field.

The fact is one could scarcely read a report from Australia, or listen to a commentary, without sighing vainly for Mike Brearley. The captaincy qualities of Brearley, both with Middlesex and England, need little underlining from me. He is a man of exceptional intellect with something akin to genius at managing people – in getting their respect and total co-operation – as well as in his tactical reading of the game.

While there is no Brearley on the horizon it is worth reminding ourselves that while he was establishing a reputation as one of our best of all England captains he batted sixty-six times in Tests, mostly as an opener, without making a hundred. His average overall was 22.88, and he picked up fifty-two catches, nearly all in the slips. As a batsman he was easily replaceable.

In theory, the likeliest candidate would be a cricketer with proved leadership qualities who was at least near the fringe of the best team. Preferably, perhaps, he should be an all-rounder who could set a first-rate example in the field. As one surveys the county ranks the name of Johnny Barclay suggests itself. At twenty-nine he is a good age. But it is asking too much, probably, to give the captaincy *in* England to someone without a Test cap.

Among other county captains Geoffrey Cook was clearly in the selectors' minds as a possible leader, and can be no longer. Roger Knight, another possible of a few years ago, now thirty-eight, is in modern terms in the sere and yellow. Brian Rose has led Somerset to great success these last five years and as a left-handed bat was by no means a failure in his nine Tests before eye-trouble set him back. He may be just in the selectors' sights still. So, surely, will be Chris Tavaré, a quiet, dedicated cricketer who is to have his first taste of leadership with Kent this summer. This may not completely exhaust the list of possibles – the names of Edmonds and Marks may occur to some – but it is close to doing so.

So one is brought back to Gower, and Willis's warning. Gower has everything, as they say, going for him. He is intelligent, popular, and, in any utterances I have noticed in print, agreeably tactful. Temperamentally he must be better equipped for leadership than Ian Botham – and yet the latter, reputedly, was Brearley's own pick as his successor. Tony Lewis, an England captain himself ten years ago and so closer to the current players than most of his fellow critics, plumps solidly, I notice, for Gower. Is it in England's best interest that the risk to his own form be taken? Well, with the Prudential Cup little more than a month away we must soon know.

THE CRICKETER
MAY 1983

Struck by Gout

Health note. Ascending to the guest room of Magdalene College, Cambridge, after a very enjoyable but far from bibulous evening, my right foot suddenly became painful. In bed it quickly got worse, as if the limb was on fire. I tried an armchair, then lying on the floor. It was torture and I slept not a wink. In the morning I rang my old POW friend, James Noble, living very close, with whom I had been watching Kent against the University at Fenner's. Thanks to him a lady doctor arrived who diagnosed gout and supplied plenty of the pain-remover Indocid. She forbade me to drive, which I was unable to do anyway because of the swollen foot. So the good James drove me home in my car, and returned by train. Humiliating. I had had attacks before, but nothing like this. My doctor prescribed the specific, Zyloric, which I've taken daily for six years now, without any twinge or a recurrence. I scarcely need to say that drink and gout have only a remote relationship, and it's only something funny if you don't get it.

DIARY
6 MAY 1983

Kent Nurseries –
Ancient and Modern

Kent throughout their history have relied as largely as possible on home-grown material, and – if one leaves Yorkshire out of consideration – their teams down the years have contained a higher proportion of native talent than those of any other county. Yet, in this age of overseas importations and freer movement between counties, it is specially notable that in 1983 the Kent staff of twenty is composed, with one exception only, of men either born or brought up in Kent or, in most cases, both.

There has been only one period in Kent's history when they could not be accounted one of the leading counties, that between 1948 and 1963. It was broadly the case then that aspiring young hopefuls came to the county for trials rather than the club looking for them. There were also some rather dubious recruitments from outside. The club has enjoyed, of course, two periods of outstanding success, the first from 1906 to 1914 and the second between 1967 and 1978, the significant thing being that each phase was the culmination of a fresh policy on the coaching front.

The establishment of the Kent Nursery, which functioned on the Angel ground at Tonbridge between 1897 and 1927, was the most important decision in the story of Kent's cricket, the foundation of the Nursery's success being the personality and dedication of one man, Captain William McCanlis. Though rich in amateur talent – as Kent have always been until the abolition of the independent cricketer in 1962 – the county club (which really meant its benevolent despot, Lord Harris) realized that for a consistent high standard a strong professional nucleus was necessary. Thus, there came under the spell of McCanlis in their formative years a youthful bevy of talent of which the most was made, so that by 1906 Kent's first Championship-winning side contained either five or all six of the following: Fielder, Blythe and Frank Woolley, famous Test cricketers all, and Humphreys, Seymour and Fairservice, a trio of sterling worth who also served the county long and faithfully.

Before McCanlis's retirement and the First World War, the Nursery had also brought out the redoubtable 'Tich' Freeman, a fifth England cricketer in Hardinge, and stout county men in

Hubble and Collins, not forgetting several such as Murrell, for twenty years the Middlesex wicket-keeper, and Claude Woolley, Frank's elder brother, who gave good service to Northamptonshire. McCanlis clearly taught the basic orthodoxies which in all departments of the game are changeless, but I recall with what gratitude and respect the greatest of his products, Frank Woolley, always spoke of him. 'Everyone wanted to please him' – a coach can have no more valuable attribute than this.

A point which both Frank and Sir Jack Hobbs used to make was how the best amateur batting of the Edwardian years shaped both their method and their attitude. In the 1906 Canterbury Week, Kent made 568 and 479 respectively against Sussex and Lancashire, each time at over 100 an hour, most of the runs scored by the amateurs, Burnup, Hutchings, Dillon, Mason and Blaker, the five who headed the averages, with a hundred also from Marsham, the captain.

The speed of Fielder and the spin of Blythe saw to it that both matches were won by an innings. Everything came together for Kent in 1906, for they were also rated by good judges – though this was pre-1970s – the best fielding side ever to play for the county. It was in those nine seasons, 1906–14, that Kent were acknowledged – as was never disputed afterwards until the decline around 1950 – the fastest batting side in England. That, too, must be attributed largely to the establishment of the Nursery.

There was no replacing the genius of McCanlis, the coaching being in the 1920s in the hands of a loveable, highly idiosyncratic, theory-ridden, umbrella-waving G. J. V. (Gerry) Weigall – of whom it was said that all his geese were swans. (But Les Ames was a swan right enough!) In 1927 the Nursery moved to Canterbury, and soon afterwards Punter Humphreys on his retirement took charge. So he continued until 1949 when he was succeeded by Claude Lewis, a slow left-arm bowler in his playing days, who has served the county now for half a century.

The next significant date in Kent's coaching story is 1960, when Colin Page, an off-spinner who had taken over 500 wickets for the county, was offered the job of taking over the Second XI by Mr Ames, the secretary/manager. To this Page gradually added a programme of winter coaching at the indoor schools which were available at strategic points within the county. This was the period of a big surge in the organization of boys' cricket throughout the country, with Kent's Schools Cricket Association and the Association of Kent Cricket Clubs, under the inspiration of Bryan Valentine, very much in the van. Today Page is president of the KSCA, which caters for boys of every age from twelve upwards. There is scarcely a member of the Kent teams of the 1970s and 1980s whom he has not spotted and helped on his upward climb. He has a way with boys and young men, just as McCanlis used to have – and, thank goodness, also like McCanlis he is firm on discipline.

Behind the ten caps currently playing in the XI there is much fine material awaiting its chance – as all the old players had to do, from Woolley and Ames downwards: Potter, Aslett, Ellison, Penn and Hinks perhaps top the list but they by no means exhaust it. It is more than just a loyal hope that, granted strong leadership, fresh Kentish honours may soon be on the way.

THE CRICKETER
JULY 1983

In Defence of MCC

It is only in the natural order of things nowadays that traditional institutions must expect to undergo regular attack. MCC is certainly one such, a target second only perhaps in frequency to the Church of England.

Last year the MCC Committee withstood by wide margins motions put by members regarding major development plans and also concerning its own constitution. Despite these votes of confidence a working party comprising members both from within and outside the Committee was at once set up to examine the way the Club functions as well as its broader role in the game today.

I write with another and more serious members' motion in the balance, that urging the sending by MCC of a team to South Africa. The result of the vote will be known by the time this issue is on sale, and one need only say here that if this proposal should succeed the question as to whether MCC should or should not continue to shoulder its public role (to which the working party have answered yes) will probably be decided automatically to the contrary.

If there is a mandate to send an MCC team to South Africa this winter the consequences would gravely affect the future public function of MCC, as the Committee explained in the circular to members published in last month's *Cricketer*.

Assuming the MCC Committee successfully wards off the attack on the South Africa matter, can any experienced, well-informed follower of cricket seriously doubt that MCC should still endeavour to play a part in the governance of the game in this ultra-commercial and competitive age?

Cricket authority in England is not, thank Heaven, as Australia's is, beholden to financial forces to whom the traditions and ethos of the game mean nothing. But with the old accepted standards everywhere under threat there surely must be value in the continued influence on the Cricket Council and the TCCB of what is at least a relatively disinterested body with a unique record of service to cricket.

There are those who take a contrary view, holding that MCC, having in 1968 presided over the curtailing of its former powers, should now voluntarily relinquish the rest. This was the line taken in the July *Cricketer* by Anthony Swainson, the retired naval captain who directs the affairs of that admirably benevolent body, the Lord's Taverners. I was puzzled by his line of argument for he seemed to be calling for MCC to be divested of its public function in one paragraph and yet going on to urge closer liaison with the other bodies (agreed!) and much increased effort in the way of fund-raising, sponsorship, public relations and 'a common secretariat'. Would patrons want to subsidize a 'private club' and if they did would its members wish to be under such an obligation?

Captain Swainson questions also why MCC should continue to act as the game's Law-makers – as they have been, incidentally, since 1788, only a year after the Club's foundation. This would indeed be a valid point if MCC acted arbitrarily in amending the Laws and making new ones. But as it is they are merely doing what they have done since the first Imperial Cricket Conference in 1909 brought together the then Test-playing countries, a body to which all countries, under its modern title (wherein the 'I' now stands for International), are members. All points of law and suggestions for amendment are directed to the Secretary of MCC, and no basic change is made without the approval of the ICC.

Declaring an interest as one of the more venerable members of the Committee, I would merely offer two personal thoughts concerning the services of members to the Club. Firstly, on the matter of age, it is obviously desirable that the nucleus of those serving on all committees should be men in the prime of life. Yet this is the age group which finds it hardest to give to Lord's meetings the time which the affairs of the Club demand: and the more successful such men are in their professional or business lives, the greater are the pressures on their day. Equally, they are probably at the stage when family demands are greatest. So which is more satisfactory from the Club's point of view – to appoint an able fellow who with the best will in the world can only be an irregular attender, or someone of ability and experience recently retired who is in a much better position to offer his time and energies?

Lastly, I would just underline the necessarily unobtrusive but valuable work which has been done over many years by the specialist sub-committees of MCC. The members of these sub-committees are experts in their own fields. Some have been the guardians of MCC's property and treasures; some have been concerned with the smooth running of its manifold activities. The exercise at present being undertaken requires a slimming-down of committee work while retaining the expertise and experience of which our great Club stands in need.

THE CRICKETER
AUGUST 1983

Lord Wakefield:
Giant of the 1920s

Lord Wakefield of Kendal, who has died aged eighty-five, was a man of boundless vitality and wide accomplishment. The basis of his long career in public life was his fame as one of the greatest rugby footballers of his or any other generation. Between 1920 and 1927 William Wavell Wakefield, popularly known as 'Wakers', won thirty-one caps for England, a number that stood as a record for more than forty years.

That this was such a halcyon period for England was even more his doing than that of several other brilliant players of the period, such as W. J. A. Davies, C. A. Kershaw, Tom Voyce and C. N. Lowe. For, besides being a forward with outstanding gifts and an apparently indestructible physique, he was a tactical thinker in advance of his time and so a notable captain in due turn of every team he played for: Sedbergh School, the RAF, Cambridge, Leicester, Harlequins, Middlesex and, of course, England.

Howard Marshall, a distinguished former rugby football correspondent of *The Daily Telegraph*, wrote of him: 'Everything about him was as solid as the trunk of a tree. He would have made a great heavyweight boxer, and in addition to his strength he was exceptionally fast. . . . He was that rare thing, the complete footballer.'

As was to be expected, he became a leading administrator with many years of service on the Rugby Union (of which he was president in 1950–1) and on the International Board. He succeeded as Harlequin president another great player, Adrian Stoop, in what has always been a life appointment.

Wakefield fought as an airman in both wars and retained throughout his life the keenest interest in things aeronautical. Elected first to Parliament in 1935 as Conservative member for Swindon, he was promoted the following year to the first of several parliamentary private secretaryships.

At the height of the war (1942–4), aged forty-four, he was made Director of the Air Training Corps, which during his tenure sent almost 100,000 cadets into the RAF and the Fleet Air Arm. In 1944 he was knighted for 'political and public services'. He represented St Marylebone from 1945 until elevated to the House of Lords in 1963.

Wakefield was a director of several companies chiefly connected with air transport and building, and served on many executives for good causes, including the YMCA, National Playing Fields, and projects involving the Lake District.

He was a competent athlete and cricketer, and took enthusiastically to skiing, winning the Kandahar Gold and other awards, and becoming president of the Ski Club of Great Britain, the British

Sub-Aqua Club and the British Water Ski Federation. After a double operation for arthritis of the hips this dedicated exponent of 'the full life' was still skiing in his late seventies.

Lady Wakefield died in 1981. They had three daughters, so there is no heir to the title.

THE DAILY TELEGRAPH
16 AUGUST 1983

Ranji's Magic Touch

The life story of His Highness the Maharajah Jam Saheb of Nawanagar, known universally as Ranji, is one that far transcended the cricket field, although it was his eminence as a cricketer which enabled him in the eyes of the ordinary Englishman to put India on the map.

The superficial picture of Ranji as the rich, bejewelled prince who suddenly took the sporting world by storm at the end of the Victorian era is only half true.

Brought to Cambridge as the secretly adopted heir to the small Indian state – and with little money – before his sixteenth birthday, he conceived a passion for cricket and a determination to excel at it.

The great open space of Parker's Piece was his training ground, as it was of Jack Hobbs a few years later. It was there that a marvellously keen eye and a shrewd, analytical brain became co-ordinated to a degree which gradually commanded more than local attention. In separate matches on different pitches on the Piece he once made three hundreds in a day.

It was in his third year as an undergraduate in 1893 that F. S. Jackson gave him a Blue, *Wisden* noting his brilliance as a slip and remarking that 'the young Indian . . . is not likely to forget the reception accorded him by the public when he played in London'. The popularity so swiftly established exploded when, having now qualified for Sussex in 1895, he came right to the front, scoring 77 not out and 150 and taking six wickets in his first match for the county, at Lord's.

There now began also the lifelong collaboration with C. B. Fry, first on the field with Sussex and later in the many other aspects of Ranji's life. On the face of it, Ranji was the natural genius, Fry the exact craftsman. But it was together that they analysed the technique of batting, each basing his play on the back-stroke, to which Ranji added his own hallmark of the leg glance and every variety of the cut.

For a decade their names were synonymous with Sussex, Ranji first taking over the captaincy and then passing it on to Fry. It was evidence of Ranji's social charms as well as his outstanding skill that within a few years he emerged as a universally acclaimed figure on the English scene. He entertained royally – though generally pressed for money. He shot and fished. If the years around the turn of the century were cricket's Golden Age it was he more than anyone who helped make it so.

In *Ranji, Prince of Cricketers* (Collins, £10.95) Alan Ross gives us a fond picture of the man in all his roles. At first disinherited, he was installed as the Jam Saheb in 1907, and promptly gave himself to the administration and general improvement of his state.

When war came he was foremost among the princes in showing his intense loyalty to the Empire. He and his Nawanagar State Lancers were soon in France, along with field hospitals and motor ambulances, Ranji being posted as ADC to Sir John French, the commander-in-chief.

On sick leave in England recovering from the asthma which persistently plagued him, Ranji lost the sight of one eye in a shooting accident. It was characteristic of him that he was hit while protecting from a notoriously erratic shot the daughter of his old Cambridge mentor, the chaplain of Trinity. Also, that he kept the culprit's name secret and to allay suspicion invited him to his next shoot.

After the war sterner matters occupied the closing years of his life. With Charles Fry beside him he represented India at the League of Nations, and when the future constitution of India became the burning issue of the 1920s he helped form the Chamber of Princes and resigned the Chancellorship immediately before his death.

The joy of his last years lay in the rich fulfilment of the batting skill of his nephew, Duleep. My own first – and last – sight of Ranji was at the Lord's Test of 1930, which he attended in full Indian dress, to see Duleep's glorious innings of 173 – a display that he himself could scarcely have bettered.

Born in India and always a Sussex man, Mr Ross has found a subject dear to his heart. He has researched it thoroughly and produced a perfect addition to the history and literature of the game.

THE DAILY TELEGRAPH
22 AUGUST 1983

Headquarters of Cricket

Now that the Committee's decision not to accede to the proposal by certain members of MCC to send a team under the Club's colours to South Africa has been vindicated by 6604 votes to 4344 (which represents a percentage of 60 to 40) the cloud that has hovered over Lord's for several months has blown away. In the first place, the chairmanship of the ICC will remain in the hands of the President of MCC, whose Secretary will continue to serve the conference; likewise the major building programme involving the rehousing of the TCCB, NCA and Middlesex behind the pavilion in or, in the case of Middlesex, adjacent to the tennis and squash block, will go ahead forthwith. The future of Lord's, in fact, is now determined not only as the ground richest in history but also as the continuing headquarters of the game.

It is worth reminding ourselves at this point that just as there were those of MCC's 18,000 members who voted for the Club to overlook its responsibilities to the Cricket Council and the bodies named above on the South African issue, so there were those who, a year ago, forced a vote on the question of whether to undertake the rebuilding. The MCC proposal then stated that 'The Committee believes it to be of vital importance both to cricket and the Club that Lord's remains the headquarters of the game, nationally and internationally, and that it is the wish of the majority of members to retain this historic character of the Club.' This was passed by 3764 votes to 645 – a figure of 85 per cent in favour.

In strictly economic terms there was certainly a case for MCC retiring into the sanctuary of the pavilion and allowing the governing bodies they themselves created to make their arrangements elsewhere. Now that the larger view has prevailed, one may hope that a happy relationship will emerge as between landlords and tenants, to the benefit of all.

As most of the reports indicated, the debate on the matter of sending an MCC team to South Africa engendered rather more heat than light after Hubert Doggart and Colin Cowdrey, in opposing the proposal, had demonstrated the futility as well as the folly of such a unilateral action on the part of the Club. John Carlisle, MP for Luton, and the organizer of the motion, deplored political interference in sport, including that of the Prime Minister and her Minister for Sport, Neil MacFarlane, but the size of the vote against him suggested that this was a case of the pot calling the kettle black. However much it may be deplored, are sport and politics any longer inseparable? Though apartheid was not directly the point at issue, it was the dominant theme. There is no doubt that some who supported the Committee did so simply because they felt that such a tour would discourage many South Africans of all races who are fighting peacefully from within. On the other side of the fence – to offer a purely personal view – among some most ardently in favour of a tour to South Africa this winter, one feels that 'hatred' of apartheid is little if anything more than a ritual phrase.

The prospect of any amicable solution to the South African question in the near future so far as the ICC is concerned seems non-existent. But international cricket attitudes could change as the picture in South Africa changes. We need not wholly despair, surely, of a multi-national tour there under ICC auspices, or at least with their acceptance, before the end of the decade. For the present, the financial counter-attraction to players has to be accepted – as, of course, it would have to be regardless of the sending of a side of insignificant strength by MCC.

THE CRICKETER
SEPTEMBER 1983

—————— As I Said at the Time ——————

As I Said at the Time published. Thanks to the admirable Louise Page, of Collins, we had plenty of reviews and broadcast interviews. I most enjoyed the one with John Dunn on Radio 2. No prior chat with him but I knew the form from listening to his programme in my bath before dinner. He uncoils to a great height from behind a large console and is completely clued up on me and the book. Very warmly done. I bracket him with Cliff Morgan as the best sound/television interviewer.

DIARY
29 SEPTEMBER 1983

Dog Has His Day

Royal St George's Autumn Meeting. Eureka! I am a poor golfer with a swing that makes Ann shudder. (She played in the Ladies' Championship in her twenties and had a lovely, long, natural swing.) Yet the humblest dog has his day, and with Stableford scores of 41 and 43 off a handicap of 20, and off the very forward yellow tees from a small entry, I won the Kirkwood Prize for the Over-70s.

DIARY
2 OCTOBER 1983

Outsider's View
Inside Lord's

The growth of cricket over the last two centuries from a country pastime to the national summer game has been synonymous with the foundation in 1787 of the Marylebone Cricket Club and the establishment by Thomas Lord of the ground that bears his name.

The history of club and ground threads its way through a wealth of cricket literature, apart from the books devoted especially to these twin institutions written by, among others, the fourth Lord Harris, F. S. Ashley-Cooper, Sir Pelham Warner, Ian Peebles and Diana Rait Kerr.

Never, though, has there been a book about Lord's and MCC written by an outsider looking in, and with the explicit co-operation of the Club. Geoffrey Moorhouse, whose authorship has covered a wide diversity of subject, has already commended himself to followers of cricket with his work *The Best Loved Game*.

His declared object in writing this sensitive and wide-ranging sketch of English cricket was to record the game as it used to be pre-Packer, fearing that it might never be the same again. No doubt this endearing credential persuaded the MCC Committee to break precedent and, at his request, allow Mr Moorhouse free access to the full range of hitherto confidential archives. The result is a comprehensive, mostly sympathetic but not sycophantic portrayal, which well repays the Committee's trust.

The reader of *Lord's* (Hodder & Stoughton, 256 pages, £9.95) will understand more, by the end of the book, about MCC and about the origins and status of their four tenant autonomous bodies, the Cricket Council, TCCB, NCA and Middlesex CCC. The reader will enjoy a tour of the ground, being introduced to its architecture, its trees, the real tennis court, Memorial Gallery, Indoor School, the gardens and much else; everything dominated by the pavilion, which stands worldwide as the apotheosis of cricket and of the Victorian age that built it. 'The whole effect is very comforting,' we read, 'as well as of something that may be called a reticent grandeur; even, dammit, a graciousness.'

With a minimum of historical background the book treats essentially of the present, with glimpses into the future. The economics of the game today and the political tensions following MCC's voluntary devolution of authority in 1968 are covered in detail.

We get a well-informed note on soils and pitch preparation. G. O. Allen's unique influence on MCC and the game today is generously and frankly appraised.

Mr Moorhouse went to great pains to establish the facts of the deplorable pavilion fracas at the ill-starred Centenary Test of 1980, even if his conclusion is in my view questionable.

He strangely demotes to a chapel St John's Wood Church, which was, incidentally, built in 1814 simultaneously with Lord's. The reception following the consecration was the first function held on the ground.

The author, by the way, thinks that a writer 'ought to be a non-joiner of any institution with a public function, the better to maintain his detachment when he writes'. Most regular cricket writers have been able to reconcile their consciences to membership of MCC and county clubs. I suppose, though, that a man who has travelled 2000 miles across the Sahara on a camel might not worry about mitigating press box discomforts by the amenities of pavilions and the fellowship to be found there.

THE DAILY TELEGRAPH
19 OCTOBER 1983

'Bodyline' Drivel

I saw the 'Bodyline' film on BBC2. One watched with mounting contempt for this crude Australian so-called reconstruction. The man playing the part of Larwood rushes up and, as he delivers, the camera cuts to a batsman who hops about as a ball suddenly whistles around his body. The ball's release and trajectory are never shown. The characterization is ludicrous. Plum Warner, a small, bald, abstemious man with a quiet manner of speaking, is portrayed as a big, bluff, hearty fellow with a drink never out of his hand. 'Bill' Fender becomes a Bertie Wooster type twanging a guitar. No Englishman is shown with any vestige of dignity or humour. It's really an exercise in the old Aussie sport of Pommie-bashing. Yet people ask one serious questions about it.

DIARY
6 NOVEMBER 1983

Portrait of Fry

Edmund Nelson's portrait of C. B. Fry is accepted by the MCC Arts and Library Sub-committee, having been offered to them anonymously, I being both the chairman and the donor. It is accounted a fine painting of Charles in old age; sad that no picture of him in his handsome prime exists. So my brother-in-law has Fry hanging in the Long Room, along with G. M. Trevelyan in the hall of Trinity, Cambridge, E. M. Forster at King's, Canon C. E. Raven at Christ's, and Michael McCrum at Tonbridge.

DIARY
29 NOVEMBER 1983

After 1984 – or
Utopia Unlimited?

Almost everything has almost always been wrong with cricket, as any historian of the game well knows. They were complaining about sterile play in the Golden Age, and efforts to reward the attacking game in a variety of ways have recurred regularly ever since. Often they have misfired, sometimes ludicrously. Yet the search must go on, especially in the domestic game, if only because of the inherently defensive sporting nature of the English. It is easier to stop the other chap than doing something positive oneself.

So much for generalizations. Let me give an airing to a few purely personal reactions to current decisions, along with some dreams for 1984 and beyond, starting on the home front.

Despite the fact of their having been founded in 1866, I had never before heard of the Britannic Assurance, who henceforward for a minimum three years are to be patrons of the one essential staple of our cricket, the County Championship. There is a good patriotic ring about the name, and I trust the investment will prove as profitable to them as has been Cornhill's, apparently, in the Test field.

Thank goodness, for the sake of all aspiring young cricketers, as also for the many thousand county members, the Championship will again consist of twenty-four matches, contested over three days; likewise, that the self-evident folly of teams up-sticking on Saturday nights, to travel hundreds of miles, often to play the same opponents on Sunday, and then returning to continue the three-day match on Monday, has at last been rectified.

A great pity that the proposal to limit county overseas players to one after 1985 failed by two votes to get a two-thirds majority at the TCCB. Great cricketers such as Gary Sobers, Mike Procter and Rohan Kanhai helped much by example in reviving county cricket. It is the proliferation and the short-term transfers which have stood in the path of the native Briton.

Talking of nationality, I am of the England-for-the-English school. It was admirable that Basil D'Oliveira should have been accepted by England since he could not play for his own country because of his colour.

Today cricketers born and taught the game in South Africa are in a different category, whatever sympathy one has for their situation. I trust and believe the TCCB are alive to the urgency of revising the qualifying period as it affects all players. Having said that, it is the unsound and sometimes weird methods prevalent among English batsmen that have made access to the Test side all too easy.

I was delighted to see Sir Donald Bradman in the new edition of *The Daily Telegraph Cricket Year Book* deploring the upright bat in the stance. He says that 'it is negative and regressive, and detracts greatly from the style and flow of batsmanship'. The truly great batsman, says the peer of them all, must 'make footwork and balance the cornerstone of his batting'.

But what changes would I most like to see? Well, first a change back to the old lbw Law whereby the ball must pitch on the line of the stumps, allowing the verdict to the bowler pitching outside the off stump only if the batsman has not offered a genuine stroke.

D. J. Insole, I see, is to talk sternly to the umpires and to the West Indians about intimidation, pointing to the provisions, ample if applied, in Law 42. Good luck to him, but the fact is that no bowler since the enactment was first made in 1935 has to my knowledge *ever* been banned for the duration of the innings.

Nor, for that matter, has the ultimate sanction for time-wasting been applied. Even if some bold umpire were to ban a bowler here in England, can anyone imagine an umpire so penalizing the home side in Kingston, Sydney or Karachi?

Depend upon it, one day, if not in mine, the bowler will be obliged to pitch beyond a line drawn across the pitch, or else. . . .

What more? Oh, yes, we must have another line drawn about 22 yards – the length of the pitch – behind each set of stumps, marking the limit of the bowler's run-up. Within three years not a bowler would be the slower or the worse – most probably the better for it.

Close fielders may not encroach within, say, 5 yards of the stumps. Nor may they wear helmets. Exit with this another form of intimidation!

Captains must be held responsible for the good behaviour of the teams under their charge – not that this should be interpreted as criticism of the average English county cricketer, who is still, as were his forebears, a good fellow and a sportsman.

We must diminish the seam of the ball to curb the 'seamer' and thus automatically help to restore the role of the spinner. We must remove all that plastic from the squares themselves and so allow groundsmen to use nature to refresh and give pace and variety to their pitches. We must give people a chance to watch another day's play free if they are denied any. We must. . . .

But I seem to have bowled my 117 overs (a ridiculous number, by the way): what a pity!

THE DAILY TELEGRAPH
30 DECEMBER 1983

1984

THE THUGGERY
OF THE BOUNCER

Captains of Surrey

The award of a benefit in 1984 to Surrey's captain, Roger Knight, encourages me to look briefly back, as far as personal memory stretches, at his modern predecessors, of whom since the First World War there have been eleven. In chronological order they were C. T. A. Wilkinson, P. G. H. Fender, D. R. Jardine, E. R. T. Holmes, H. M. Garland-Wells, N. H. Bennett, Holmes again, M. R. Barton, W. S. Surridge, P. B. H. May, M. J. Stewart and J. H. Edrich: a colourful band, containing, as might be expected, many and diverse talents and, incidentally, six Test cricketers.

'Wilks', the first, actually led Surrey to the Championship truncated by the war, in 1914. He was a skilful and dedicated cricketer who was still running them out from cover point at Beckenham in his sixties. He might have carried on longer as county captain had not Fender, his deputy in 1920, shown such an obvious zest and flair in the job. He was full of ideas, and if brushes with the opposition were not unknown, his own players responded 100 per cent to his democratic, sympathetic handling of them.

Douglas Jardine's more aloof approach to the job in his two-year tenure was appreciated less perhaps on the county scene than the value of his batting. Only Hobbs, May and Edrich have better figures than he for Surrey.

Errol Holmes from 1934 brought to Surrey a cheerful and enterprising spirit both in his leadership and in his play. I once saw Errol at The Oval with more elegance than effort stroke a hundred against Sussex in 65 minutes.

Monty Garland-Wells, a useful all-rounder, carried on the Holmes tradition in the one summer Hitler allowed. When peace returned Surrey somehow got The Oval ship-shape after its wartime requisitionment, but they were at a loss to find an amateur captain – who at that time was deemed necessary. Nigel Bennett was appointed for 1946, but it was really asking far too large a leap from an amiable middle-order club batsman of the 1930s fresh out of the Forces.

Holmes next bridged the gap admirably for two years until Michael Barton, the fourth Oxford Blue among the last five, arrived to add substance to the batting in support of the bowling quartet of Alec Bedser, Peter Loader, Jim Laker and Tony Lock. In 1950 Surrey shared the title with Lancashire – the first time they had finished top since 1914, near though they had come in the Fender years.

The side that Stuart Surridge inherited was well equipped at all points – except in high-class batting when Peter May was needed by England. What Surridge infused, besides a daring example as a close fieldsman, was a tougher, more authoritarian rule, and Surrey responded to it with a string of successive Championships that not even Yorkshire, still less any individual captain, ever surpassed.

There were five running, whereupon Surridge handed over his conquering band to May, who already had two years' successful captaincy of England behind him. As the best of the post-war breed of English batsmen, Peter led from the front. An unrelenting determination lay behind that courteous manner. He held on to two more Championships before the decline of the great bowling quartet, coupled with an illness that took almost a year off his playing life, enabled Yorkshire to come into their own once more.

May's retirement coincided, as it happened, with two fundamental changes in the county scene: the abolition of the amateur, and the introduction of the first (and best) of the one-day competitions, the Gillette Cup. Micky Stewart in 1963 and his successor, John Edrich, who took over from him from 1973 to 1977, were obliged therefore to tackle the responsibilities of leadership without the independence of spirit and decision enjoyed by their predecessors. As leading batsmen, going in first, of a side with whom they had grown up on the staff, they must have found a greater difficulty in adapting to their role than most of those previously named.

In 1978 Surrey were lucky indeed to find an ideal captain for the times in Roger Knight, a man dedicated to two professions –

schoolmastering in winter, cricket in summer. After a quiet start Surrey these last five years have had their share of success, culminating in the Nat West Trophy in 1982 after appearing at Lord's in three previous finals, two of them in the B & H.

Surrey's future loss is the gain of Cranleigh, where he is now a housemaster, but the school has given him leave in this summer of 1984 to reap the fruits of a well-earned benefit.

ROGER KNIGHT BENEFIT BROCHURE
JANUARY 1984

Umpiring –
the Feminine Touch

I suppose the idea of feminine umpires in masculine cricket may strike many, at first impact, as strange, to say the least. One can imagine that in club bars the very thought might well excite ribald comment. The fact is, however, that in a small way it is already happening. There are a few women, so Philip August of the NCA tells me, who have been standing in club cricket of a good standard, and I hear from Tom Smith, Hon. Sec. Emeritus of the Association of Cricket Umpires and the doyen of his kind, that in 1982 a teenage girl won the Arthur Sims Prize, open to all, as the candidate who in examination showed the best knowledge of the Laws. Naturally she is a Fair Maid of Kent. Her name is Lorraine Baker, and in company with her parents she came up from Sittingbourne to Lord's to the Association's AGM to receive her award.

Nor is England the only place where women have officiated in men's matches. It happens in Australia, and I am assured that at least two young women stood, a year or two ago, in Sheffield Shield matches. Whether either or both were called upon to withstand the combined appeals of Dennis Lillee and Rodney Marsh – and, if so, what effect such a drastic experience had on their keenness for the job – I cannot say. Perhaps they were mercifully preserved from such a fate. But the mere possibility brings one to the thought that the presence of women umpires in men's cricket might prove a restraining, civilizing influence in a game which in parts is badly in need of it.

There is certainly keen interest in the game and knowledge of it existing among women. That they have played it among their own sex for upwards of two centuries is, of course, a matter of history, as is the fact that the father-figure of cricket, the great W.G., first learned the arts and skills from his mother in the orchard at Downend.

Women are already greatly involved in the cricket of their menfolk – whether they like it or not, in many cases – washing the shirts, pressing the flannels (so one hopes), and making endless pavilion teas. There is so often a shortage of umpires. Might not more be attracted by the thought, especially if they have played the game at school, of qualifying to wear the white coat out there in the middle? As Mr Smith says, sex is quite irrelevant so far as the Association is concerned. Due qualification is all that matters, and any cricket club should be able to put anyone interested on the right track.

My interest in the idea of women umpiring men's matches came from a young friend who has taken an umpiring course and, although she has not yet been able to sit the examination, has been standing at Oxford in college matches. Teresa McLean (though she will not thank me for saying so) is no ordinary person. She played in the Women's University Match, first for Oxford where she took her degree, and then, when reading for her Ph.D. at Trinity, Cambridge, captaining Cambridge in the year that 'the wonderful Cyril Coote let us play at Fenner's'.

It has always been the measure of cricket's charm that it has attracted 'all sorts and conditions of men' – and women. I find it fortifying, therefore, that Teresa McLean can write of umpiring: 'I love it. In my dreams that is what I'll be.'

THE CRICKETER
JANUARY 1984

A Great Groundsman

I attend the Institute of Groundsmanship's Jubilee Dinner at Goldsmith's Hall, a grandiose affair, the central figure of which was the founder, later secretary, chairman and now the president, William Bowles. He and ten other groundsmen from London clubs met in a City pub in 1934, each chipping in £1 towards what they named the Association of Groundsmen. The thing grew quickly and flourished, so that today (renamed the Institute) it has its own ground and offices at Milton Keynes, its own magazine, runs its own courses, with a bank balance of close on £1 million. The top table was full of nobs, including the Provost of Eton, a former Minister of Sport, Denis Howell, and the Chief of the Defence Staff, Field Marshal Sir Edwin (now Lord) Bramall. A proud night for William, who is still a few months short of his retirement, aged eighty-four, from the Eton post he has held for forty-eight years.

DIARY
10 JANUARY 1984

The Thuggery of the Bouncer

I had intended this month to tell readers something about the great celebrations attending the Jubilee of the Institute of Groundsmanship and about the man who founded it, W. H. Bowles, still (until the end of the summer) the Eton head groundsman at the age of eighty-four. But the subject will be topical for a while yet, and I feel I must hasten to underline as best I can the admirable contributions in last month's *Cricketer* from Peter Roebuck and Bomber Wells on the pressing evil of intimidation.

Mr Roebuck, writing from Australia, told how the home side, playing four fast bowlers, softened up the Pakistanis, who – with Imran Khan unfit – had no counter of their own. Mr Wells, noting that simultaneously the West Indians were engaged in a Test series in India using four fast bowlers and not a specialist spinner, talked of batsmen having had to face 'a barrage of intimidation'. He feels that the English national games of cricket and soccer face the danger that skill is becoming more and more subordinate to physical threat: hence the great rise in the popularity of individual games such as golf, snooker and, indeed, darts. 'The present four-man pace attack will make rubbish of the skills of cricket.'

Both men believe that every country would restrict their attack to speed if they could find enough of it. In England, batsmen are often reprieved by the slowness of the pitches. Likewise the long grind of the county season itself discourages the aspiring bowler from concentrating on speed alone. Nevertheless, says Mr Roebuck, umpires are more than shy of applying the Law, and 'tail-enders are regularly greeted by a bumper first ball'. The picture illustrating the article showed Lillee, characteristically, bowling a nasty one last winter in Perth at Cowans, England's number eleven, and I was reminded how, eight years earlier, Lillee's first ball to England's then number eleven, Geoff Arnold, flew past Arnold's head and over Marsh's for four byes.

That ball might certainly have been fatal and, if it had been, Lillee could have been charged with manslaughter. Prosecuting counsel could have condemned the accused out of his own mouth, for in Lillee's *Back to the Mark*, then recently published, was the essence of his creed:

> Why can't fast bowlers be honest and say: 'I bowl bouncers for one reason and that is to hit the batsman and thus intimidate him.' I try to hit the batsman in the rib-cage when I bowl a purposeful bouncer, and I want it to hurt so much that the batsman doesn't want to face me any more. . . .

I have quoted these words before and offer no apology for doing so again. In all the tributes paid to this great bowler with the sadistic streak and uncontrolled temper, the Londoner's Diary in the *Standard* made the most cogent comment when he wrote that Lillee was remarkably lucky to have been allowed to retire in his own time.

That his example persists, at least in the immediate future in Australia, Mr Roebuck gave sad evidence. 'In my last two school matches in Sydney,' he wrote, 'batsmen have retired after being hit on the head amidst a hail of short balls.'

It is encouraging and salutary that a modern cricketer such as Somerset's accomplished batsman should address himself to cricket's most serious problem – which gives me, incidentally, the chance of thanking him, if belatedly, for his hilarious 'Journal of the Season' in the *Winter Annual*. But he does not suggest a cure for intimidation, and neither does Mr Wells, except to the extent of his novel idea of allowing only three bowlers in a side to run up more than 6 yards.

As I have been saying for a long time umpires will never – except possibly in the grossest cases – apply a Law which involves the necessity, on their part, of judging intent. They will adjudicate as to fractions of a second or to within inches, but not otherwise. The provisions and penalties regarding intimidation, time-wasting, damaging the pitch and other forms of cheating are explicitly laid down in the Unfair Play Law, now No. 42 and the longest in the book. But they are never applied, and to this extent the Law is brought into disrepute.

As regards intimidation, the umpires have to be given a matter of fact to determine, and the only one that occurs to me is the line across the pitch, any ball short of which would be a no-ball with perhaps an ascending scale of penalties. This would be in addition to the present Law which might then be applied in the case of persistent offenders, of whose deviations there would be a record in the scorebook.

I am delighted that Sir Donald Bradman favours the line. I believe that Sir Pelham Warner advocated it after 'Bodyline', though I fear I have looked in vain among his writings. (Can anyone oblige?) The umpires would need to instruct groundsmen where the line should be drawn, according to the pace of the pitch – which means there might often have to be two lines, one for each end. A thin strip of tape or plastic held down at the ends by a couple of pins is all that would be necessary. To those who would object to such a defacement on aesthetic grounds I would say, 'yes, I sympathize with you, but which is preferable: this attempt to abolish something that is repugnant to the traditions of the game and which at the highest levels is endangering its survival as a contest of skill and chivalry; or to allow the evil to continue unchecked?'

THE CRICKETER
MARCH 1984

Authors of the Year

Authors of the Year party at Hatchards. My presence should be put down to my being a Collins author and to Collins owning Hatchards. As I Said at the Time, my fifth book with them, had been published in autumn 1983. Quite a distinguished company, naturally – so a little name-dropping! Hosts were Ian Chapman, the chairman who had steered Collins from crisis to prosperity; Philip Ziegler, who had finished his Mountbatten book, and having been en passant in-house editor of Barclays World of Cricket; *and Tommy Joy, managing director of Hatchards, proud that old Sir*

Arthur Bryant had dedicated his last book to him – The Lion and the Unicorn. *Sir Arthur (in the loo) quoted for my enjoyment verses from one of the Harrow Songs about Stanley Jackson.*

The Queen's Secretary, Sir Philip (now Lord) Moore voiced his relief at being back from Jordan. King Hussein was an excellent fellow, but he didn't think the Queen should be exposed to Middle East political situations. Agreed on all sides. Frank Taylor of the Daily Mirror *was there, the only press survivor of the Manchester United air crash at Munich. It killed twenty-three out of forty-four. They saved him a rear seat, but he preferred to go up front; he suffered twenty-one fractures and eighteen months in hospital.*

A trim, smiling chap said he'd read every word I'd written, and quoted Ian Wooldridge's Daily Mail *piece on my retirement, back in 1975! Flattering stuff. When he had gone Ian Chapman relieved my sorry ignorance. It was Jeffrey Archer.*

DIARY
4 APRIL 1984

The Changing Face of May

Time was when May used to usher in the cricket season on a note of quiet welcome, as restrained as the delicate hues of spring. We scribes used to motor up to Worcester through the fruit blossom there to see the summer's tourists test out their skills in a cooler climate and milder light and on a more yielding turf than they had known at home. There was time for the public gradually to identify the new faces from overseas. The counties lined up to flex their muscles against the aspiring undergraduates of Fenner's and The Parks. For the club cricketer May meant stiffness and the scent of new-mown grass and the thought of a string of happy weekends ahead.

Sometimes the truly extraordinary had everyone sitting up and taking notice. There was Don Bradman's explosion on to the scene, first, unforgettably, in 1930 and, indeed, whenever he arrived thereafter. One cool day at Hove K. S. Duleepsinhji, sweatered throughout, greeted the first appearance of that comely scoreboard on the far side of the field by making 333 before close of play. In 1938 a fine May gave Bill Edrich the chance, never to be repeated, of scoring 1000 runs before the end of the month, all at Lord's.

By contrast, the cricket season of the 1980s strikes from the start a more urgent, competitive note. The county staffs have been half-killing themselves since the beginning of April doing their circuit-training indoors under expert torturers. Hard and continuous net practice, once thought to be an essential way of both bringing the cricket muscles into play and of getting the respective techniques into full working order, is now almost an optional extra. The counties plunge straight into hard, competitive combat – this year the Britannic County Championship, as we must learn to call it, bursts into life on 28 April, the Benson and Hedges stages its first round on 5 May and the John Player League the following day. Everything at once begins to matter a lot.

As to the touring team, or teams, of the summer it is no use pretending they excite the old speculative thrill because we know most of them already as staple characters on the county scene. In any case they arrive later now, being rushed from yet another Test series almost straight into another. Our 1984 visitors, the West Indians, do not start their tour until 19 May, and after three games find themselves plunged into a new round of one-day Internationals (Texaco is now the name) and Test matches. May they stimulate us as always, may they bowl their overs at a respectable speed, and may they use the short fast ball as a variant rather than the rule.

THE CRICKETER
MAY 1984

——————— *O'Reilly Sparkles* ———————

Tony O'Reilly, at the invitation of the President, Alex Dibbs, proposed the toast to Cricket and MCC, as he would do, in a sparkling speech at the Anniversary Dinner. It mattered not at all that, strictly speaking, he should not have been there, not being a member. Quite unabashed, Alex pleaded ignorance of the restriction.

A. J. F. O'Reilly has always seemed several sizes larger than life from the moment when as an eighteen-year-old he first pulled on the green jersey of Ireland. Winning twenty-nine international caps as a wing-three-quarter, he outshone all in his day. On two Lions tours to South Africa and Australia/New Zealand he picked up a record thirty-eight tries. In Sydney he also picked up a stunning Australian girl, Susan Cameron, perhaps his most important capture and far from his easiest. Married in 1962, she produced six children within less than four years of one another; yes, the last three were triplets.

The O'Reilly dynasty being now secure, Tony resumed his picking up habit – directorships galore, including (since 1979) the presidency and chief executiveship of H. J. Heinz Co. Inc. and the chairmanship of Independent Newspapers of Ireland. Her children now pursuing various glamorous careers, Susan has time to cement Irish–Australian interests and friendships, and to chair the Tyrone Guthrie Centre, an Irish haven for artists of all sorts and nationalities.

Every winter at Sandy Lane Hotel, Barbados, where Tony holds his annual Heinz convention, Ann and I enjoy hospitable evidence that Tony is as full as ever of his native zest and wit.

DIARY
2 MAY 1984

Bill Voce: Prince of Bowlers

The name of Bill Voce, one of the best of all left-arm fast bowlers, who died in Nottingham yesterday aged seventy-four, will be associated for ever in history with that of his great partner for Nottinghamshire and England, Harold Larwood. Together they had the chief part in winning the County Championship of 1929; together, under the stern instruction of their captain, D. R. Jardine, they perfected in the 1932–3 Test series in Australia the fast leg-theory attack which came to be known as 'Bodyline'.

Larwood so injured his left foot on that tour that he could never again recapture anything approaching his phenomenal speed, though he soldiered on for several more seasons of county cricket at fast-medium pace in company with Voce, his junior by five years.

Both before and after the 'Bodyline' tour the Nottinghamshire bowling, on the orders of the captain, A. W. Carr, sometimes overstepped the margin of fair play, and it was not until Nottinghamshire put the leadership into more acceptable hands that relations with several of the counties were repaired.

Happily, too, though Larwood's Test days were past, the breach with Lord's that had prevented Voce's selection for England for four of his prime years was healed, and he sailed for Australia again with G. O. Allen's team for the 1936–7 tour.

With twenty-six wickets at 21 runs each he headed England's Test bowling averages, and such was the paucity of talent after the Second World War that in his thirty-eighth year, he made a third tour to Australia in 1946–7. The spirit still was as willing as ever, but of the fire and elasticity of that bounding run and classical delivery only spasmodic vestiges remained.

Circumstances, then, prevented Voce from building up over a long but interrupted career the sort of figures his excellence as a cricketer deserved. However, in first-class cricket he had 1558 wickets at 23 runs each. His dangerous batting brought him four hundreds and an average just short of 20. In twenty-seven Tests he took ninety-eight wickets at 27 a time. He was an admirable fielder with a formidable throw.

Voce as a tall, slim lad walked from the colliery town of Hucknall to Trent Bridge in the late 1920s in search of a trial. There his natural talent was at once recognized. He had a long loose arm and a natural flowing action, with the ability, bowling over the wicket, to swing the ball either way in the air. He was indeed an artist and an athlete quite out of the ordinary.

Bill, after his retirement, was in much demand as a coach, and at the age of seventy was still wheeling away at Lord's at the MCC Indoor School and enthusing the boys with his humour and friendliness.

THE DAILY TELEGRAPH
7 JUNE 1984

———— *Committee and Players Meet* ————

The customary Lord's Test drinks party in the Committee Room after play for the two teams and their ladies. The President is supported by a few members of the Committee. These things can be a bit sticky and are never prolonged. But Alex Dibbs is nothing if not convivial in a cheerful, bantering way, and with two sociable captains, David Gower and Clive Lloyd, the West Indian father-figure, all passes off well enough.

DIARY
29 JUNE 1984

Underwood's Maiden Hundred

In a week's cricket news which has taken us through the whole gamut of surprise, one happening has given lovers of the game a special degree of pleasure. Derek Underwood's first hundred came in his 22nd season with Kent and in his 618th first-class innings. He made it in 3½ hours, going in at number three as night-watchman.

He batted through while all around him were failing until he found his most fruitful partner in Terry Alderman, at number ten. His 111 at Hastings saved his side from an otherwise certain defeat in two days and made the prelude to a palpitating climax and the first tied match in this Championship for a decade. It was not, perhaps, wholly incidental that his innings followed the day after his taking 6 for 12 in the John Player League, for he had gone strangely wicketless in this competition for half a dozen matches and was duly elevated when his 300th Sunday victim ended the drought.

Only Bob Taylor, so thinks William Frindall the cricket statistician, may have needed more innings to reach his first and only hundred which was made in 1981 at Sheffield against Yorkshire in his 744th innings and his 21st season with Derbyshire.

It is a happy coincidence that has coupled these two senior figures in the limelight, for each has been an ornament to his profession both on and off the field to a degree that has marked them out in an age when the brash and undisciplined attitudes of a few of their fellow Test cricketers have driven many to despair.

What endeared almost all the great figures of the past to their public – and in so doing helped to give cricket a unique place in the sporting world of England – was their innate modesty. Hobbs, Woolley, Tate, 'Duleep', Hendren, Verity – the names of my generation roll off the tongue as do those of a later age – Hutton, Compton, May, Cowdrey and many more.

It so happens I recently came by a copy of a document produced by the publicity concern that now 'markets' Australian cricket, the philosophy behind which is the complete antithesis of the historic spirit of cricket. Listen to this:

> Consumers of all products and services today are increasingly fickle and prone to change. Above all they are easily bored and are constantly

seeking entertainment and spectacle.

Tradition, gentlemanly conduct, inviolable unchanging rules and formality are increasingly meaningless in today's society.

Large audiences are far more vulnerable to the excitement of a gladiatorial clash, colour, noise and constant activity.

Poor Australia.

But back to Derek Underwood, whose name I first heard from Ronnie Bryan, one of the three Kentish brothers, who after his retirement took and gave much pleasure coaching the young idea at that venerable home of the game Beckenham Cricket Club.

Derek, like so many fine cricketers, owed much to an enthusiastic father, Leslie, who for many years captained the village of Farnborough. There was a net in the garden, and winter visits to a Croydon indoor school where Ken Barrington, Arthur McIntyre and Tony Lock saw great possibilities. Hence went word to Leslie Ames, the Kent manager, and the introduction to county cricket shortly before his eighteenth birthday.

There followed an auspicious start: 5 for 42 against Yorkshire in his first match, 101 wickets in his first season, his county cap at nineteen (the youngest ever for Kent, bar Colin Cowdrey who awarded it) and, when just twenty-one, the first of his eighty-nine England caps.

Having seen as much of his cricket as most people, I can recall no single gesture of dissent at a decision nor any moment when the slightest slackening of effort could be detected either when bowling or in the field. Indeed, it is possibly in his fielding that Underwood most clearly expresses himself, for he is no born athlete and has had to make the very best of what nature has given him – including a pair of rather flat feet.

His cheerful, wholehearted endeavour over so many years has endowed him with a rare charisma. The world of cricket will, therefore, be particularly glad to know that all he wants to do – and all, of course, that Kent want him to do – is to go on wheeling away with that strong left-arm as long as his legs will carry him. Furthermore, at the age of thirty-nine, he has by no means given up the ambition to play again for England. I should think not, indeed. Wilfred Rhodes, let me remind him, headed the MCC bowling with forty-one wickets at the age of fifty-two in the West Indies.

THE DAILY TELEGRAPH
6 JULY 1984

Denis Howell and Cricket

I go to see Denis Howell at the House of Commons in connection with my biography of Gubby Allen. He was the first Minister of Sport, appointed in 1964 by Harold Wilson, and some would say the best. He approved in 1968 the scheme for the MCC devolution of power to the TCCB, NCA and the Cricket Council, which had been largely the work of Gubby as Treasurer and Billy Griffith as Secretary. The constitution of the governing Council, comprising equal representation to MCC, TCCB and NCA whereby no one body could out-vote the other two, was satisfactory to him, thus making cricket eligible for government aid. (The balance was upset in favour of the TCCB in 1982, whereupon Gubby resigned on principle.)

DIARY
24 JULY 1984

Saluting the West Indians

I had the honour of proposing the toast to the West Indies team at the traditional dinner in their honour. Aged seventy-seven, was this a record? It was Clive Lloyd's fifth tour of England, his third as captain, yet he was coming up to only his fortieth birthday. His retirement had been announced, but not to be effective until after his fourth tour of Australia in the coming winter. How about W.G., I asked, who called it a day at fifty, and Wilfred Rhodes, who in the West Indies in 1929–30 bowled nearly 500 overs and topped the bowling with forty-one wickets at a tender fifty-two? Clive was coming up to his sixty-ninth Test as captain, and of the last thirty-six he had lost only one. I tried to keep it fairly short and lighthearted, and thought it not the occasion to say that an attack of undiluted speed had transformed Test cricket over the period of his leadership, and not for the better.

DIARY
6 AUGUST 1984

Clive Lloyd, the Father Figure

By any yardstick Clive Hubert Lloyd, the West Indies captain, is, and must always be, an immense figure in the world of cricket. This is patently true in terms of physique and performance. It is true – though not quite without reservation – as regards leadership. It is true, too, in a sense that gives him a special esteem among old crustaceans like me who so hope to see the game's traditional courtesies observed and who, when some of the modern players write or talk in public, shrink from what they may read or hear. Clichéd banality is normally the best to be expected.

By contrast, a general benevolence lies behind the slow smile and those gleaming specs. In twenty-odd years as a first-class cricketer I cannot think he has made an enemy. He personifies West Indian good nature and with it the not easily ruffled temperament that these exuberant, volatile cricketers particularly need at the helm. Worrell, the first regular black West Indian captain – and, incidentally, just about the best of any shade, in my experience – had this quality to the point, at times, almost of aloofness. His teams would do anything for him, just as today they will do anything for the man they know as Hubert.

His seniority, of course, is unchallengeable. No one has led his countrymen as many as sixty-nine times if he plays today. Nor, needless to say, has any man captained in thirty-six consecutive Tests and met with only one defeat – a narrow one on a difficult Melbourne pitch in 1981–2. The West Indies under Lloyd have been the strongest side in the world for the best part of a decade. England have won one match against them out of the last twenty-six and lost thirteen. Australia have won twice out of sixteen and lost nine.

It is not difficult, it may be remarked, to present a benign exterior when one is backed up by a seemingly endless supply of fast bowlers. Indeed no, but Lloyd's nature has been clear for all to see ever since he was capped by Lancashire in 1969. When he was selected as one of *Wisden*'s Five Cricketers of the Year two years later he explained to John Kay, his biographer, why he moved across from league to county cricket: 'I had settled down so well at Haslingden. They are a great bunch of fellows and Jack Bond is a captain in a million.' For his part Bond declared that 'the very fact of playing alongside Clive has been an inspiration'.

This mutual admiration has not diminished with the years. Lloyd is a Guyanese-Lancastrian who has absorbed a dual culture in the same way as his two illustrious predecessors, Learie, later Lord Constantine of Maraval in Trinidad and Tobago and of Nelson in the County Palantine of Lancaster, and F.M.M., later Sir Frank Worrell, of Barbados and Radcliffe. Clive would readily subscribe to what Constantine wrote on Worrell's untimely death: 'There is much to learn in the field of human relations from the kind, friendly and warm people of the North of England.'

Lloyd, then, naturally and unself-consciously, fulfils an ambassadorial role as between the West Indies and his adopted country. But the binding influence he exerts is at least equally important among the several island territories of the Caribbean with which, for cricket purposes, is associated his South American homeland, Guyana.

Considering the political and economic rivalries of the Caribbean, and the ultra-sensitivity of some of the governments, it is remarkable that the West Indian Board of Control, despite many alarms and pressures, still manages to hold together its member boards, scattered over some 1700 miles from Kingston down to Georgetown.

With the emancipation from Empire, love of cricket and pride in the play of their heroes are today the only strong common bonds. There is some evidence that the various heads of government now are increasingly conscious of the coalescent value of cricket in this respect.

The qualification I have made as regards Lloyd's leadership must be mentioned here. While the loyalty of his side has been absolute, he has sometimes allowed his fast bowlers on past tours if not, to my knowledge, in the current one, to run on too loose a rein, leaving it (in the manner of most modern Test captains) to the luckless umpires to apply the Law without any visible help from him. There have been breaches, notably at Old Trafford in 1976 and in New Zealand more recently, when in retrospect he probably regrets he did not act more firmly.

There are the ingredients of friction when one side has a near-monopoly of fast bowling. Having said this, one must also deplore certain English forecasts of trouble ahead written before a ball of this 1984 tour had been bowled. These have not gone unnoticed or unresented in the Caribbean.

These disciplinary instances apart, what a decoration Clive Lloyd has been, and still is, to the wide world of cricket. There have been few harder hitters than this large, ambling fellow who learned to play as a boy in the streets and backyards of Georgetown. Nor, though he has now retired to the slips, should his fielding be forgotten as with cat-like tread he patrolled the off-side. Considering the vast amount of cricket he has played it is extraordinary how over so long a span he has retained both his form and his zest for the game.

He will be forty at the end of August, and last year he announced his intention to retire. He not only had second thoughts but has now accepted for this coming winter the captaincy of the West Indies in a full tour of Australia which, both physically and mentally, is the most exacting of all. One can only admire, and wish him well.

THE DAILY TELEGRAPH
9 AUGUST 1984

─────────── *Committee Farewell* ───────────

My last MCC Committee Meeting as full member. Much history made, of course, since 1975, including the long 'Packer' saga; the Laws revised; staging of the first World Cups; MCC working party reforms; rebuilding, including my two special responsibilities for the Indoor School and the new Library; a mass of detail from the ten sub-committees, all to be approved or otherwise. We sit down at 3.45 and finish often nearer seven than six o'clock.

I have loved it all, except for much of the time consumed as a result of MCC Secretariat–TCCB friction. Little in the way of tension, apart from this. There is a tradition of courtesy in debate, of which one must be conscious, looking at those famous paintings on the walls – of Aislabie, Lacey, Cobham, Findlay, Christopherson, Harris, Hawke and Altham.

DIARY
21 AUGUST 1984

────────── *Last-Ball Kent Defeat* ──────────

Kent lose the Nat West Final for the second year running. This time John Emburey settles it for Middlesex, almost in the dark, by hitting the very last ball for 4, up to the Grandstand, Richard Ellison having overpitched an intended yorker. One trudges up to St John's Wood station in the rain, drained of all emotion, suddenly very, very tired.

DIARY
I SEPTEMBER 1984

Martin-Jenkins
Reviews the Modern Game

On May Day 1963 at Old Trafford in a game extended by rain into a second day Lancashire beat Leicestershire by 101 runs in what was then known just as The Knock-out Competition.

In greatcoat and muffler Frank Woolley, just coming up to his seventy-fourth birthday, scorning pavilion comforts, sat among the empty benches behind the bowler's arm and at the end presented the first Gold Medal to Peter Marner, whose 121 and three wickets had ensured the victory.

Such was the inauspicious beginning of 'one-day' limited-over cricket which within the next two decades spread itself worldwide and transformed the game to a degree unimagined by the English counties who had so tentatively given the idea a trial.

The Gillette company contributed a mere £6500 in that first year for distribution among the counties, an amount which today would just about cover the summer's wages of one capped player. It was the warm public reaction for this more concentrated version of cricket which brought home to the authorities its financial possibilities.

From 1963 the bandwagon began to roll, slowly at first, more rapidly when the quick-fire John Player Sunday game and the instant registration of overseas players coincided in 1968. The Benson and Hedges Cup followed in 1972, with the unfortunate consequences of a further diversion of interest from the County Championship.

Still, the game was being played for the most part with the time-honoured conventions of good sportsmanship, and a more adequate wage was beginning to come the way of English cricketers when the Packer bombshell erupted in Australia in 1977.

The evils which now inflict the game, its over-riding commercialism, the decline in so many standards, date and derive from the split contrived by Kerry Packer and his marketing minions. Christopher Martin-Jenkins underlines all this in *Twenty Years On: Cricket's Years of Change 1963–1983*, published today (Collins Willow, £8.95).

Writing of floodlit cricket, the author considers that 'played in a warm climate it is an exciting experience and a thrilling spectacle, but I loathed then, and still do, the razzmatazz which went with it. Coloured clothes were the visible symbol of Mr Packer's new, commercial cricket, and they became, too, the symbol of the aggressive, "liberated" player. By wearing them Australia's top cricketers – and the many players from West Indies, England, South Africa and Pakistan who also signed secret and lucrative contracts to play unofficial cricket in opposition to official Test matches during 1977 – were saying, it seemed, "To hell with dignity and tradition. Pay us enough and we will wear anything, or, if you wish, nothing."'

Mr Martin-Jenkins is no septuagenarian reactionary but a broadcaster, journalist and author still in his thirties who both in *The Cricketer* and over the air has won general respect for the sincerity and moderation of his interpretation of the cricket scene over most of the critical period he has surveyed.

He is strongly against the over-exposure of Test and one-day International cricket with the same players pursuing the same tactics in match after match. In 1981–2 West Indies, Australia and Pakistan played nineteen one-dayers and six Tests, and seventeen Internationals two years later. The novelty had completely gone, and as Ijaz Butt, of Pakistan, observed, '. . . players will soon start objecting to being treated as financial bait and want to be treated as human beings'.

The misdeeds of the arch-offender against cricket standards, Dennis Lillee, get their proper censure, and the moral duly drawn – to have banned him as he deserved would have drawn the anger of both the sponsor and his vociferous public. This player, for a while, was, thanks to Australian marketing, bigger than the game.

The author deplores the 'appalling pressure put upon the umpires by the players', and thinks that 'in each bonanza there will be several who would stop at very little to get their share of the gravy'.

He has a number of positive ideas; would like to see, experimentally, bowlers required to bowl with the front foot behind the back crease rather than the popping crease, pointing out that present dimensions were decided when the average man was much smaller than today. He would lessen the menace of helmeted and padded close fielders by forbidding them to encroach within 6 feet of the cut portion of the pitch.

There are other positive suggestions in a thoughtful book, well documented, which, outspoken as it is on the crucial issues, is not wholly pessimistic about the future. In a phrase it is a plea for strength and moral courage at the top, and for the control of the game not by the men of business but by those who have played it, and who have its spirit in their bones.

THE DAILY TELEGRAPH
6 SEPTEMBER 1984

Jack Ikin:
The Model Sportsman

The sudden death of John Thomas Ikin, aged sixty-six, will be much mourned in the cricket world beyond the boundaries of his native Staffordshire and of Lancashire, of whose team he was a leading member in the first twelve summers after the war. For apart from his considerable merits as a player – and they brought him eighteen Test caps – he was in every respect the very model of a sportsman, modest, courageous, cheerful and conspicuously unselfish.

Jack Ikin's varied career spanned nearly forty years from his first appearing for Staffordshire at sixteen in 1934 on the same side as the great S. F. Barnes (then sixty-one) until in 1972 he managed the first England Young Cricketers side to the West Indies which was led by John Barclay.

As a steady left-hand bat, brilliant close fielder and on his day a tolerable leg-spinner, he showed sufficient promise to be chosen for the first two post-war MCC tours to Australia and the West Indies. Out of necessity he was thrown in at the deep end with the minimum of experience, and was at his best for England a few years later.

Those who saw it will always recall the battering he stood up to at the hands of Cuan McCarthy of South Africa as Len Hutton's opening partner in the 1951 Test at Old Trafford.

Having made nearly 18,000 runs (average 36), including twenty-six hundreds, Ikin returned home, aged forty, to captain Staffordshire, which he continued to do until he had turned fifty. In this last phase he was not only his side's leading batsman but also a regular wicket-taker.

He went as Assistant Manager to S. C. Griffith on the successful MCC tour to Australia and New Zealand in 1965–6 and on his playing retirement devoted himself to coaching the young of the Midlands and North.

THE DAILY TELEGRAPH
18 SEPTEMBER 1984

A Lesson from Sri Lanka

I enjoyed the unexpected chance of a talk with Peter West on television during the tea interval on the Friday of the Sri Lanka Test even if my old colleague, with whom I first appeared on television more than thirty years ago, was obviously obliged by the present plight of English cricket to steer my thoughts in that direction rather than allowing them to wander nostalgically in the past.

One of the viewers who was impelled to write, however, remarked, 'not much of a Test, more a lesson' – which prompts me to repeat and underline my appreciation of the spirit and the technique of the foremost Sri Lankan batsmen.

The methods of Duleep Mendis, the admirable captain, of Sidath Wettimuny, of Roy Dias, and of Ranjan Madugalle impressed those good judges one met at Lord's or who derived their opinions from watching on the box. The fundamental things were observed.

Apart from the minimal tapping of the bat such as most of the great players have found helpful as the bowler approached the crease, the head and body remained still until the stroke was decided upon and effected. The pick-up of the bat was generous and in or near the vertical plane. Not least, the feet were properly adjusted to the length of the ball, whether forward or back.

Plum Warner used to quote Tom Emmett, calling out in the Rugby nets: 'Smell 'er, sir, smell 'er!' Harry Altham used to talk about 'leading with the head', which is the same precept differently expressed. One was put in mind of those great purist teachers watching Wettimuny and Mendis stretching into those lovely strokes to either side of cover point. It was gratifying to hear, by the way, from the Sri Lankan manager, Neil Chanmugam, when he brought the team to Canterbury, that five of them, including Wettimuny, had flown to England several weeks before the start of the tour to practise and polish up their technique under Don Wilson at the MCC Indoor School.

They also (through the TCCB) recruited the old Sussex and England cricketer, now the coach at Lancing, D. V. Smith, to travel with them as adviser and with the idea of helping especially those new to English conditions. In other words, Sri Lanka's first Test tour of this country was thoroughly well planned, and congratulations are due to all concerned, and not least to Gamini Dissanayake, MP, president of their Board of Control, who spoke with such modest charm at the dinner given to the team before the match by MCC in the Committee Dining Room, and also to their resident coach, that attractive Leicestershire batsman of former days, Stanley Jayasinghe.

I write this before England's team for the winter tour is chosen – which is one reason why I forebear to comment on the immediate prospect. The choice is important in all respects, and in particular as regards the identity of the two men to make up the management, the assistant to Tony Brown and the vice-captain to David Gower. Strength, judgement and real authority are urgently needed in these two positions. Pray goodness they are forthcoming.

In any case I do not feel disposed at this range to add to the censure – some of surely unprecedented severity – which has been meted out to the successive England XIs of the summer of 1984. John Woodcock's reports of the Sri Lankan Test in *The Times* were clearly the words of a man at the very end of his tether, written from the depths of the heart. To no one is the good name of English cricket more precious than the Editor of *Wisden* and the cricket correspondent of *The Times*, and if there had been any remaining complacency as to the state of English cricket at the top, his polemics must surely have removed it. An interview with Ray Illingworth in the *Daily Mail* a few weeks earlier was equally condemnatory. One can only hope that the brighter dawn that must follow the present darkness is not too far below the horizon.

THE CRICKETER
OCTOBER 1984

─────────── *Prestigious Occasion* ───────────

My first dinner as president of the Forty Club. As usual at the Hilton, and as usual we eat river trout, saddle of lamb and Welsh rarebit; only the starter varies. We are within two years of the Jubilee of this club with a worldwide membership of 3600, started back in 1936 by that gregarious personality of robust humour to whom everyone warmed, Henry Grierson. The dinner is the biggest annual assembly of cricketers, this year 627 of us, the same total as England achieved at Old Trafford against Australia, I remind them, fifty years ago. Our speakers are the Editor of The Daily Telegraph, *the Rt. Hon. Bill Deedes; George Mann, President of MCC; Humphrey Tilling, perpetual manager of the Old Stagers' Dramatic Society and the voice behind the scenes at the Remembrance reunion at the Albert Hall; and William Douglas-Home, the playwright. It is always a good audience, and there is much laughter. We hear from the last of them of the Scottish umpire in the Borders who gave seven successive lbws. On his day he was reckoned unplayable.*

DIARY
26 OCTOBER 1984

Don Tallon:
The Best 'Keeper of Them All?

─────────────

Donald Tallon, who died in Brisbane on 7 September aged sixty-eight, occupies an honoured place in the list of great wicket-keepers.

Indeed, Sir Donald Bradman, in whose post-war Australian teams he was an integral part, has rated him even above the legendary Bertie Oldfield.

Not far short of 6 ft, Don Tallon was tall for a 'keeper, but he folded himself down low on his haunches as the bowler approached and was a model of stillness until he had judged the speed and length of the ball. In his lack of ostentation he resembled Oldfield, from whose sound advice he profited in the 1930s.

As a country boy from Bundaberg, Tallon played first for Queensland at seventeen in the 1932–3 season and was considered highly unlucky not to have been chosen for the 1938 tour of England, especially as he had developed by then into a reliable batsman. The following season he equalled Ted Pooley's ancient record of twelve victims in a match, a number still unexceeded. When at length he was chosen for Australia in 1946–7, he had twenty wickets in the series against England, which was then a record number. At Melbourne, he also made his best Test score of 92, he and Lindwall turning the game in an eighth-wicket stand of 154 in an hour and a half.

Lean and deeply sun-tanned, Tallon was a man of characteristically dry laconic Aussie humour. Nicknamed 'Deafy' from a slight affliction, he caught almost every snick whether he heard them or not, and no one was quicker to the bails when a stumping chance offered.

Of his 432 victims, 129 were stumped, a proportion probably exceeded, among the best of those who have kept post war, only by Leslie Ames and 'Tich' Cornford of Sussex. His diving left-handed catch in the Oval Test of 1948 to dismiss Sir Leonard Hutton off Lindwall from a leg glance truly hit is remembered still as a classic of its kind.

THE CRICKETER
OCTOBER 1984

The Father of Games-writing Brought to Life

No one of my sporting generation – nor, surely, any still with us from the one before – would dispute the distinction commonly accorded to Bernard Darwin of being the father of modern games-writing. He was not specifically the first of identifiable sporting journalists. There were the Pardon brothers, whose editorships had already shaped the character and authority of *Wisden's Cricketers' Almanack*. Sydney Pardon, Editor from 1891 to 1925, to whom at The Oval I was once introduced, found time both for sports reporting and dramatic criticism. There was a certain 'Sporting' Ward, so called, who made a fair fist of describing several different games as a daily reporter. F. B. Wilson, father of Peter and grandfather of Julian, a triple Blue at Cambridge, took at once to games-writing, first in a racy, idiomatic style for 'the populars' soon after the turn of the century and just about when Darwin cast away his barrister's wig and gown and assumed the mantle of golf correspondent.

Darwin humanized the reporting of golf, suggesting the ebb and sway of battle, the agonies and the successes, in a way that attracted to the game those who had little or no knowledge of it. He was never too technical, though a very fine player himself. Indeed, he had the luck of achieving the ultimate in that he travelled to the United States to report the first Walker Cup match in 1922, was called upon to play in the place of the British captain who fell sick, and in the Singles won a famous victory.

For all but half a century, between 1907 and his retirement in 1953, he wrote copiously about golf, not only for *The Times* but weekly also for *Country Life*. Though his work for the newspaper remained unsigned according to the tradition of the day, his easy, flowing style, sprinkled with quotations and allusions and with occasional wicked shafts of humour, was unmistakeable.

A characteristic that marked him out was that though he wrote passionately about the drama of what he saw he was restrained in both his praise and his censure of the players. In his book *Life is Sweet, Brother* he records with pleasure how in an after-dinner speech Charles Whitcombe said that he did not present them with bouquets when they won but with nice little buttonholes.

Darwin went on to remark that 'if we let ourselves go too unrestrainedly about him, there are no words left for the man who wins the Victoria Cross'. This echoes the feelings of old codgers like me who, as the air becomes thick with superlatives *every* time a goal is scored, ask themselves what language is there left to portray the truly great moment, the unforgettable achievement.

Darwin, in short, was a beautiful writer – whether about golf or any other human activity that took his interest. He was great on prizefighting, murder trials. He was thought to be the greatest living authority on Dickens. He wrote a perfect short biography of W. G. Grace.

A fresh anthology of his work twenty-odd years after his death comes therefore as a great bonus which, one hopes, will not only bring back memories to the elderly but convey to younger golf addicts something of the flavour of the man and of the game as played in his time.

The latter generality may well find food for thought in the contrast Darwin makes between the reporter to whom putts were always missed 'carelessly' or 'unaccountably' even though he could almost see the club trembling in the delinquent's hand, and his successor today who has 'gone all psychological'. Surely we get too much nowadays, especially from players of games and their ghosts, about the appalling stress and strain of it all.

Prospective purchasers must be warned. Darwin was both a vivid reporter and an incomparable essayist. Miss Hughes, friend and confidante of another great games-writer, Neville Cardus, not being herself a golfer, has ignored the reportage and concentrated exclusively on Darwin's imaginative, philosophical articles.

I trust that Peter Ryde's admirably varied Darwin anthology may be next for republication for as a reporter he was supreme. Meanwhile, *A Round with Darwin* has conjured for me memories of so many good men and true who in my early years followed in his train: such names as Robertson-Glasgow, Wakelam, Croome, Owen, Pullin, Henley, Ward-Thomas, Peebles, Cardus and a host more. Most, and probably all, of these would have admitted the debt owed by all games-writers to the example of Darwin, and would have acknowledged him, in the words used by Belloc of P. G. Wodehouse in a wider context, as 'the head of our profession'.

THE DAILY TELEGRAPH
9 NOVEMBER 1984

A Word
for the Cricket Writers

By the time these words are in print the England team will be making their farewells and a few days later the scores and reports from India will be beginning to lighten our breakfast reading, and so compensate in some degree for the absence of news of the daily county scene.

The end of the home season is a melancholy time for the great army of cricket readers, and it struck me as I digested the cricket pages of *The Daily Telegraph* and *The Times* recording the happenings of the penultimate day how well we were served by both. Here was John Woodcock in a full three-column spread analysing in some depth the fruits of his summer's observation in anticipation of the new England team due to be picked that evening. A Gatting man and hopeful of his choice as vice-captain, he made the point that Bobby Simpson, who went on to such great things for Australia, was a year older than Gatting and had likewise played fifty-two innings before he made the first of his Test hundreds. (He added another nine.) Thirteen of his personal sixteen choices agreed with those of the selectors announced next day.

Woodcock confessed 'a soft spot for Williams. He spins the ball, and he can bat, and he fights like a terrier'. Marks was preferred, as were Moxon for Benson and French for his Bairstow. In his report from Taunton the *Times* correspondent doubted the current theory that the wicket-keeping standard is unusually high. There are goal-keepers, yes, but 'the art is standing up to the wicket'. At Old Trafford Richard Streeton was reporting 'a riveting day on which 534 runs were scored and 19 wickets fell' – and which ended with Essex in dreadful light forcing the two-day win which proved to have retained for them the Championship, and deservedly so.

How would the *Telegraph* coverage compare with that? I need not have been anxious. There was plenty to enjoy and likewise to think about. Michael Carey and Derek Hodgson reported fully and with discernment the decisive games at Taunton and Old Trafford. After a day of missed chances it was 'French without tears' in the end as Carey told us how the Nottinghamshire wicket-keeper equalled his predecessor Geoff Millman's records of eighty-five victims in a season and six in an innings. Hodgson found room to applaud two youthful batting successes – of Michael Watkinson for Lancashire and the nineteen-year-old Paul Prichard who made a maiden hundred going in first for Essex.

Rex Alston's father was a bishop and he surely earns the honorary title of Venerable as he still follows the game as keenly as ever round the southern county grounds. Those who think he must be getting on can look up his age in *Who's Who*, and I would only add that he doesn't look it and never has. Another not-so-old faithful, D. J. Rutnagur, also provided one of the eight signed reports, as did the Oxford, Lancashire and Gloucestershire batsman, David Green.

Further, Green contributed an article which I found myself heartily applauding, entitled 'Heavy bats and early back-lift in question'. It came well from a man who was striking the ball good and hard in first-class cricket not many years ago to query the fashion condemned by Sir Donald Bradman in the last *DT Cricket Year Book* of 'standing like sentinels with bats in mid-air', as the bowler's arm comes over. Notwithstanding that Graham Gooch adopts this method, and that he has such followers as Broad and Moxon, it remains true that 'it is essential in all ball games for the striker's head to be as still as possible at the moment of impact, whether the ball be large or small, round or oval'. There have always been batsmen who have successfully defied the orthodox, but surely the art of batting is difficult enough without making it more so.

As to the modern fad of the heavy bat – Green thinks that the average weight has increased by as much as half a pound since the days of Bradman and Denis Compton – my belief is that it has changed batting methods very much for the worse, especially against fast bowling. It is a subject to which I hope to return.

THE CRICKETER
DECEMBER 1984

1985

NEW LIBRARY AT LORD'S

Giving Spectators
Their Money's Worth

One of the sure things about cricket is that reform is always in the air. Within recent memory, the MCC, in each case at the counties' request, set up five full-scale inquiries within thirty years. And since December, C. H. Palmer's working party has been looking into the reasons for England's 'dismal' showings in Tests – an adjective which, incidentally, could certainly not be applied to recent happenings in India.

Simultaneously, ideas which are only indirectly connected with Test performances are being paraded as usual. A conservative-inclined administrator such as C. G. A. Paris, president of Hampshire, for instance, supports a school which would oblige the bowler to deliver with his front foot behind the bowling rather than the popping crease. He would have the bowler propel the ball 4 feet further, thus giving the batsman extra time to decide upon and execute his stroke.

Mr Paris tied this theme to a general proposition that 'spectators are no longer getting their money's worth' – as to which, viewing the phrase literally, the TCCB have at last taken the plunge to the extent that in next summer's Tests against Australia spectators can claim a refund on their tickets if there has been no play.

My mind goes back to a question asked me once by Charlie Chaplin late in his life when he was reminiscing about Tom Hayward, Bobbie Abel, Tom Richardson and other Surrey heroes of his Kennington youth. 'Tell me,' he asked, 'have they got around to giving a raincheck yet?' As a young comedian playing at a Nottingham music hall he had gone to Trent Bridge to watch his team, splashed out half-a-crown on a stand seat, and seen not a ball bowled. The injustice had rankled for upwards of half a century. 'So I had to go over to America and watch baseball,' he added.

At present the TCCB say their experiment will last two years and be confined to Tests. There may be difficulties of implementation at first, and one can understand secretariats being less than enthusiastic at an increase of work. I hope, however, that the principle will be extended to all first-class cricket with an inevitable if intangible increase of public goodwill.

This winter has seen other welcome evidence of concern for the paying spectator. Next month in Melbourne Fred Bennett, the Australian Cricket Board chairman, is to press all ICC countries to agree a minimum over rate of 90 per day in Tests – something obviously desirable which has hitherto stuck on the refusal of West Indies to comply. In such matters surely the say-so of the home authority should be obligatory.

Again, the TCCB has tightened up on county over rates and reinstituted for 1985 realistic fines, despite the opposition of county captains. The captains stood self-condemned last year when, on the fine system being lifted, the seasonal over rate dropped more than 2 overs per hour. The crowd were robbed of 40 minutes play each day.

I cannot believe that Mr Palmer's experts will fall for the notion often pushed by certain players and critics that England's Test performances would be improved if the County Championship were confined to sixteen four-day matches. There are too many counter-arguments to parade them all here. I can imagine nothing more disastrous to the county clubs less likely to improve the technique or mental outlook of potential Test cricketers. Let it be sufficient, so far as the theme of value for spectators is concerned, that they would be the losers. Parkinson's Law would apply: 'Work expands to fill the time available for its completion.'

Lastly, on the matter of restoring the tempo of the game, whatever happened to the reform put forward and accepted for trial of limiting the bowler's run-up? It was in the early 1960s that Sir Frank Worrell at an ICC meeting, speaking for himself rather than for the West Indies board, proposed a limit, if I remember rightly, mentioning 22 yards. Coming when it did, the idea was specially noteworthy – and, incidentally, Wes Hall and Charlie Griffith were still in their heyday.

England among other countries then promised to 'use their best endeavours' to discourage exaggerated run-ups – and promptly picked an opening bowler who began his approach not far short of Lord's pavilion.

The 'advisory' county committee, as it then was, announced that they would press for a limitation 'in all grades of cricket'. They were empty words. Sixteen years later the TCCB agreed, at the instigation of the ICC and through the Cricket Council, that bowlers' run-ups should be limited to 25 yards. That was in 1980 – since when, what?

Much guff is talked about the sin of depriving the game of the glorious rhythm of a Holding or a Lillee. But most great fast bowlers have generated their speed from a run of 20 yards or a shade more.

Those who really know are sure that after a short period of acclimatization no bowler would be the worse for a limitation and most would be the better. If cricket were to deprive itself of the sight of quickish bowlers lumbering up from 35 yards or so in the present fashion the tempo of the game would be much accelerated with great benefit all round. The TCCB *might* even be able eventually to discard their at present necessary fining system.

THE DAILY TELEGRAPH
12 FEBRUARY 1985

─────────── *Rugger Writers Revisited* ───────────

The Rugby Union Writers' Club celebrate their Silver Jubilee with a gala dinner at the Press Club. Would I, as the first chairman, attend and speak? *Did so with some foreboding, but found a very good audience and got it all in in about 12 minutes – surely the maximum for any after-dinner speech. I went back to my first season as* Evening Standard *correspondent in 1928–9 (when England under R. Cove-Smith won all five Internationals – five because the Waratahs from NSW were over). The attitude to writers by the authorities was traditionally friendly except for the Scots, who in my day (1927–64) made few concessions either to press or public. For instance, they didn't even number their players. Jock Aikman-Smith, their formidable supremo, died in the train on his way to watch Wales v Scotland, but for some years afterwards, presumably out of timid respect for his memory, their players remained un-numbered and the forwards, therefore, all but anonymous. His verdict had been a gruff: 'Our men are no' cattle.'*

Of the founders of the RUWC three committee members had died – Ross McWhirter, murdered by the IRA, Pat Marshall of the Daily Express, *and the one and only Owen Llewelyn Owen, who carried a triple responsibility as the number one* Times *man on rugby football, athletics and boxing, all for a reputed salary of less than £1000 a year. Ross, of course, is for ever associated, along with his twin, Norris, as founder of about the most successful book since the Bible,* The Guinness Book of Records. *But he was also the co-author and guiding hand of two exemplary publications, the centenary histories of the RFU and of the OURFC.*

Owen's flow of reminiscence beguiled many a long train journey, recited with utter blue-eyed assurance. Whether playing one code of football for Swansea or the other for Bristol City or Ipswich, going a round or two as sparring partner to Gene Tunney, reporting the Boxer Rising, fighting in the First World War or the Second, or relating something exciting happening at one of the nine Olympic Games he had covered during his forty-two years on The Times, *we could never catch him out. He had seen it all, and went on doing so until he died in harness at seventy-nine. With other senior games-writers of his generation he was extremely kind and helpful to me.*

DIARY
14 MARCH 1985

Lyttelton/Hart-Davis Bons Mots

Resuming my recent ramble among the *Lyttelton/Hart-Davis Letters* one finds G.W.L. writing scathingly in 1957 (during the editorship of Norman Preston) about the *Wisden* of that time: 'The letterpress is very poor stuff compared with that in the *Wisden*'s of cricket's Golden Age (1892–1912).' My feeling is that Lyttelton might not be so disapproving of the *Wisden* of the 1980s, though what he would have said about one-day cricket and the utter dependence on sponsorship one dares not think.

Yet he was not altogether blind to frailties in his youthful heroes:

It is disillusioning to one with my youthful loyalties to realise that the majestic MacLaren, with his 'superb crease-side manner', was an extremely stupid, prejudiced and pig-headed man, even in cricket matters. Plum always says he had the worst fault of a captain, viz pessimism about his team, expressed in their presence: 'Just look what they've given me – half of them creaking with old age, George Hirst fat as butter' etc., etc. But let us remember that when Wainwright gave him a long-hop to leg to get his century off in a Gents and Players, he kicked it away and sternly ordered him to bowl his best.

I would say that this judgement by the founder of *The Cricketer* was, as they say, spot on. Neither MacLaren nor Jardine had the instinctive understanding of human nature which is just about the most important quality in leadership. Both, surely, were over-rated as captains, and Jardine at least undervalued as a batsman.

Lyttelton's memory is keen but not infallible. He writes that the Grandstand has not altered except for Father Time at the top, noting in passing that

> The first Eton *v* Harrow I saw was from a box above the Grandstand in 1895; a waiter had an apoplectic fit just outside. We – my brother and I – felt we were seeing life.

No doubt he was right about the poor waiter, but Hart-Davis had to remind him that the Grandstand was completely rebuilt. Furthermore and by the way, it has been alleged that Sir Herbert Baker's present building, comely though it is, is reckoned in relation to its bulk to contain the lowest possible number of saleable seats – i.e., those with a view of both sets of stumps. The architect, however, made a surprise gift of the Father Time weather vane, which disarmed criticism.

C. M. Wells, apart from being Gubby Allen's housemaster, was a famous Eton figure, the embodiment of the scholar-sportsman. He was talking about great hams he had eaten, one at Bembridge in 1899 and another at Aberdovey in 1904. It was not easy, says Lyttelton, to steer him on to cricket, though primed with claret he will

> tell you of his best innings, viz nine runs on a ruined and crumbling pitch, in the dark, against Richardson and Lockwood – and of course no protector. 'I needn't have had a bat; I was hit all over from chin to heel, but I didn't get out that night. I was bowled first ball next day.' By Tom Richardson, whose genial way it was to say as his victim passed him pavilion-wards: 'Best one I've bowled this year, sir.' All old cricketers of any sense will tell you that Tom R. bowling in 1894–8 was the finest sight in the world.

How right was G.W.L. about the habit of comparing cricketers of different generations:

Apropos of cricket, I was browsing in an *Ego* last night and found that C. B. Fry's order of merit over the ages was Ranji, W.G., Trumper, Bradman, Hobbs, on which I make two comments: (1) How can anyone be *above* W.G. or Hobbs, or alternatively, as the lawyers say, how could either have done more than he did? and (2) Ranji and Fry always over-estimated each other, both apparently blind to the stark fact that each was found wanting in too many Test matches, which after all is *the* test of the *whole* cricketer – body, mind, and heart. . . . Those lists in order of merit are silly; there are too many candidates. It is a case of 'there is no measuring the precedence between a louse and a flea' at the other end of the scale.

Hart-Davis concurs:

We shall never know whether Irving was a greater actor than Garrick, and who cares? Let Trumper and W.G. sleep in peace with their deathless and unclassifiable fame.

Ego was the autobiography, in umpteen separate parts, of James Agate, another literary man attracted to cricket. G.W.L. gives this aside about him:

Yes, old Agate was at Giggleswick. Tuppy always alleged that he knew a man called Wigglesworth who lived at Biggleswade and was educated at Giggleswick. But I don't think we believed him. I fancy the clientele is mainly local.

Lyttelton quotes Gubby Allen:

He had just seen Statham who told him that Hall, 6 ft 5 in, was *much* the fastest bowler he or anyone else had ever seen; not even Cowdrey really enjoyed facing him.

He adds that G.O.A. regarded himself as much the same pace as Larwood. With the subject very recently in my mind, let me say G.O.A. never thought so, though Larwood himself thought that he was the faster in Australia, Allen in England. The latter disagrees.

Just occasionally G.W.L. is well wide of the mark. Writing of perhaps the greatest of all Test series, Australia *v* West Indies in 1960–1, he says:

With Bradman as captain that black team would have won the rubber – or M. A. Noble. Both of them, they tell me, immensely superior to any English captain.

But decidedly not superior to Frank Worrell in the context of that tour.

By the spring of 1962 George Lyttelton's health failed fast. He dictated his last letter, saying of the last cricket book Hart-Davis sent him, *Great Cricket Matches*, edited by Handasyde Buchanan:

> That cricket book is full of interest and also strange omissions. Fancy leaving out Jessop's great match at The Oval in 1902, and the famous, though possibly apocryphal, 'Come on, Wilfred, we'll get 'em in singles.' Uncle Edward on Fowler's Match I find a little prolix in places and I think there are better accounts, but it is all right. It calls up numberless memories, and as you may imagine I live during the day largely on reminiscence.

His last recorded comment was, 'Oh, the boredom.' Well, he never bored anyone. I select this tail-piece:

> Cousin Oliver reported his father's eulogy of W.G.'s neck. Well, I don't suppose the doctor's rivalled driven snow, but in sober fact the remark was made about E.M.'s.

Cousin Oliver's father was in the best position to make a judgement – he was Alfred, the great wicket-keeper. Driven snow indeed!

THE CRICKETER
MARCH 1985

George Cox: Man of Sussex

Few cricketers in his day were more popular with the crowds than 'Young' George Cox, who after many months of illness died following a severe heart attack on Saturday at Burgess Hill, Sussex, aged seventy-three.

Cox the younger, cherubic of countenance and full of enthusiastic intent whether batting or in the field, was the son of George R. Cox, an austere figure by contrast. George senior was a slow left-arm bowler of guile and accuracy, who at the age of fifty-one took seventeen wickets in a match for Sussex against Warwickshire at Horsham, a mile or two from the village of Warnham where both were born.

Together, with only two years, 1929 and 1930, intervening, the Coxes spanned the period 1901–60. In the county of families – notably the Parkses, the Langridges, the Tates, the Griffiths and the Gilligans – no one could quite match this record.

Young George did much to sustain the reputation of Sussex as an attractive batting side in the early 1930s when, in search of the Championship for which they were runners-up three years running, their play sometimes wore a dullish look.

Maybe Cox's cricket, though it came very close to England standards, was considered a shade too lighthearted for Test purposes. It says much for the quality of his method, however, that he enjoyed his best season, with 2369 runs and an average of 49, in his fortieth year. The following summer, 1951, his benefit amounted to £6620, at that time a Sussex record.

In all he made 22,949 runs, including fifty hundreds, with an average of 32.

In his younger days he was a dashing centre-forward for three professional clubs, Arsenal (in their heyday of the 1930s), Fulham and Luton Town.

On retirement, he remained immersed in cricket, first as coach at Winchester, then with Sussex, and later for many years on the county committee.

Always in much demand as an after-dinner speaker of the driest humour, he was an active president of the Sussex Cricket Society, and the moving spirit of the flourishing Sussex Junior Cricket Festival. As an antidote to all that is sad in modern cricket, the annual Festival Dinners under George's chairmanship, attended by both sexes and all ages, were hard to beat.

THE DAILY TELEGRAPH
I APRIL 1985

How Headley's Genius Paved the Way

Headley was not the first West Indian batsman to be designated 'great'. That distinction, according to the sure judgement of the senior West Indian historian C. L. R. James, belongs to George Challenor, who so impressed the English critics when he came over with the West Indian teams of 1906 and 1923. But he was certainly the first great *black* West Indian batsman, and the extraordinary thing is that he learned the game not in one of the traditional strongholds of Bridgetown, Port of Spain and Georgetown, where inter-colonial rivalry had flourished for more than half a century, but in faraway Jamaica, cut off from the south by a thousand miles of sea. Until, after the war, they became connected with the rest of the Caribbean by air the Jamaicans' experience of first-class cricket was confined to visits by MCC and privately organized teams, notably the three brought between 1927 and 1932 by Lionel, Lord Tennyson.

Headley was a natural genius, almost self-taught, who as an eighteen-year-old suddenly announced himself with a succession of very high scores against Tennyson's second team of 1927–8. As historians know well, he was due to have left Jamaica for the United States in order to be trained as a dentist before the first match against the touring side was due, and it was only the delay in the issue of a visa that allowed him to play – and to announce himself with an innings of 71. When this was followed by 211 against the Englishmen in the second representative match, dentistry's loss became cricket's gain.

Two years later in his first Test match in Barbados Headley made 176, the first of the ten Test hundreds he had built up when the war came. Throughout the pre-war decade this wiry but short, slight fellow, coming in at number three, more often than not with next to nothing on the board, held Test innings after Test innings together. At the end of a tour or a series he had averaged, as like as not, more than double the next man. In England in 1939, aged thirty and at his peak, he scored 1745 runs, averaging 72. No one else reached 1000 or averaged more than 30. He stood alone.

In the Lord's Test of 1939 George made 106 and 107 out of totals of 277 and 225, and since this was the first Test I broadcast in England the picture of his batting still remains clear in the mind. His stance was distinctly two-shouldered as he stood there, stock still, sleeves buttoned at the wrist and the plum-coloured cap jauntily askew, a model of wary concentration. Like all the great ones, he played the ball very late yet without any suggestion of hurry. He was strongest off the back foot and on the on-side. Perfect timing and wrist-work propelled the ball sweetly through the whole segment from mid-on to fine leg with little suggestion of force. But he also had all the off-side strokes at will, being, like nearly all the best of the smaller men, a beautiful cutter.

If the key to his batting was a determined avoidance of risk it was simply that he – unlike his illustrious successors – knew that he could not afford to get out. If he failed, the end was always in sight. Jeffrey Stollmeyer, writing in his biography *Everything Under The Sun*, is quite unequivocal: 'He was the greatest batsman that the West Indies produced. Of this I have no doubt, and my association with Test cricket in the West Indies spans a period from 1939 to the present day, during which I have seen and/or played with the three "W"s, Gary Sobers and Rohan Kanhai in their prime: also Viv Richards of the present crop, great players all.' To this list of those within measurable distance of Headley one might perhaps today add Clive Lloyd but surely no one else.

Whether or not one goes all the way with Stollmeyer's judgement, it must be acknowledged that he is in a position to speak parallelled only by his great friend and youthful contemporary in the West Indies side of 1939, Gerry Gomez. But what of the famous batsmen in Headley's descent who have held the West Indian flag high now for the best part of forty years? Well, the only sure thing about the batting quality of the immortal trio from Barbados, Frank Worrell, Everton Weekes and Clyde Walcott, is that there was precious little between them in terms of achievement. Between 1949 and 1960, playing around fifty Tests apiece, the three Ws in their widely separated styles scored thirty-nine hundreds: Worrell all grace and elegance; Weekes stocky, punchy, full of the killer instinct; Walcott, towering physically above them both, a driver of awesome power. Throw in Worrell's distinct utility as a bowler and Walcott's as a wicket-keeper, and the old cliché 'a host in themselves' scarcely meets the case.

Until Worrell's last glorious phase as a captain, by which time the other two had retired, each drew strength from the presence of the other two. Likewise Sobers was never called upon to bear the weight of the West Indian batting unaided. He began with the three, and played most of his long Test career in tandem with Kanhai. These were latterly joined by Lloyd, who in these last ten years has been fortified by the genius of Richards.

Of the last four mentioned, three are a little less easy to place than their predecessors. Kanhai (the only East Indian under consideration, although some may well argue that Alvin Kallicharran should be) combined a rare natural talent with an admirable technique. Lloyd hits the ball just about as hard as anyone who ever played, but one sees him predominantly as a fighter whose easy manner belies a degree of determination second to none. Richards possesses an almost unequalled brilliance, and his finest innings are incomparable. If he fails more often than the others under review it is because he is a victim of the modern overexposure of the top players. He will make no secret that he and his contemporaries, wearied by perpetual travel and the limelight, are often merely going through the motions.

There remains the inimitable Sobers. That no one can approach his record as an all-round cricketer goes without saying. What one wonders is, if he had not taken 235 wickets for the West Indies over a span of ninety-three Tests, and if in consequence he had batted a couple of places higher in the order, how many more runs and hundreds would he have scored than the figures of 8032 and 26 which, as they stand, tower high above everyone else's? Not that anyone ever cared less about the arithmetic of his cricket. If I had to choose anyone to play for my life, as the saying is, I would name Gary without hesitation. In him genius based on strictly orthodox principles found almost perfect expression.

To sum up: Headley enjoyed a lonely pre-eminence in his day, though it must be allowed that the bowling opposed to him was less formidable than much that his successors had to face. Paraphrasing Plum Warner, who used to say, 'No one has ever batted *better* than Jack Hobbs', I would suggest that no West Indian has ever batted better than Headley and Sobers. And a final reflection: how extraordinary that within modern times a few scattered communities with a combined population roughly akin to the 3 million or so of Sydney or Melbourne should have produced a string of memorable batsmen at least equivalent to the combined output of England and Australia.

WISDEN
APRIL 1985

———————— *Bajans at the Abbey* ————————

Attended Memorial Service at Westminster Abbey for the Rt. Hon. Tom Adams, Barbados Prime Minister, who had died suddenly aged only fifty-three. He and I had been talking cricket (on the history of which he was the island's prime expert) only a few weeks earlier. These occasions show the Bajans for the dignified, proud Christian people they are. This was much in evidence at the Independence celebrations on the Savannah in Bridgetown in 1966, in the Abbey service of thanksgiving ten years later, and here now. Fancy the immigrant community of so tiny a country – the island population is fewer than 300,000 – coming, sober-suited, on a working day, and filling the transepts and most of the nave of the Abbey to honour one of the family, so to say. When racial troubles flare up in England those from the Caribbean islands concerned are lumped together as West Indians. I'm sure that precious few of them come from Barbados.

DIARY
20 MAY 1985

Brearley Examines Captain's Art

Is there a full-length cricket book (288 pages) likely to hold the attention of the average reader on the one basic theme of captaincy? It is a fact, I think, that amid all the 10,000 or so books listed in the *Bibliography of Cricket* nothing on this scale has been hitherto attempted.

But it is also true that (with the possible exception of C. B. Fry) there has never been anyone fitted to tackle the job with such glittering credentials as one of the most successful of all England captains, who happens to be a high-class scholar specializing in psychotherapy. Yes, John Michael Brearley, OBE – I give his full name and honour since it is not to be found in the book – has given us the fruits of four years of preparation in *The Art of Captaincy* (Hodder & Stoughton, £12.95), and the jacket blurb scarcely over-states when it claims 'the result is sure to be regarded as a classic in the game'.

True, the theory of captaincy is palatable only in small doses. A chapter on the art is to be found in many a textbook. What Mike Brearley has done is to illustrate his eleven chapters or sub-divisions with a heap of more or less relevant anecdote, much culled from the past, more picked up at first hand.

The index contains several references to all the captains prominent since he first put on his pads for Cambridge in 1961, but he also comments on and evaluates household names from the past.

This is a modestly told book with little of the personal pronoun, which nevertheless says a lot about Brearley. He was an outstanding leader for the reasons that matter most. He was popular with his players, so that authority came easily and naturally. Also he was a close student of the game and in consequence a sound tactician whom his teams accordingly trusted and followed.

He comes near to saying that he was not always worth his place in the England XI. 'I knew what it was like to be regarded as a liability in the team one week and as the Duke of Wellington a week later.'

I would submit there has been scarcely an England Test performance in the four years since his retirement which would not have been improved, and sometimes transformed, by his leadership.

Though himself richly endowed with it, Brearley is strangely dismissive of the captaincy value of charisma, which my dictionary describes as the 'capacity to inspire followers or disciples with devotion and enthusiasm'.

It is a pity there was no longer anyone available to give him a personal assessment of two of the most famous and successful of his predecessors, Plum Warner and Percy Chapman.

Sir Donald Bradman is quoted without contradiction as saying that captains should ideally be batsmen. Certainly I never saw a better one than Bradman. But what about all-rounders? My own list would include Benaud, Illingworth, Worrell, Robins and Fender at first hand, and by repute Jackson, Armstrong and Noble – all-rounders all.

To understand the mind of a bowler is greatly important. It is rare to find a modern captain who has a clue as to the proper use of spin. This is one reason for its decline.

The author rates Illingworth, Greig and the Chappell brothers as four of the best of his time, even though Ian, the elder, 'nudged cricket in the direction of gang warfare'. Against Tony Greig's pre-Packer triumph in India must surely be set his failure with Sussex.

Clive Lloyd is a delightful man but 'I never felt he had a cricketing brain'. Peter May gets high marks, Brian Close scarcely fewer. 'Cowdrey's problem was himself . . .', Benaud was 'one of the greatest captains', and Keith Miller (surely the ultimate purveyor of charisma?) 'the best captain never to lead Australia'. The best of all touring managers was, for him, Douglas Insole.

On more general matters Brearley believes that players are much too reluctant to take advice, and coaches too reluctant 'from modesty or lack of confidence' to impart it. The condition of most county nets is a scandal.

Over-indulgent, surely, as regards intimidatory bowling, he finds the modern curse of abusive talk aimed at the batsman 'a totally unwelcome aberration in the game, inane, humourless and unacceptable'.

The book is informative and entertaining reading for all sorts and conditions of cricketers. It is sad, though of course understandable, that Mike is at present so absorbed in the work of psychiatry that he can afford no time for the administration of the game he has adorned and which has formed so large a part of his life.

THE DAILY TELEGRAPH
7 JUNE 1985

———————————— *Scare at Lord's* ————————————

Bomb-plot scare at Lord's during Queen's visit? Well, that might have been the headline. There I was, enjoying lunch in the President's Box, when a police officer asked to see me urgently. Round we went to the office behind the Committee Room in which Her Majesty was shortly due. An accusing finger pointed at a briefcase with my initials thereon. And why, pray, was a soft, regular ticking sound issuing therefrom? So sorry, officer, I'm staying the night, and the noise came from my alarm-clock. Apparently a sniffer-dog had thus earned his keep, and they had only just stopped short of evacuating the pavilion. Of course, some mischievous fellow told the Queen, who was tolerably amused.

DIARY
28 JUNE 1985

One-day Cricket Under Fire

I hate basketball and baseball and have been busy establishing that baseball and cricket are in every way different. Having watched an hour or so, Isabel said, 'But, my dear man, it's exactly like baseball. They swish at everything that comes along and if they get a touch they run like crazy regardless of where the ball goes!' I muttered something about cricket being philosophically different, but had really nought to offer! It was so true – and so awful!

Who wrote that to me and from where might make a teasing quiz question. The answers are that the lament came from a former first-class cricketer now domiciled in the United States and married to an American. On a visit to England they had tuned in to the so-called World Championship relayed from Australia, and my old friend's wife had seemingly found the goings-on rather less mystifying than he had. He had only ever seen one Gillette final many years ago, and 'was astonished at the white ball, coloured clothes and, in fact, the whole thing including the field-setting and strokes'.

It scarcely needs a retired cricketer back from abroad to remind us how far 'the meadow game with the beautiful name' has strayed from its origins. I write as one who in the early 1960s welcomed the first knock-out cup more readily than most, and who saw the Sunday League, coupled with the counties' simultaneous import in 1968 of leading cricketers from abroad – one would not have happened without the other – as an economic necessity at that time.

The limited-over game is with us for good, whether we like it or not, and in the right proportions its place in the season's pro-gramme would today be accepted by most. It is Australian commercial interests which have both magnified the thing to a ridiculous extent and multiplied the offence by vulgarizing the game at the same time, so that all concerned – public, players, cricket writers and their readers – are thoroughly disenchanted.

In Australia I suspect that a decrease in the number of one-day Internationals may only come if the countries touring there resolutely insist on a more balanced programme – which, among other advantages, would tend to bring State cricket back at least a little way into the limelight.

So far as one-day Internationals in England are concerned, this summer's rubber of three, acting as an aperitif to the Test series, would seem about right. As to our domestic cricket, we must await the recommendations of the C. H. Palmer working party in the hope they may advise a judicious revision of the county programme. (Generally speaking, the greater the number of overs the better the game, and my personal preference would be for the John Player League matches to begin at noon with a maximum of 50 overs and a 22-yard run-up.) Meanwhile, I hope my correspondent from America, if he comes over this summer, strikes lucky with a well-fought match before a well-behaved Lord's crowd. Something like the Nat West Final of 1984 might suggest to him that the game has not gone completely to the dogs.

THE CRICKETER
JUNE 1985

Sandy Lyle's Open

How lucky to have the Open Championship on one's doorstep! Royal St George's, as in 1981, proved too tough for most, though weather conditions were not unduly difficult, only the winner equalling the par of 280.

As one of the 18th green stewards I saw much drama and, of course, Sandy Lyle's victory, the first by a Briton since Jacklin sixteen years ago, this despite his famous fluff when leading by a single stroke at the last. The pin was at its most testing placement near the top of the slope leading down to where Lyle's ball finished in Duncan's Hollow. The most delicate of pitches is called for. He fractionally underhits his wedge from the thick apron and the ball comes back most of the way to his feet. Agonized cries. Deliberately he tries again and this time gets safely down in two. Almost at once a roar announces fours on the leader board for both his nearest rivals, Langer and Graham at the short 16th. Another difficult pin position tempted both into error. Such are the strains, so narrow are the margins between triumph and sickening disappointment. Lyle has since shown himself the stuff of a champion, wearing his fame with modesty and Scottish good manners.

DIARY
21 JULY 1985

Wyatt the Fighter

R. E. S. Wyatt was, I think, the best amateur batsman to play for England between 1919 and the prime of Peter May in the 1950s, save only K. S. Duleepsinhji, with whose genius, in that tragically brief career, scarcely any could compare.

Bob Wyatt was as indomitable as Douglas Jardine and a much better player of slow bowling. If he did not aspire to the brilliance of A. P. F. Chapman in his prime their durability was in sharp contrast.

Gerald Pawle's well-researched, smoothly flowing *R. E. S. Wyatt, Fighting Cricketer* (Allen & Unwin, £12.95) gives a valuable insight into the game as it used to be between the wars and just after. The subject has been lucky to find such a sympathetic and widely experienced author living near at hand. No one could better deserve the epithet 'fighting'. He captained England through the 1934 Test series against Australia with a metal shield giving only partial protection to a badly fractured right thumb.

Of his seven broken bones the worst occurred in the West Indies where a fast ball broke his jaw in four places with a noise like a revolver shot. 'He came to as he lay on a stretcher in the pavilion and gestured for a note pad. He then rearranged his batting order.' He next sent a message to Martindale, the bowler, assuring him it was a perfectly fair ball. On his return home he answered prophecies that his nerve might be affected by scoring hundreds in the first two matches of the English season.

Wyatt had been the all-round backbone of Warwickshire cricket for sixteen years and county captain for eight when a sinister combination of secretary and treasurer manipulated his removal. The fact that an aloof, undemonstrative exterior concealed a real concern for his players and a burning devotion to the game gave them their chance. The last of his 39,470 runs were accordingly made after the war for Worcestershire in a far more congenial atmosphere.

Wyatt's judgement on Jardine in Australia is surely the right one. 'In my opinion he was much maligned, but I felt it was rather sad that such a fine cricketer and captain should ever have chosen to return to a country which he fundamentally disliked. His previous very successful tour there had left him with deep-lying prejudices which he was never to overcome.'

THE DAILY TELEGRAPH
27 JULY 1985

──────────── *Arab Jubilee* ────────────

The Arabs, the club I started almost by chance in 1935, celebrate their Jubilee at Hurlingham, with a keen inter-Arab match, followed by a dinner-dance attended by fifty-eight of us with forty-four (headed by Ann) of the most beautiful, best-dressed and altogether stunning partners you ever saw. Founding the Arabs was the luckiest thing I ever did. It really has given pleasure to all over its long span, and no one has more cause to be grateful than I.

DIARY
27 JULY 1985

McGilvray: Voice of Australia

When Alan McGilvray takes his final turn at the microphone at the Oval Test match the last of the first generation of sporting broadcasters will have passed into retirement. The Voice of Australian cricket will sign off, I expect, in a quiet professional way, just as John Arlott did – was it as long as five years ago?

For McGilvray it will be the end of a long, long road, on which he trod the first steps back in 1938. In his early days he took to the air in two ways, with first-hand running commentary for the Australian Broadcasting Commission and also for a commercial company, as it were synthetically.

The latter exercise, for listeners far away beyond the range of pre-war transmitters, involved a studio, a plan of the ground, a continuous stream of cabled information and an effects man to synchronize sound noises with the commentary thus realistically manufactured. I cannot recall whether we actually heard the noise as 'the ball rapped the pickets', but the similitude was such that the unsophisticated audiences of those days thought they were listening to the real thing. It cannot have been an easy assignment.

When in the late 1930s summaries at intervals and close of play were first augmented by periods of running commentary, the respective 'inside men' at the BBC and ABC evolved, with the co-operation of the commentator, a style of cricket description which depended on certain rules. The most important of these was that the listener must be given a mental vision of the bowler's run-up, his delivery, and the batsman's stroke as they all happened, or within a second or two thereof. You coloured the general picture in intervening moments as best you could, so long as you did not commit the cardinal sin of being late on the strokes.

Alan, as we all did, followed this technique, which was thought to give a basic pattern to play in the mind of the listener, and while, over the years, other styles have evolved around him he has stuck with it. That is one reason why I personally have found him so easy to listen to.

A retired performer must tread carefully here lest he seem to imply that we did the job better than it is done today. I do not presume to say any such thing. The more relaxed, free and easy 'Test Match Special' style of presenting cricket introduces the game to an enormous following – including, by the way, many who combine the radio commentary with the television picture.

Too many in-jokes and thank-yous for the chocolate cake, do I hear? Maybe occasionally, but think of the extra time which today has to be filled by the slower pace of the play, and the effect on the commentaries on the much greater accent on fastish bowling from over-long runs as compared with spin.

Returning, however, to McGilvray, his work at the microphone has had for me other admirable qualities beyond his basic style, and the chief of these is a complete objectivity and absence of bias. Were it not for the Australian inflexion, one could not tell where his personal sympathies lay. His critical judgements have been not only sound but eminently fair and consistently generous.

He is the enemy, thank goodness, of all that cheapens the game or threatens the values which were taken for granted in every generation before Packerism cast its ugly shadow on it. In Australia the last eight years his cricket generation have been fighting a particularly tough uphill battle. How pleased he must be, therefore, that his last series is being contested in a chivalrous, sporting manner – for which Allan Border and David Gower deserve the gratitude of all.

Whatever happens in the Ashes-decider at The Oval – and in the hope, I must add, that there will be no further comments in the heat of the moment on umpires' decisions – one Alan will be able to say of the other that he had led the most popular Australian side to have come to England for a very long time.

THE DAILY TELEGRAPH
23 AUGUST 1985

──────── *General Tamed the Aussies* ────────

An Australian note: this is the eightieth birthday of my old friend John Grimwade, who has been entertaining visiting Poms at Mount Eliza with gusto and humour ever since the war. John's father, whose kindness in 1946 started me on a long and hospitable association with Peninsula Golf and Country Club (which he founded), was a grizzled general from the First World War. When, after the Armistice, the Aussie troops did a bit more than grumble at having to hang around northern France in the 1918 winter until ships were available to take them home to sunshine and plenty, the Military Police proposed that they should provide him with an armed escort as he attempted to tackle the situation. The general knew his countrymen better. He strolled in to the hornet's nest unescorted, with his hands in his pockets, and gave them the facts in the vernacular. Son John used to sound a bit chippy in a half-serious way, saying in his war he had been promoted only as far as company sergeant major. However, he was proud a few years ago to be awarded an AM – that is, a Member of the Order of Australia.

DIARY
16 SEPTEMBER 1985

Haute Couture at Canterbury

The wettest Canterbury Week for ages had redeeming days and at least one moment of comedy much enjoyed by our near-octogenarian (3 December), Leslie Ames. Enter a guest in a Rolls-

Royce who pokes his head out to the gateman and announces, 'I am a guest, will you please direct me to the Hardy Amies stand?' 'Sir', he might have been told, 'Mr Ames is a cricketer, not a couturier.' Or did he think he'd come to a fashion show?

Even Ladies' Day is not exactly that.

THE CRICKETER
OCTOBER 1985

─────────── *Alston All Alive-O* ───────────

The BBC celebrated sixty years of Outside Broadcasts with a gala dinner. Arlott, Alston and Swanton found themselves at Patricia Ewing's table, all being rather senior in the business. John, having got to work seriously on the claret, was moved to some sotto voce criticisms of a ridiculously long speech. Rex was chirpy as ever, so I was surprised as well as rather cross to be woken up only a few days later by The Daily Telegraph *and told that* The Times' *first edition contained his obituary, written by John Woodcock. Could they use the one which I had written of him? Having suffered once in the past in this respect, I said a firm 'no', unless they could get confirmation. Rex was duly located next morning fit and well, and* The Times *had, of course, to print an apology. Rex had the rare pleasure of pointing out to them several inaccuracies in the obituary. His revenge was complete a while later when as a widower he inserted on the social page a notice of his second marriage. As I write he is eighty-four and still going strong.*

DIARY
14 OCTOBER 1985

─────────── *In the Arms of Sister Agnes* ───────────

To Sister Agnes's (otherwise known as King Edward VII Hospital for Officers) to undergo transurethral prostatectomy and litholapaxy (otherwise known as the Old Man's Op.). It was reassuring that at the prior consultation the distinguished surgeon J. P. Williams (not J.P.R.!) had worn an MCC tie.

Sister Agnes's is the friendliest place possible. The founder's spirit permeates it from top to bottom, the top then being personified in the hospital chairman, Sir Mark Baring, and the famous Matron, Miss Shipsey. Sir Mark (who has since died of cancer after innumerable operations), a devout Anglican Catholic, bypassed St Paul's,

Knightsbridge, for once and most kindly drove me to All Saints', Margaret Street, where Ann and I were married, for Sunday High Mass.

The operation was completely successful, but the popular idea that it is a push-over nowadays I found wide of the mark. It was two months before I again trod the links. The new World of Cricket *therefore had my best attention.*

DIARY
26 OCTOBER 1985

Books and Bouncers

Everyone who came to the opening of the new MCC Library, performed as his final Presidential duty by Mr George Mann, made very satisfied noises about it. It is reasonably spacious, well furnished, and the upper of its two rooms looks out onto a particularly civilized corner of Lord's, the Coronation Garden. The only criticism, and a valid one, concerns the size of the curator's and secretary's offices – and there are ideas to remedy this.

The shelves contain most, if not all, of the books likely to be in general demand, including the *Wisden* set, and others of special value safely under lock and key. There is a lending section for members, composed of duplicate copies, and if this catches the eye of a well-disposed publisher or two let me add it is capable of expansion. The Library is open, as it has always been, to genuine researchers, by prior arrangement with the curator. That was a condition of a generous contribution to the cost made by Agatha Christie Ltd through the person of her grandson, M. C. T. Prichard, captain of the Eton XI of 1962 and now chairman of the firm.

The status and positioning of the Library (as an adjunct of the pavilion reached by way of the bridge on the first floor) must bring to an end the at best equivocal MCC attitude to books which stretches back the best part of a century. One of the archival show-cases, indeed, contains a copy of a committee minute of 1893 noting that an offer of books could not be accepted 'at present'. Victorian sportsmen were not, perhaps, great readers. At any rate the reputed comment of the greatest of them, W.G., rings true enough when he diagnosed a young cricketer's failure to make runs to too much reading: 'You don't catch me that way.'

But now to sterner things. The England tour to West Indies approaches, and I suppose that the advance feelings of most with first-hand experience of cricket in the Caribbean will be mixed – relish at the prospect of a continuation of the old rivalry; real apprehension at the prospect of intimidation by fast bowlers.

I hope my credentials as a friend and admirer of West Indies cricket are sufficient to discount any suggestion of chauvinistic motives in writing at a time when the West Indies have several fast bowlers capable of posing a dangerous threat, while England have none.

The fact is, however, that there have been numerous occasions when their bowlers have bowled at a highly dangerous length, apparently unchecked by the captain, and eliciting, at most, ineffectual murmurings by the umpires. Nor has this only happened in front of excited home crowds. Old Trafford, 1976 and The Oval, 1984 will be stark, unhappy memories for many. Clive Lloyd, captain on both occasions, made no secret of his philosophy that it is the umpires' job to administer the Law without intervention from him.

Now Viv Richards has succeeded Lloyd and it was under his captaincy that in May last year, in the last Test in Kingston, Jamaica, the West Indies bowled in a way that evoked bitter complaint from his opposite number, Geoff Howarth, and from Jeremy Coney, who suffered a broken forearm.

It may have been mere coincidence, but that match followed directly on a Reuter interview with Richards, who was asked to comment on criticism of West Indian fast bowling by John Woodcock, Editor of *Wisden*, in the 1985 issue. Richards was quoted as saying he did not disagree with his fast bowlers bowling bouncers to tail-enders, particularly if they showed resistance. 'If you have guys who are going to stay around and be stubborn, and obviously make fast bowlers look like they are not fast bowlers, I can't see why they shouldn't be softened up a bit.'

'Softened up a bit' is a mild euphemism for what seems to have gone on in Kingston, and the first Test of David Gower's team is due to be played there on 21 February, on a pitch that traditionally encourages fast bowling and where the crowds are apt to be more volatile than elsewhere. It seems to me that before the series gets under way the authorities owe it to the game, in the light of recent events, to face the facts of the situation. These are, surely, that Law 42 against Unfair Play, including, of course, intimidation, should be explicit enough and a sufficiently strong deterrent if its provisions were enforced.

But it has hardly ever been applied to the extent of a bowler being warned off for the remainder of an innings. It is completely unrealistic to suppose that it would be applied – indeed, *could* be without the prospect of disorder – against West Indian fast bowlers by West Indian umpires in front of West Indian crowds.

That is to say the Law is unworkable. I have maintained for several years that the only *practical* preventive against intimidation is a line across the pitch. In the absence of that, and with the Law in this regard in disrepute, what action can the West Indies Board and the TCCB take to try to ensure that the forthcoming series is played, as was that between England and Australia, in proper spirit?

I believe that the ICC should propose a meeting of the two boards, before the First Test, with managers, captains and umpires present, to try to arrive at a concordat based on mutual liking and respect. If it achieved little, so much the worse for the game; at least those responsible would have tried.

THE CRICKETER
NOVEMBER 1985

Leslie Ames – Still Going Strong

Cricket is seldom forgetful of its favourite sons. Even so, it is a signal mark of the affection in which Leslie Ames is held that his eightieth birthday tomorrow should be marked by three celebrations. Kent supporters' club gave him a dinner at the weekend; there is a dinner tomorrow night, restricted by space to 120 of his friends and Kent colleagues in the Canterbury pavilion; and there is also to be a reception at the House of Lords.

Apart from a tiresome difficulty in following the flight of his shots on the golf course (and he scarcely need worry for they are almost always down the middle), Les Ames is the fittest eighty imaginable, a blessing he attributes to a daily diet of walking, whether on the links at Deal or the 9 miles from his Canterbury home to his native village of Elham.

Let me then, with the help of his clear memory, note a few of the Ames milestones, beginning with his first visit, aged eight, to the Canterbury Week with the family the day before war was declared in 1914. When Arthur Fielder bowled Vallance Jupp of Sussex he broke the stump, and Les plainly recalls the umpire having to fetch a new one.

Les learned his cricket at Elham, a strong side playing on a good pitch and rarely beaten. In the post-war years it was said among opponents that the young kid hits you all over the place, then either father bowls you out or grandfather gives you out.

The crucial milestone was the day at Hythe when Gerry Weigall, the Kent coach, told him after he had seen him bat that if he had ambitions to be a professional he must be 'double-barrelled', and promptly made him keep wicket, which he had only ever done occasionally at Harvey Grammar School, Folkestone. A place on the Kent staff soon followed, and he was only nineteen when in the Tunbridge Wells Week he made 35 in his first innings for Kent.

The following year, 1927, he became the regular 'keeper, made 1200 runs and scored the first of his 102 hundreds. *Wisden* thought he would soon be playing for England, and so he was.

He played in forty-seven Tests before Hitler brought the sequence to an end, by which time his record among the world's wicket-keeper batsmen was one to which only Alan Knott (subsequently) could hold a candle. He did not 'keep after the war, Kent having found a promising lad called Godfrey Evans.

A milestone with a personal touch: I broadcast the Middlesex match in the 1950 Canterbury Week and happened to be on the air at the moment he reached his 100th hundred. Les was in his favourite role, chasing runs against the clock, and one can see him now going yards down the pitch to Jack Young and Jim Sims and hitting them sweetly past extra cover. He made 131 out of 211 in 2 hours, and Kent won by four wickets and 7 minutes.

It was his fifth hundred of the summer, and there seemed surely more in the bag. But in the first match of 1951 his back 'went' badly. That was the end, the Kent committee being thus frustrated in their intention to offer him the captaincy in 1952.

Since then Les Ames's service to the game (rewarded with the

CBE) is a saga on its own: for seventeen years secretary-manager of Kent before becoming the club's president; Test Selector; manager of three MCC teams abroad; first professional elected to the MCC Committee. To each post he has brought the virtue of plain-spoken, completely unprejudiced good sense.

His memories in these days of stress are refreshing to listen to, happy, all of them, full of warmth for help given – starting with dear old Weigall – and friendships made.

He had 'a marvellous time as a player', batting with the great Frank Woolley, which he loved doing, not to mention 'keeping to 'Tich' Freeman – perhaps the most lethal partnership in cricket history. 'It was a privilege,' he says, 'to play alongside such wonderful people and tremendous characters as Bryan Valentine, Percy Chapman, Hopper Levett and Gerry Chalk.' He saw the amateur-pro relationship develop in his time from a reserved mutual respect – 'friendly but formal', he calls it – to a more relaxed attitude all round.

There are aspects of modern cricket that he hates, as do all the older generation – and not only they. Intimidation, whether by bowlers or close fielders, 'is not in my book of cricket'.

He has always opposed covered wickets in England, and believes the game would lose something of its dull uniformity and become far more entertaining if the covers were removed; if they are not, what future can there be for the spinner?

Ames is far from denying merit to the modern game. He thinks England now have the right batting order and a pretty good one, and is enthusiastic about the fielding, which is 'streets ahead' of what it used to be.

When exactly ten years ago I saluted L. E. G. Ames in these pages on his seventieth birthday, I mentioned that the E. stood for Ethelbert, an old family name. Now Ethelbert was King of Kent for fifty-six years, AD 560–614. Well, it is fifty-six years since our Kentish Ethelbert first played for England – and he's still going strong.

THE DAILY TELEGRAPH
2 DECEMBER 1985

——————— *Judge Faulks, RIP* ———————

Memorial services are plentifully sprinkled through my diaries. Today's in the Temple Church was for my boyhood friend, Neville Faulks. Winning scholarships to Uppingham and Sidney Sussex, he was always destined for the Bar, and was in high demand as an advocate before becoming one of those High Court judges apt to enliven the proceedings with quotable bons mots. *There was frequent 'laughter in court'. He was a prime authority on libel and divorce. No man better merited a comfortable retirement, but, twice widowed, he was for many years a martyr to the hateful, incurable skin disease psoriasis. It was rated an eccentricity when he walked about in court, but it was to get relief from pain, for sitting still could be agony. His* Who's Who *hobbies, listed before the second bereavement, were surely unique: the company of his wife and* The Times *crossword puzzle.*

DIARY
11 DECEMBER 1985

1986

STRIFE IN SOMERSET

Statistical Niceties

Amid the profusion of books published in 1985 Collins Willow have produced two which any serious collector must regard as integral to his or her library. For following *Double Century*, the fascinating anthology of 200 years of cricket in *The Times*, edited by Marcus Williams, there appeared in time for Christmas (price £25) *The Collins Who's Who of English First-Class Cricket, 1945–1984*, compiled and edited by Robert Brooke.

The world of the statistician is one into which the average person can only peer in wide-eyed astonishment. The sheer volume of work involved must have daunted anyone contemplating such an idea before the Society of Cricket Statisticians got busy, since nothing of the kind has seen the light of day since the third and last of Sir Home Gordon's *Cricket Form at a Glance* took the record from 1878 to 1937.

As it is, hail to Robert Brooke, and hail once more to Philip Bailey, Philip Thorn and Peter Wynne-Thomas, whose *Who's Who of Cricketers*, published in late 1984, claims to include all who have played in an English first-class match since the beginning of time.

In his foreword John Woodcock calls Brooke's *Who's Who* 'a book to stand alongside the great works of sporting reference, precise and unopinionated, informative, definitive, evocative and timeless', and in so doing does not claim too much for it. What, of course, is fascinating is to compare both the general format and individual entries of the two *Who's Who*s. By abbreviation according to a clear formula the Brooke method conveys more fact than that of the triumvirate in a given space. A basic difference is that whereas the latter include career figures within each entry, with Brooke these – both first-class and Test where applicable – are concentrated alphabetically in 80-odd pages at the end.

Mr Brooke is 'unopinionated', whereas the triumvirate make judgements. They tell us, for instance, that Alan Ealham was a good outfield. Their rival records the fact that he 'took five catches in field in one inns, Kent *v* Gloucs, Folkestone, 1966, all at either long-off or long-on and all off bowling of D. L. Underwood'.

Such detail apart, there is a clear and important divergence in the respect for previously accepted figures, as Mr Brooke explains in his introduction. He, in fact, founded the Society of Cricket Statisticians in 1973, and in doing so publicly stated that 'one of our express purposes was the "correction" of long-accepted figures and records'. While a process of 'correction' still marks the Bailey-Thorn-Wynne-Thomas book (which is published by Newnes 'in association with' the ACS), notably in respect of three cricketers of imperishable fame, Mr Brooke has seen the light on the road to Damascus. The 'youthful revolutionary', he says, has become 'the middle-aged reactionary'. For him the accepted records of great men are inviolate.

The three authors – and by implication the ACS itself – have had the effrontery, by contrast, to tinker with the career records not only of Sir Jack Hobbs and Herbert Sutcliffe but – wait for it – of W.G. himself. The Champion has been deprived of 600–odd runs and sixty-odd wickets, *and of two hundreds*. Not 126, it seems, but 124. With the great opening pair it is the other way round, their figures being raised by the acceptance of matches in India and Ceylon in 1930–1 which were regarded at the time, by them and everyone else, as in the nature of missionary exhibitions. (There is not a line about them in *Wisden*.) Hobbs, it would seem, scored not 197 hundreds but 199! Thus is history stood on its head. Needless to say, the Editor of *Wisden* in his foreword does not mince his words. 'Standardization of cricket records is obviously desirable; but it is best based, I think, so far as the status of a match is concerned, on contemporary rather than latter-day opinion.' There are some people, he adds, who, given half a chance, would rewrite the Church's Table of Kindred and Affinity.

I would venture to suggest to the ACS trio that they purge their blasphemy. Can they not, like Robert Brooke did earlier, have a rethink? By attempting to perpetuate the untenable they only disparage their own credibility and devalue a remarkable feat of industry and scholarship.

THE CRICKETER
JANUARY 1986

—————— *Harold Macmillan Remembers* ——————

An annual treat! When Harold Macmillan came over from Birch Grove to stay with Julian and Carol Faber (she being his daughter) at Sandwich Bay, Ann and I used kindly to be asked to meet him for drinks or dinner. He was now ninety-one and had become the Earl of Stockton. Refreshed with a whisky and soda, his talk flowed so swiftly and easily.

We spoke of Fowler's Match of 1910, which he saw. This brought him on to talk of Alexander who, of course, played in it. Then I heard how the last war generals were better than those of the First World War. Why? Because they were up there and saw it all, not lying miles behind as in France and Belgium. Otherwise how could they have been so stupid as to launch the futility of Passchendaele? What was Passchendaele like? Well, if you can imagine the lowlands of Lincolnshire after the dykes had over-flowed you have an idea. It was the most impossible country to fight over, and casualties were bound to have been enormous. Anyone who knew the ground would have known that.

So in a moment or two we proceeded from Eton v Harrow to the mud of Flanders, all in that quiet, conversational voice. Magical!

DIARY
8 JANUARY 1986

Mixed Emotions as Australia Suffer

At least nine out of ten of *Cricketer* readers, I feel sure, hailed with the utmost pleasure the historic victory of New Zealand in the three-match series in Australia, while ten out of ten must have applauded with wonder as well as admiration the achievement of Richard Hadlee in taking thirty-three wickets. Of that more anon.

Our sentiments were compounded of pleasure that New Zealand should have 'broken through' with their first success in Australia against neighbours who for more than forty years up to the early 1970s had ignored them deplorably; that and a feeling that the Australian authorities, in having allowed the whole pattern of their cricket to be transformed by commercial interests, had got what was coming to them.

Yet, though Englishmen, not unnaturally, take more than ordinary satisfaction when the colours of their ancient enemy are lowered, the low state of Australian cricket ought to be greeted not so much with even modified rapture as real alarm. It is good, no doubt, that the other Test countries have come up in the world and are no longer easy prey for England and Australia, but to beat either of them on their own pitches has always been the touchstone. At this moment of writing Australia, home and away, have won just three of their last twenty-two Tests and lost eleven.

I recently quoted Bill O'Reilly's strictures on the post-Packer-intrusion scene. Another distinguished Australian critic recently expressed the view to me, more in sorrow than in anger, that he feels a recovery will only come when the administration is 'restructured' with new men at the top.

The revelations in our December issue of Kim Hughes, a man of high repute in England who feels passionately about Australian cricket, will have alerted many to the current picture, even if some allowance should perhaps be made for his personal situation. Let me only add that I never hoped nor expected to see such a decline in batting techniques, such an absence of variety in attack, nor such a dilution of that traditional fighting spirit, as was in evidence in England last summer.

Now, what about Walter Hadlee's boy? As Maurice Leyland might have said, 'Has't seen owt like it?' The short answer is that, in the scorebook at any rate, there has been no parallel to a man taking thirty-three wickets in three Tests on Australian pitches. Indeed, the only betterment in figure terms might well turn out to be Sydney Barnes's forty-nine victims on the responsive South African mat in the first four Tests against South Africa in 1913–14. The nearest modern approach to Richard Hadlee's performance was Michael Holding's twenty-four in three Tests in 1981–2. Whatever the limitations of Australia's batting, the example that Hadlee's bowling conveys to young aspirants lies primarily in mastery of the basic essentials of length and direction. Add ability to move the ball when conditions allowed, both in the air and off the pitch, plus a full allowance of determination, and they have the recipe.

★

Finally, Rex Alston assures me he has quite recovered his equilibrium after being shown his premature obituary in *The Times*, embarrassed though he was at first. At least he had the opportunity of telling his old public over the air that at eighty-four he is still alive and kicking. Indeed, he still reports in *The Daily Telegraph*. I reminded him that *The Cricketer* once slipped similarly in the case of H. L. V. Day, and it fell upon me to ring him and apologize. He took the thing well, and to underline his continued health and strength wrote us an agreeable article on his happy days with Hampshire.

That was in the summer of 1968. Four years later, when both of us happened to meet as fellow guests at White's Club, we joked about it. On arriving home that evening I found a message from the *DT* asking me for an obituary of him. He had died in the afternoon on a station platform. The chance meeting in White's was, I think, the most uncanny coincidence of my life.

THE CRICKETER
FEBRUARY 1986

Alex Dibbs:
A Forthright President

The death of Arthur Henry Alexander Dibbs, CBE, at the age of sixty-six following a massive stroke is not only an unwelcome shock to his friends in many quarters but a distinct loss to cricket administration, to which he came from an unusual background.

When Alex Dibbs was nominated President of MCC in May 1983 by his predecessor and fellow banker Sir Anthony Tuke, his only contact with Lord's was as a member of the Finance Sub-committee. With the experience of 'sitting-in' on committees during the summer he chaired his first full Committee on assuming office in October, and impressed all by his quick grasp of affairs and the skills, fair-mindedness and, at times, bluff humour which he brought to the Club's business.

Chairing the International Cricket Conference of 1984 he so impressed overseas delegates that he was asked to undertake important ICC liaison work. When taken ill he was involved not only in this but in certain commercial negotiation on behalf of MCC.

From Whitgift Middle School, Croydon, he joined the then Westminster Bank aged sixteen in 1935 and apart from war service spent his working life with them. He rose from the managership of the Croydon branch in 1960 to the deputy chairmanship of Nat West in 1977. From there he was appointed (1981–5) deputy chairman to British Airways.

Alex rose steeply from the ranks by dint of a sharp intelligence and a singularly bluff, forceful manner. He was not as careful of himself as he might have been. If he took rather too much from life for his own good, he certainly gave generously to it.

THE CRICKETER
FEBRUARY 1986

Under Fire in the West Indies

To have toured the West Indies with G. O. Allen's team all but forty years ago and to have returned again this spring is to realize how complete has been the change in the flavour of England–West Indies cricket.

There has always been something special about the Anglo–West Indian relationship, and it is cricket, more than anything else, that has given these diverse Caribbean islands a common identity. To those of us who know the West Indies well, who have an affection for the people and presume to some insight into their philosophy, the realization that future England visits are under threat is hard to bear.

Let me lighten the picture by recalling my first impressions of West Indian cricket, written in Barbados for *The Field* early in 1948.

They seem, from this distance, to have been happy, unsophisticated days, albeit darkened by a casualty list until Len Hutton finally came to the rescue. At the Marine Hotel, Barbados, where there was, of course, no travelling physiotherapist, our venerable captain conducted a morning clinic in a room next to his own.

England inevitably lost the series with that experimental side, but in accepting the urgent invitation from the West Indies MCC set the islands on the path to that further success which has given so much to world cricket ever since.

But what now? This is an exceptional tour, surrounded as it is by intense propaganda about the apartheid issue – particularly in Trinidad and, of course, in Guyana, which declined to receive the England team in the first place.

For so long as the cricketers who are under the control of the TCCB are allowed to pursue their profession in a South Africa still violently divided, the circumstances of the current England team's unhappy situation in the West Indies will remain.

There will always be the risk that politicians like the President and Prime Minister of Trinidad will make provocative statements to a public already, and not unnaturally, outraged by the sight on television of members of their own race attacked by sjamboks. Equally, there will always be a radical press eager to whip up strong passions.

In the event, thanks in part no doubt to the excitement engendered by the phenomenal happenings in the one-day International and England's last-ball victory, the pull of cricket to the Queen's Park Oval proved stronger with the public than the counter-argument. But the tensions created by heavy security precautions and the attentions of over-intrusive journalists must have created an atmosphere that would have made the team's enjoyment almost impossible, even without the ordeal by fire of England's batsmen.

Fast bowling with intimidatory intent has been the most serious menace to cricket on the technical side ever since Dennis Lillee and Jeff Thomson exploded on to the scene in the early 1970s. English bowlers have not always been guiltless. It is, however, the West Indies who have made the short fast ball the basis of their attack. By selecting a battery of four and dispensing with even a single spinner, they determine a pattern of play which precludes the arts and graces of batting and makes courage the prime requisite.

The TCCB have this month published for consideration by the International Cricket Conference a slightly stronger wording of the relevant section of the Unfair Play Law. I doubt whether, if passed, it would make the slightest difference.

Robin Marlar tells us that relations between the two teams off the field are 'excellent' – which says much for the players' instinctive decency and much, too, I am sure, for the managership of Tony Brown. If ever there was a taxing assignment in sport, surely his is it. And if he can bring back the side next month more or less intact and not all murmuring that they will never tour in the West Indies again he will deserve a decoration.

THE FIELD
22 MARCH 1986

Unwarranted Intrusions

It is sad for an old hand to read of the sorry state of press–player relations in the West Indies: sad, but in all the politically inflamed circumstances and in respect of certain elements, not surprising.

There is apt, at the best of times, to be a degree of tension between touring teams and journalists (or at least some of them), especially when things are going badly on the field – and when, indeed, have they gone as badly as now?

What, of course, has made a delicate relationship infinitely more bitter is the presence on the spot of a corps of newsmen and feature writers sent to cover the activities of those who object to the team's presence because of the South African connections of some members of it.

Having recently returned from Barbados, I can attest that the percentage of those who think the tour should have been cancelled, or who proclaimed that they would not watch the cricket, in that admittedly most stable and law-respecting of all the territories, was infinitesimal. The one West Indian flash-point was, and perhaps remains, Trinidad.

Faced with a political non-story for weeks on end, the news and feature element have been intrusive and inquisitive to a degree which the team have found intolerable. More or less confined to their hotels, confronted by press and security officers round every corner, they have sought the laager of their own rooms, there to rest limbs bruised by the eternal fast bowling, to read what has been written about them, off the field and on, and to hear about it on the telephone from their anxious families at home.

It is not for me to comment on the cricket, having merely seen some of the high spots on the box and watched only what certainly seemed a somewhat desultory practice while they were acclimatizing before the first match – except to lament that there can be no enjoyment in it.

Without enjoyment it is difficult indeed for any captain to maintain among his troops a proper zest for battle, much more so when the disparity between the two sides begins and ends with the fast bowling, with its ever present physical threat.

David Gower's laconic attitude in the face of adversity may irritate some, but that is his style. It is something that he can still keep a cheerful face, and that in his comment humour sometimes still breaks in.

As to the bona fide cricket writers, I need scarcely say they have my sympathy. Having just after the war reported eleven English defeats against Australia before, at the fifteenth time of asking, victory came to Freddie Brown's side at Melbourne, I know too well how difficult it is to present a fair and plausibly optimistic story to readers hungry for good news.

The phrase 'cricket writers' describing our calling became general when the fourteen of us who accompanied the 1946–7 MCC team to Australia promptly formed, along with the Australian colleagues we found awaiting us at Perth, the Cricket Writers' Club.

The degree of mutual cordiality has had some ups and downs since those early days, depending considerably on individual personalities, both managers and captains on the one hand and writers on the other. Where each party has its job to do it is, however, plainly to the good all round that a basis of respect and co-operation be established.

This point is forcibly made from the West Indies by Frances Edmonds, wife of Phillipe, who in an article due to be published in *The Cricketer* after the tour is over, has thus referred to the professional cricket writers: 'This is the gentleman's club of cricket correspondents. Here we have journalists who have spent twenty years establishing links of friendship, honour and trust with successive England touring teams. They are links which are currently being strained to breaking point by this tour's inundation with a totally different *genre* . . . .'

Mrs Edmonds goes on to describe the antics of this other *genre* in terms which suggest that when it comes to polemical writing, no holds barred, the female of the species can be more deadly than the male.

It was therefore all the more welcome to hear a day or two ago from the doyen of our craft, John Woodcock, that relations between the players and the 'serious' cricket writers are perfectly friendly. Frances Edmonds's worst fears at least have not been realized.

THE DAILY TELEGRAPH
29 MARCH 1986

Woodcock's Last *Wisden*

For the true lover of cricket keen both to be informed of topical happenings and to see them in historical perspective, *Wisden* has always been a 'must'. Despite the current spate of books, unparalleled in number, an inspection of the latest issue, out yesterday, prompts the thought that its reputation has never been more secure.

The price of this 123rd edition of *Wisden's Cricketers' Almanack* has jumped from £11.95 to £14.50 hard-cased and from £9.95 to £12.50 in limp covers, the size remaining roughly constant at 1300 pages. But for ghosted biographies of minimal merit publishers ask as much.

In *Wisden* 1986 the match coverage and records, births and deaths, obituaries, Five Cricketers of the Year (particularly well portrayed), and all the usual annual features can be taken as read, with presumably only the rarest fact or figure needing amendment.

The 1985 errata lists just six minor items, two of them concerning a catch made by Ian Gould (Sussex), wrongly credited to his captain, standing no doubt at his elbow: a venial slip indeed.

The distinctive features this time include Sir Donald Bradman's second contribution, 'Whither Cricket Now?' coming forty-seven years after his first, and articles on appropriate themes by J. M. Brearley, Jack Bannister, E. M. Wellings and John Kitchin.

Mike Brearley writes a warm and characteristically perceptive tribute to Alan Knott. Mr Bannister, who is the secretary of the Cricketers' Association, analyses the financial revolution of the past ten years as it has affected the game and the players.

There is a relation between Mr Wellings's survey of pitch covering over the years and Mr Kitchin's meteorological researches into the wettest summers. We learn that 1985 was the eighth wettest of the century, notwithstanding which runs were infinitely cheaper than ever before and, not surprisingly, despite every sort of collusion among captains, the proportion of unfinished matches at 62.7 per cent was the highest in history.

Mr Wellings echoes the Editor and most intelligent critics when he says, 'Both as player and spectator I am in the uncovering lobby.' Yet the TCCB have just decided to turn down (along with almost everything else) the recommendation of C. H. Palmer's expert Inquiry Committee which proposed a limited uncovering in the Championship.

There are no more revealing or depressing figures in the book than this contrast between now and thirty years ago, 1956 having been the fifth wettest summer:

	Batsmen averaging over 50	Bowlers averaging under 20
1956	0	29
1985	19	4

Will the counties ever learn? Or will those with black fast bowlers decree misguidedly for what they imagine to be playing and financial advantage that their first-class squares are to be deprived of sun and rain and dew by tarpaulin and plastic while the natural life and sap is drained away and the precious arts of spin and flight recede to a distant memory?

John Woodcock in his 'Notes' is sound on this issue as on all the pressing problems of cricket, as he has been since taking over the editorship six years ago. Cricket authority will indeed echo the comment of the publishers that the appearance of this edition is 'tinged with sadness' in that he has announced his retirement.

Mr Woodcock, who has found doing two jobs too heavy a burden, has put a firmer individual stamp on *Wisden* than any Editor since Sydney Pardon. The consolation is that the appointment has gone to Graeme Wright, his right-hand man, and that his long experience will still be available in a consultant's role.

The Editor makes yet another plea for strong government and greater support for umpires. He notes that within a fortnight three past or present Test captains, Botham, Fletcher and Imran Khan, were charged for bringing the game into disrepute, and all they got was a TCCB warning. 'What Botham does on television one day, his country's fans do on the recreation ground or the school playing field the next. Had he been up before the Professional Golfers' Association or the Jockey Club he would have paid for it. Had it been tennis he would probably not, and we know what tennis has come to. After much agonizing, Lord's just admonished him.'

Of Australian cricket we read that too little of the vast revenue the game produces there goes back into it – Packer promotions see to that. As to the 1985 Australian team, the Editor doubts whether they would have finished among the first four in the County Championship.

THE DAILY TELEGRAPH
18 APRIL 1986

David Macindoe

David Henry Macindoe, Vice-Provost of Eton, died suddenly there on 3 March following a heart attack. He was sixty-eight. The news will have come as no small shock to his friends, for with that strong, craggy physique and eager energy he had seemed almost indestructible. David was an all-round sportsman who, aside from his cricket, played in the Oxford scrummage without winning a Blue, and for Christ Church represented the college in three Cuppers finals (at both codes of football and also hockey) in the same term. He was a formidable exponent of the Eton Field Game. In his later years he was a keen antagonist on the golf course.

He not only won his Blue as opening bowler in his freshman's year, 1937, but as such had the rare distinction of being chosen for the Gentlemen at Lord's. An even more unusual distinction was, and remains, his when in 1946 he became only the second man in this century to play on three winning Oxford cricket sides against Cambridge. (The other, A. G. Pawson, pre-deceased him, aged ninety-seven, only by a matter of days.)

After war service with the Royal Artillery, during which he won the Military Cross, Macindoe returned to Oxford where as captain – and fortified by the invaluable presence of Martin Donnelly – he restarted University cricket in The Parks on a wonderfully strong note. It was in 1946 that he accomplished his most striking performance: 10 for 146 in 61 overs against the full Lancashire side, who were beaten by 76 runs.

David bowled medium-fast with an in-swinger's somewhat front-on delivery, and like the best of his type could sometimes get movement off the seam from leg to off. He had life off the pitch, and was seemingly tireless. In his four undergraduate years he took 152 wickets at 28 a time. With the bat he was no duffer. After one August with Buckinghamshire in 1947 he turned to club cricket and was the manager and mainspring of the Harlequin tour until a long way into maturity.

Returning to his old school to teach, he ran Eton cricket with cheerful zest, became a housemaster, and after thirty-three years on the staff was in 1979 elected Vice-Provost. Thus he returned to the Cloisters where – his father having been bursar – he had been born and brought up. Incredibly his family had served Eton for seven generations in unbroken succession. Many, both Etonians and other visitors, will have enjoyed the stimulus of his company for he was a generous-minded, outgoing person and withal a man of humour and dry wit.

THE CRICKETER
MAY 1986

Great Contemporaries

What a melancholy accident it was that two such famous cricketers should have passed on within a few hours of one another! There was a warm kinship between those of that war generation, and Bill Edrich and Jim Laker were always close friends even though, as it happened, they never toured together with MCC.

In terms of temperament and personality they were, of course, as diverse as could be: Bill outgoing, pugnacious, cheerful, gregarious; Jim quiet, canny, a man of few words and a dry humour. The word laconic could have been invented to describe him. Economy of words was one of his virtues as a television commentator, in which capacity he will be, to younger followers, the better known. He talked over the air rather as he bowled, precisely, accurately, shrewdly, with no fanciful flights. The only time he ever raised his voice – remembering, so to speak, that he was a Yorkshireman – was when he appealed for lbw. That was a not infrequent occurrence.

One usually gets to know a man pretty well on tour, or did in my time when any natural barriers of reserve between players and writers were negotiable, granted tact and good manners. For Bill Edrich and me the 1938–9 tour to South Africa was our first such adventure, and a lively customer he soon showed himself to be in that hospitable and, in those days, untroubled country. The MCC side were amply strong for their purpose, and manager and captain, A. J. Holmes and Walter Hammond, ran them on a loose rein. Bill scored well enough in the provincial matches, but in the Tests the run of failure which he had endured against Australia the previous summer still persisted. When it came to the last ('Timeless') Test at Durban his ten innings for England had yielded just 87 runs. If he had not been a great favourite of the captain's he could hardly have played.

As it was, on a pitch like an old carpet and against an attack weakened by injury, he made 219, in 7 hours and 40 minutes when only rain prevented England from getting the fantastic 696 they needed before they had to begin the journey home on the tenth evening.

Bill Edrich's part in the later stages underlined his combative spirit, which was all too soon being tested to the hilt as a bomber pilot. He emerged with flying colours and a DFC, and in the autumn of 1946, with six precious seasons lost, was sailing to Australia, again under Hammond's leadership, with MCC. (It was a 'dry' voyage in an overcrowded government-chartered ship, but Bill's romantic nature – of which his whole life bore ample evidence – was more than compensated by the presence of some 200 'war brides' on the way to join their Australian husbands in the New World.)

Greeted everywhere as a war hero, Bill in Australia emerged as a cricketer of true Test stamp. He was indispensible to England over the next four series until in 1950 a disciplinary brush with authority helped to lose him his Test place against the West Indies and probably cost him selection for Australia the following winter. 'Many . . . would have preferred W. J. Edrich,' wrote the *Daily Telegraph* cricket correspondent, I notice, when F. R. Brown's MCC side was completed, and retrospectively it looks even more as though the selectors made what in the old *Wisden*s used to be called 'a sad blunder'. However, a personal comeback was in store, and the old stalwart was brought back to play a worthy part in England's regaining of the Ashes under Len Hutton in 1953 and in their retention of them eighteen months later.

What Edrich lacked in technique against the highest class of bowling he strove like a tiger to make up in resolution and courage. Such a man was always sure to make a leader, and the last phase of his career was a conspicuously happy and successful one. He ended his great services to Middlesex with seven years as a captain whose key qualities were optimism and enterprise. Finally, in 1959, he returned to Norfolk, the county of all the Edriches, leading them with flair and undiminished zest for ten years. He was fifty-five when he gave up, having the previous summer topped the Norfolk batting averages and finished second in the bowling. Game to the last!

As Bill played before full houses at Lord's – and who will forget his great partnerships with Denis Compton that helped to attract them? – so Jim Laker was a leading character in those famous Surrey sides of the 1950s which brought big crowds to The Oval. His achievements against the 1956 Australians – nineteen wickets in the Old Trafford Test, forty-six in the series and all ten against them for Surrey – are a legend that will never fade. On English pitches there has surely been no finer off-spinner.

Yet one feels, looking back, that fate did not always deal kindly with him. Considering his own inexperience with that raw side of G. O. Allen's in the West Indies on those plumb pitches, his Test debut was propitious indeed. Yet in the following nine years he was chosen only once to go overseas, to the West Indies again in 1953–4. If he was not perhaps the easiest bowler to handle it could be argued for him that there were times when he might have been more sympathetically led. It rankled with him that not until his thirty-seventh year, his fingers arthritic and calloused from the taking of 1700 wickets, was he put to the acid test of Australian pitches. The fact that he allowed his frustration to spill over into a ghosted autobiography which for a time alienated him from the cricket world was something which he soon came greatly to regret.

Happily, though, this episode became forgotten in the light of his fair and balanced presentation of the game over the air, while all who saw him bowl in his heyday will retain a lasting memory of the perfect artist at work.

THE CRICKETER
JUNE 1986

Trent Bridge
Past and Present

On few of England's traditional grounds have recollections of the past and practicalities of the present been more happily blended than at Trent Bridge, where the Second Test against New Zealand starts on Thursday.

Yes, there is the multi-storey block on the north-east corner. By selling the site of this the late, much lamented Frank Gregory rescued Nottinghamshire from financial crisis and directed the club to a prosperous future.

In front is the elaborate electronic scoreboard, and above the pavilion the executive comforts, the existence of which helps so greatly to attract the business world. But most of the old landmarks are much as they were when I first remember them.

A new stand over deep mid-wicket at the pavilion end melds agreeably into the contours of the ground, facing across on the river side the Trent Bridge Inn, from which William Clarke raised and ran those missionary All-England teams that spread the gospel of cricket.

In the cricket sense Nottingham was the gateway to the North, its seniority a fact of which we shall be reminded when the 150th birthday of the ground is celebrated two years hence.

I know of no pavilion, apart from that at Lord's, whose walls portray its heroes and its history more fully and in better taste than that of Trent Bridge. There they all are – Alfred Shaw and Arthur

Shrewsbury, the Gunn family, the Hardstaffs, Harold Larwood and Bill Voce, men of Nottinghamshire all of them, alongside the contemporary stars, Randall, Rice and Hadlee.

The club are properly proud of Richard Hadlee, of New Zealand, who has been and still is a wonderful servant, as were two earlier pre-eminent all-rounders, Bruce Dooland and Gary Sobers. More than half of the Nottinghamshire XI of today are, however, Nottinghamshire born and bred.

A recent visit sharpened old memories: of Grimmett and O'Reilly spinning England to defeat on a dusty pitch in 1934; of Graeme Pollock in 1965 making one of the best Test hundreds I ever saw; of England under Ray Illingworth somehow beating that marvellous Rest of the World side in 1970.

On my last visit I saw Kent (in the Nat West) sadly out-batted, out-fielded and out-bowled. Yet I was glad again to breathe the Trent Bridge air and to sample afresh the hospitality of a club run by men who from the president, Jack Baddiley, downwards understand the game and live to serve it.

THE DAILY TELEGRAPH
4 AUGUST 1986

Ronnie Aird

Ronald Aird, who died on Saturday aged eighty-four, served MCC as Assistant Secretary from 1926 to 1952, the Second World War years excluded, then from 1952 to 1962 as Secretary, and in 1968–9 as President. He was also many years latterly a trustee.

He was in many ways the perfect Secretary; he had the blend of charm and courtesy proof against the crustiest of members, and equally the guarantor of a loyal, devoted staff. Lord's was never a happier place than during his long tenure of office.

Ronnie Aird grew up in the sparkling post-First World War sporting days of Eton and Cambridge, playing at Lord's three times for his school and once for his university, and, as a stylish bat with the wrists of a rackets player, soon showing his worth for Hampshire.

It is doubtful, though, whether he enjoyed any subsequent innings more than the hundred with which in 1921 he assured Eton of victory against Winchester after they had fielded out to J. L. Guise's 278, the highest score ever made in a schools match.

After leading by 198 on first innings Eton needed to make 184 against the clock on the second evening. Aird's share was a debonair 112 not out.

Coming down from Cambridge, his opportunities for county cricket were limited, but he played off and on for Hampshire from his schooldays to the Second World War, made four hundreds, and shared with Phil Mead in a stand of 266 against Sussex.

At rackets he reached the final of the Public Schools Doubles Championship, played first string for Cambridge, and was always in his years at Lord's a great supporter of rackets and real tennis.

During the Second World War he served in the Royal Tank Regiment and in 1942 won the MC in the Middle East. In his years of retirement he was in demand as a National Hunt steward.

THE DAILY TELEGRAPH
18 AUGUST 1986

From Grace to Arlott

Wine and cricket! Let me give more serious affairs respite for a change and pursue the happy connection for a paragraph or two. We know, of course, that when visiting cricketers stayed with him at Bristol, W.G. used to have a bottle 'down the well'. And there was the story of how at Cambridge when the redoubtable S. M. J. Woods and his fellow undergraduates thought they might dull his appetite for runs by offering him champagne for breakfast W.G., by habit an abstemious man, took all that was offered. He then went out at Fenner's with W. L. Murdoch and gave the University side a rare run-around, crying, 'Come on, Billy, we'll champagne 'em!'

Not that Woods and his friends were starting anything new, for the MCC President, Jack Davies, the authority on all things appertaining to Cambridge cricket, has told how the Rev. A. R. Ward, the benevolent despot of Fenner's, used to offer earlier generations an unvarying breakfast menu of eggs, sausages, salmon cutlets and Bollinger. As a concession to the demands of the game ahead the champagne was apparently diluted with Apollinaris.

In more modern days amateurs used to find ready openings in the wine trade where firms used their 'contact' advantages rather as happened with others on the Stock Exchange. P. G. H. Fender became something of an authority on sherry, and Ian Peebles on hock. His city lunches were famous, whereat, if one's luck were truly in, would be present Ian's favourite guest, Jack Hobbs. And in whom is affection for both wine and cricket better exemplified than John Arlott, whose retirement from commentating was announced by the *Standard's* Londoner's Diary in the headline: JOHN ARLOTT DECLARES AT 4000 BOTTLES? The head of Christie's wine department, Michael Broadbent, was quoted as saying before the bulk – but far from all – of this collection came up for auction that it was 'probably the most wide-ranging' he had ever handled, in particular the clarets.

THE CRICKETER
AUGUST 1986

Cruising On Canberra

Ann and I embark on SS Canberra for a fortnight's Mediterranean cruise, senior members of a cricket party comprising also Tom and Jackie Graveney, Dennis and Jill Amiss, Christopher and Judy Martin-Jenkins and Christopher Cowdrey. They called it a cricket cruise, and there was a mixture of talks (not compulsory!) and a quiz, much deck cricket and two brief games ashore. The cricketers very agreeable and popular with all; also, like all the moderns, accustomed as they are to public speaking, highly articulate.

I love nothing in the world better than life on a great ship in congenial company and here it all was – a nostalgic trip for me especially, since I had been aboard with the 1962–3 MCC team to Australia on Canberra's maiden voyage.

The itinerary this time was Gibraltar, Naples, Itea, Corfu, Palma and home. Scarcely a cloud, never a drop, just blue skies and sunshine. Made positively my last appearance on the field as umpire on that khaki-coloured surface at Gib, and as public address commentator at Corfu, that ancient outpost of the game, the ground in the town square, with the spectators under the acacia trees, drinking ouzo or ginger beer and offering vociferous comment in Greek. The Canberra team paraded on time but due to an administrative hiccup their Corfiot opponents did not. However, there was a game of sorts and the lively matting on concrete pitch put one in mind of Bermuda. The coarse grass field consists of a profusion of humps and hollows, on which on a previous holiday I had seen some Corfiot fielding which was an astonishing revelation of the virtue of keeping your eyes on the ball in the interests of self-preservation.

DIARY
28 SEPTEMBER 1986

A *Guardian* Anthology

Any book is to be welcomed today which presents cricket both as it is and as it was through all its adult life at a time when, for many followers, love of the game is being so rudely threatened by all about it that is increasingly mercenary, self-seeking and vulgar. An anthology of cricket writing in *The Guardian* over the last century or more promises a rich feast to the connoisseur, and with one clear reservation expectation is well fulfilled.

Matthew Engel is a worthy successor in the line of *Guardian* cricket writers. He is one of the reasons why some people order two serious daily papers in the summer months – why, perhaps, other discriminating folk, but for the cost, might even order three. He has clearly enjoyed his difficult labour of selection, and from the same ample reservoir might no doubt edit another volume equally fascinating.

Should we read again of Neville Cardus's one scoop, the romantic first defeat of the Australians by MacLaren's XI at Eastbourne? Or of Lancashire's bloody but unbowed emergence from Nottinghamshire's 'Bodyline' mauling at Trent Bridge, when at the finish Ernest Tyldesley, least demonstrative of men, flung the ball triumphantly into the crowd, after which a nude George Duckworth's bruises were photographed as forthcoming evidence by order of the Committee? Or of A. P. F. Chapman's imperial 260 against MacDonald at the Mote ground, Maidstone? Answers: yes, no, no.

We can't have everything, but Mr Engel has given us one of the best of the Cardus classics. It begins: 'Yesterday was the gladdest I have spent on a cricket field for many years. The cricketers of Grace's lovely county – O the orchards of Gloucestershire and the ancient peacefulness of the Cotswolds! – came to dour Old Trafford and brought with them tidings of comfort and joy. The summer game is not dead, but is alive and returning to us, still the prodigal bearer of handsome sons who will grow up in the likeness of the men of old – the MacLarens and the Trumpers.'

'Too flowery' reputedly was my old friend for the taste of Dick Tyldesley and the warm, loveable Lancashire generation of cricketers he immortalized.

As 'the perfect example of cricket reporting as idyll', Mr Engel prints all three days of a fine match at Dover between Kent and Lancashire. Cardus was happy in Kent: 'To my dying day I shall remember gratefully these afternoons in Kent, afternoons full of the air and peaceful sunshine of imperishable England.'

When the older generation thinks of *The Guardian* they think automatically of Cardus. The editor gives us nearly twenty of his pieces, but succeeds in emphasizing that 'Cricketer' from his emergence in 1920 was the originator of a school of individual writing, often idiosyncratic, at times inimitable, occasionally irritating, which has informed and entertained discriminating cricket readers ever since.

The successors to Cardus as cricket correspondent, Terence Prittie, Denys Rowbotham, John Arlott, Paul Fitzpatrick and (too briefly) Engel himself, are duly paraded, and there is room for the second-stringers and essayists, notably Brian Chapman, Henry Blofeld, Ian Peebles (shortly before his death), Frank Keating and a special favourite of mine, Eric Todd.

C. L. R. James contributes a piece full of careful observation on the great S. F. Barnes in a League match. Don Davies also treats delightfully with League cricket. Keating on Alec Bedser and, on his death, Ken Barrington are not to be missed.

The book is well laced with short pieces, readers' letters, and a number of leaders, all divided by headings of haphazard size and style. It is partitioned into compartments of a kind, but – and here is the weakness – there is no adequate list of contents. An anthology is almost by definition a dipper-in book and as such particularly needs direction posts. It is irritating not to be able to find what one may want. May this book run to further editions with clear signs to all its treasures.

THE GUARDIAN
SEPTEMBER 1986

—————— 'Duke Hussey Defended ——————

The Spectator *diary is usually good reading, and Peregrine Worsthorne has hit the nail on the head on the subject of Marmaduke Hussey, whose recent appointment as Chairman of Governors of the BBC has been conspicuously ill received by much of the media. Worsthorne wrote that the media nowadays is only interested – apart from royalty – in bastards:*

> *And if they are not bastards, then the media does its best to make them seem so, as happened to poor Dukey Hussey last week. The truth about Dukey is that he is about as splendid and decent a man as ever lived and something of a war hero to boot, having lost a leg at Anzio. Time was when disabled warriors could expect a bit of kid-glove treatment from scribblers. No longer. Courage beyond the call of duty no longer seems to impress or be thought at all relevant. Dukey and I were in the same officer cadet squad at Pirbright in 1943. He was much stronger and bigger than the rest of us and used these advantages to stop the NCOs picking on the weaklings. Has this anything to do with whether he will make a good chairman of the BBC? Possibly not much. But rather more, I suspect, than all that bitchy tittle-tattle that has appeared elsewhere.*

Strong stuff! Before those Pirbright days 'Duke Hussey played for the school in the Tom Brown Centenary Match at Rugby in 1942 and won a wartime Blue at Oxford. As an undergraduate in the late 1940s I recall him as one of a remarkable Trinity generation which also included Robin Leigh-Pemberton, Ossie Newton Thompson, Robin Fletcher, Ian Campbell, Dick Hornby and John Woodcock, to name just a few sportsmen with successful careers in a variety of fields ahead of them. As a resident of Pusey House I was lucky to be a peripheral part of those happy post-war Oxford days wherein several generations mingled, to the benefit of all.

DIARY
11 OCTOBER 1986

RC Ecumenist

The Very Rev. Canon Dennis Corbishley, a delightful and distinguished RC priest whom I first knew from his writing to me about Lancashire cricket, a subject close to his heart, came to stay and to preach to us at St Clement's, as he had done before. He was secretary to an RC–Anglican ecumenical committee, combining that with the chaplaincy of a girl's school at Woldingham. He seemed in perfect health yet within a few weeks was dead. At the Memorial Mass in Westminster Cathedral later the eulogy was given by an Anglican, Canon Martin Reardon. There were other Anglican clergy in the sanctuary, including Bishop Knapp-Fisher from the Abbey, and others among the congregation, including the Archbishop of York and General Synod members.

What a contrast in atmosphere there is between the churches today and yesterday! Why, when Pusey House celebrated its Diamond Jubilee in 1946 there were plenty of beards and shovel hats representing the Orthodox, but not a Roman in sight, not even a priest from the Dominican house of Black Friars next door. Come to that, I doubt if any Nonconformist was honoured with an invitation.

DIARY
18 OCTOBER 1986

XL Club Gala Night

Had the honour to preside at the Jubilee Dinner of the XL Club – 769 present, the second highest turn-out since 1962 when the ticket cost £2 as against the current £24. Seven England captains graced the top table: in order of seniority, Wyatt, Allen, Mann, May, Cowdrey, Dexter and Lewis. Illness kept away Sir Leonard Hutton, whom I announced as the committee's choice as my successor as president. The speakers were Field Marshal Sir 'Dwin (now Lord) Bramall, proposing the traditional toast to Cricket and MCC, replied to by the President, Colin Cowdrey. The club and their guests were in the inimitable hands of John Warr, to whom Tom Harvey, past captain of the Royal and Ancient, had the difficult job of response. All four batted admirably and with decent brevity (shortest innings 9 minutes, longest 15), even if none quite achieved the standing ovation spontaneously accorded at the 1985 dinner to the Archbishop of Canterbury.

The Jubilee was marked by the publication of a short history of the club and by the institution of the Henry Grierson Trophy. In his foreword our

Patron, the Duke of Edinburgh, hit the ball plumb in the middle of the royal bat when he wrote: 'Cricket can only flourish if it is played by civilized people with the highest standards of sportsmanship and good humour.'

Yes, it's that sort of game. It was no doubt with such a sentiment in mind that the committee decided to perpetuate our founder's name by offering the Trophy to the school opponents who annually put up the best performance both in the various arts of the game and in the equally important things such as sportsmanship, turn-out and good manners generally. Nearly all our 130 fixtures are against schools, most of whom entered for the Trophy, which was won by Canford.

DIARY
24 OCTOBER 1986

Somerset of Fond Legend

There is a Somerset of legend and fond memory, and, whatever the outcome of their malign revolt, old faces and past deeds have honoured places in the history of English cricket.

The Somerset story is of a county numerically small – only Northamptonshire of the first-class seventeen is less well populated – offering cricket of courage and character by dint of the efforts of outstanding men. One thinks of tough ones – S. M. J. Woods, John Daniell, Tom Lowry, Bill Alley and Brian Close; of eccentrics such as R. J. O. Meyer, creator of Millfield, and R. C. Robertson-Glasgow, known as 'Crusoe'; of men to be heroes – Arthur Wellard, Harold Gimblett and Jack White, the farmer; of the county's historian, the late, lamented Ron Roberts.

Sammy Woods, loveable, lion-hearted, thirsty Aussie, I never met, but Daniell I knew, who like Woods before him, led the county for thirteen seasons, a master of robust English. He got a hundred in both innings at the age of forty-six. They lasted well without the trouble of Sunday cricket. Alley was well over forty when he totted 3000 runs one summer and in the next took 100 wickets and scored almost 2000. Close, indestructible and with a vocabulary matching that of Daniell 'the Prophet', also soldiered on till he was forty-six. Lowry, who led New Zealand into Test cricket, was the archetypal Antipodean. He is remembered for having got the better of Lord Harris, who queried his qualification. 'I was born in Wellington – isn't that good enough?' Which Wellington his Lordship did not enquire.

White, with his slow left-arm bowling – an art which he demonstrated as rewarding flight as generously as spin – took many more wickets for Somerset (2166) than anyone else. He is remembered not least for one of the most memorable of Test bowling figures, at Adelaide of all places: 124–37–256–13. 'I used several shirts and a few whiskies and soda.'

White and Daniell, moving spirits for so long, were Somerset born and bred, and so, indeed, was the local boy from Watchet who burst so explosively on the cricket world in the 1930s, Harold Gimblett. But of necessity with such a restricted area from which to draw its talent, the county had to recruit largely from beyond its boundaries and, indeed, from abroad.

Of its two famous past all-rounders Len Braund graduated via W.G.'s London County at the turn of the century while Arthur Wellard only qualified, in 1929, for Somerset after his promise had been strangely overlooked in his native Kent – whose bowlers he took special pleasure in punishing. In 1938 at Taunton he hit Frank Woolley (who dealt in the commodity quite extensively himself) for five sixes in an over and was missed in front of the screen off the sixth ball. Arthur hit about 500 sixes, a quarter of his total output.

Somerset's cricket was not all about hitting sixes, need one say. Indeed, two of their successful imports from the Lord's groundstaff, F.S. and J. W. Lee, were batsmen distinctly on the sticky side. They have generally been, however, an attractive side and one with a special personality and flavour which their immigrants have seemed readily to absorb.

This has been not least true of their Australian recruits from Woods onwards. Alley, the cheerful Sydneysider, soon seemed Somerset through and through; Colin McCool likewise. A pity, perhaps, that Greg Chappell did not stay long enough to be imbued.

The charm of Somerset cricket was first instilled into me by the inimitable Crusoe, who surrounded his Somerset contemporaries with an affectionately humorous aura all his own. Playing in university and school vacations, and on occasional leave from the *Morning Post*, he could have fitted no other county. 'Come again next year,' Daniell would say, 'and don't bring that ruddy straw hat.' The late Robertson-Glasgow in-swing confounded the best on his day. He took five wickets against the 1926 Australians and 9 for 38 against Middlesex at Lord's.

No word about post-war Somerset cricket could be adequate without mention of Maurice Tremlett. It so happened I saw his very first performance in May 1947 at Lord's against the coming county champions. With bowling akin almost to Maurice Tate, ex-trooper Tremlett, just demobilized, scattered the stars, then with six into the pavilion won the match with number eleven at the wicket. Thirsting as England were for young bowlers he was overpraised by some of us too soon, and on MCC tours to West Indies and South Africa failed to fulfil hopes. However, as a batsman, as a captain who pulled Somerset out of a trough, and as a man respected by all and held in much affection by those who knew him best, Tremlett has an honoured place in the story.

Now, in 1986, with a strong Millfield contingent in the van the fact is that the Somerset staff, from the captain Peter Roebuck downwards, probably has more players locally born and/or educated than any county bar Yorkshire and Kent. Victor Marks and Brian Rose, Test cricketers both, come into this category, along with most of the younger element. Anyone in the slightest familiar with the workings of modern county cricket will have had the utmost sympathy with Roebuck in these recent months, and, indeed, for all concerned. It will be a bleak day indeed for English cricket if, by the time these words are being read, the authority of the Somerset committee has not been fully vindicated and upheld.

THE CRICKETER
NOVEMBER 1986

Introduction to *Batter's Castle*

I must emphasize to the average reader of this new edition of *Batter's Castle* – and only those far gone into the sere and yellow could have a first-hand memory of him in his prime, nor can it be detected from his charmingly modest writing – that for at least three seasons Ian Alexander Ross Peebles was a truly great leg-spin and googly bowler. Otherwise he would not have played in thirteen Test matches for England at a moment in history when at least five other famous practitioners of the art – R. W. V. Robins and F. R. Brown (both high-class all-rounders), Richard Tyldesley, Tommy Mitchell and, above all, 'Tich' Freeman – were also at their peak.

I watched, and reported on, the greatest of his achievements in his golden summer of 1930: the thirteen wickets for 237 in 81 overs in the University Match (despite which, Oxford went down in the end to headlong defeat); his mastery, temporarily at least, of Don Bradman at Old Trafford (c. Duleepsinhji, b. Peebles 14); and his marathon 6 for 204 in The Oval Test while Bradman made hay and the one wicket apiece of Harold Larwood and Maurice Tate was costing a little matter of 285!

Ian spun the ball enough, if not quite as sharply as some of this quintet. Where in his heyday he had the advantage of all of them was in that precious, mysterious, elusive quality known as 'flight'. All too often the ball was not quite where the batsman thought it was. He played, mostly, a shade too early or, sometimes, in a hurry – and not even those with the soundest techniques were proof against error. I am thinking now of Ian's bowling on the plumb pitches typical of his time. When they had grown a bit dusty, and sometimes after rain, he could be a holy terror.

Aubrey Faulkner, with his wonderful flair as a teacher at his Indoor School of Cricket, had fashioned the talent that descended upon him in the shape of the raw youngster from Scotland. Ian was just eighteen when, in early 1926, he came south to work for Faulkner, nominally as his secretary but principally to bowl, bowl and go on bowling to the clientele who thronged to his school. For a full two years many hours a day Ian followed the routine. In order to relieve his tiredness he even taught himself to bowl left-arm – I once in a match caught a slip catch from a quickish ball bowled with the wrong arm. It was the strain on those teenage shoulders which built up a legacy of trouble. Though at first Ian remained hopeful that time would do the trick, it never did. When he captained Middlesex to second place in the Championship in 1939 he took forty-nine first-class wickets at 27 runs apiece. With that action, and an ample supply of determination, he could never be under-rated.

But though he still derived much joy from all that the game had to offer, there was a melancholy underlying feeling that his great potential had been only partially fulfilled.

It is time to move on from Ian's playing days to the literary side of his cricket career, which covered the years from the end of the war even beyond the publication of his autobiography in 1977 to a number of distinctive, perceptive biographies written for *Barclays World of Cricket* during his last illness and within a few months of his death in February 1980.

To his regret the *Evening Standard* had failed to renew their invitation to contribute in 1932, but there was just one slim volume of 100 pages which I remember for a literally vivid reason. At the last moment the publishers of *How to Bowl* wanted a picture of the famous arm at the point of delivery and, the weather being inclement, Ian had to don a cricket shirt and pose, rather unwillingly, in the sitting-room of 8 King's Bench Walk. The photographer in far-off 1933 had to ignite a white substance (magnesium?) on a tray adjacent to the camera. The result was a blinding flash, clouds of smoke billowing out of the windows, and the clattering arrival of the Temple fire brigade. They were not best pleased.

Ian was such a good talker and reminiscer, and had such an individual turn of phrase, that all the makings of a writer were there, as *Everybody's* discovered, a magazine boasting at one time 1 million circulation to which Ian managed to contribute regularly, even when he was busily rebuilding, from small pre-war beginnings, what became a highly prosperous wine firm, which he ran in partnership with Hans Siegel. (This charming man was the 'H.J.G.S., a non-cricketing but long-suffering business partner, entrapped in *Batter's Castle* these twenty years', to whom he dedicated this book.) When one takes account of the fact that in this full period of his life the budding wine merchant's ardent courtship of the ladies – over two decades – culminated in 1947 in his marrying Ursula Boxer (née Tulloch) and so taking on the responsibilities of family life, the evidence suggests that he really enjoyed writing, and indeed he did.

He became, in 1949, the *Sunday Graphic* cricket correspondent, and four years later was promoted within the Kemsley Group to the top cricket job on the *Sunday Times*. For them, he covered the Australian visit of 1953 and England's recovery of the Ashes, and went on the MCC tour of Australia in 1954–5 wherein we retained

them. This was the first of three tours abroad, those to Australia in
1958–9 and to the West Indies in 1959–60 being the others. Increasingly, Ian grew less happy at these long absences from family and
business, and thereafter he confined himself to covering the home
season and to book authorship, while much of the overseas reporting was undertaken for the *Sunday Times* by his old friend, and
professional journalist, Jack Fingleton.

Ian was always an entertaining reporter and his critical assessments of players and tactical situations were read with respect. The
fact was, however, that his particular skill lay in the short essay – on
any cricket subject, and especially one which allowed an outlet to
his wit. Henry Longhurst, who for a while shared our Temple flat,
and who was for many years Ian's colleague on the *Sunday Times*, as
golf correspondent, was likewise a master of the brief 'boxed'
piece, which Henry consciously kept to a length convenient for the
golfer to absorb during his visit to the loo prior to the Sunday
round. Ian and Henry formed a formidable pair both on and off the
printed page.

In their company the badinage passed to and fro at speed, and
they made an even match. It isn't easy to put across the flavour of a
'genial insult' relationship among friends, but maybe this example
will convey a hint of it. Henry was one day wearing a flag in his
buttonhole and, seeing Ian did not have one, suggested in that
unique, gravelly voice that so worthy a charity surely deserved
some support even from a tight-fisted Scot. Ian promptly inspected
the reverse side of Henry's flag and remarked laconically, 'As I
thought – press.'

From the later 1950s the books flowed. This collection of essays
was an early one and it reflects Ian's cricket philosophy as well as
any. The first edition was marred, by the way, only by his positively medieval indifference to spelling, an idiosyncrasy which no
conscientious publisher should have allowed to go through
unchecked. Otherwise *Batter's Castle* fully lives up to the general
verdict on his writing of the late and great Lord Cobham: 'He
writes about cricket beautifully and with knowledge, and above all
wholly without rancour; Ian is sometimes critical but never
unkind.' Charles Cobham would have greeted this reissue with the
warmest approval.

BATTER'S CASTLE, BY IAN PEEBLES
DECEMBER 1986

1987

BICENTENARY YEAR

Run Rabbit, Run . . .

Kent's senior capped player after Derek Underwood, Kevin Jarvis, has given his utmost service as a fast-medium bowler since he came first into the county team as a tall, slim, fresh-faced twenty-two-year-old back in 1975.

If he has not very often hit the headlines – though there are some fine performances in the scorebook – he has been a cheerful trier in the best Kent tradition, so often making do with the upwind end, so often answering his captain's call when the bat is on top and no one else shows any keenness to turn his arm over.

Cricket crowds spot these things over a period, and their estimations are generally pretty near the mark. In the last twelve summers, Jarvis has averaged fifty first-class wickets, twice reaching the eighties. He has been of great value to Kent, and I have no doubt that his benefit will be generously supported.

So much for his bowling. I venture, now, trusting in our hero's abundant good nature, to share in public a hitherto quiet private joke between us about his batting. Of course, batting as he does in the fast bowler's number eleven place, he could well point out that his opportunities have been limited. Similarly, his successive captains could argue that his performances with the bat have given them little encouragement to push him up the order.

The solemn facts are that in his first year his batting average worked out at 3.50 – and that at the time of writing, far from its improving with experience, it stands over his whole career a shade below that at 3.25. In 1977, boosted by a sparkling 12 not out, he averaged a giddy 6.6, but next year down he went to 3.14. Twice it has descended to one point something.

Even in 1984 the figure was only 3.41. I say 'even' because in that summer, against Derbyshire in the second match of the Maidstone Week, as all loyal Jarvis fans will recall, he made his highest score so far – 19 no less, scoring almost run for run with Terry Alderman in a last-wicket stand of 42.

Were runs cheap that afternoon? Decidedly not. The partnership took Kent's score only to 279, and it could be argued quite plausibly that this was one of the turning points leading to an eventual Kent victory.

I can find only one reference in *Wisden* to Kevin's batting: it concerned the Benson and Hedges tie in 1982 against Surrey at Canterbury that helped to decide which side should go on to the quarter-finals. Off the final over of the game, bowled by the formidable Sylvester Clarke, the last pair of Jarvis and young Chris Penn needed 8 runs. A tall order. Finally, 'Jarvis steered the winning 4 off the penultimate delivery.' Spectators afterwards disputed the exact nature of the victorious stroke. It was likened by some to the old-fashioned 'draw' which deflected the ball neatly between the right pad and the leg stump. In any event, all agreed that the ball flew past the wicket-keeper with wonderful precision down to the pavilion boundary, leaving long leg sprawling and helpless.

Alas! It would need a violent turn of events if, when Jarvis retires, he is not to be numbered among those who have taken more wickets than they have scored runs. It is a select company among whom, with figures appended, may be mentioned the following:

	WKTS	RUNS	AV.
B. J. Griffiths (Northants)	348	290	3.33
H. D. Read (Essex)	219	158	3.67
J. N. Graham (Kent)	614	404	3.84
C. S. Marriott (Kent)	711	574	4.41
W. E. Hollies (Warwicks)	2323	1673	5.00

Compare with these the current figures of Jarvis – 606 wickets, 325 runs, average 3.25 – and it will be noticed not only that his average is just a little below even that of his contemporary, Griffiths, but that, alone of those listed, he has taken nearly twice as many wickets as he has made runs.

A lean time with the bat in his remaining career might mean his going down to history as the only English cricketer who has played an appreciable amount and for whom this distinction could be claimed.

THE DAILY TELEGRAPH
21 JANUARY 1987

───────── *One's Only Eighty Once* ─────────

In Barbados as usual for my birthday, this one being the eightieth and therefore the signal for numerous articles, messages and a pre-recorded Radio 4 interview with Cliff Morgan which, thanks to him, I was pleased with. England this day were narrowly winning a one-day International at Sydney, and Richie Benaud kindly took occasion to wish happy returns over the air and mention the magic name, Bollinger: result, one bottle from him and one to go with it from Anthony Leschallas, the boss. There seemed plenty of space for sporting features, for there were long pieces in The Daily Telegraph *by Doug Ibbotson, the* Observer *by Michael Davie (heading was 'Happiness is eight million words at eighty') and* The Guardian *by Frank Keating. The last had a rather unusual setting since I took the London call at the pool bar of the Buccaneer Bay Hotel. A lighthearted interview ensued, me up to my waist in water with the telephone in one hand and a rum punch in the other.*

DIARY
11 FEBRUARY 1987

'Bothamania' – an Affliction of Our Time

ITN News, Saturday before Christmas: 'England are set to thrash Tasmania'. Such were the evening news announcer's words which brought welcome anticipation of some light about to be shed on the second day's play at Hobart. 'Thrash' seemed an extravagant word to describe the expected elimination of the Cinderella state not long accepted into the ranks of the Sheffield Shield. However, over-emphasis is the order of the day. The losers are never just beaten: they are flayed or flogged or thrashed. What now?

What now indeed? On the screen was flashed the bare score line without a single individual score or analysis, while the presenter, making no further mention whatever of the match, announced that Botham had had a doubly successful day, winning several thousand pounds in some gamble or other *and also catching a 3 lb trout.*

Ian Botham had broken down with a muscle injury in the left side, a quite common bowling misfortune, when bowling on Wednesday 3 December, seventeen days earlier. From then on there were more daily yards of column space in the way of surgeons' diagnoses, progress reports from captain, manager, team manager, physiotherapist and, not least, the victim himself, than about the operations of the whole of the rest of the tour party, both on the field and off – aside, that is, from the actual reporting of the Third Test itself. Even with that, the common refrain, both before and during this Adelaide Test, was – how can we struggle on without him?

The media obsession with Botham found abundant material even during his two-month suspension in the summer. Then, as soon as he had asserted that he proposed to sever his ties with Somerset following their decision not to renew their contracts with Richards and Garner, came endless speculation about which lucky county would secure his services.

The press invented a mythical 'chase' among them. There never was a chase, nor was there likely to be, for to most county committees the price, measured in several crucial respects, for his all-round talent was plainly far too high to pay. The result of boundless rumour was that there were only two counties to announce they were in the market – Worcestershire and Derbyshire. The 'winner' of this two-horse race, barring some late financial intervention, will probably be known by the time these words are being read. All that is established at present is that Botham has contracted to play for Queensland henceforth, and has therefore put himself out of court for future England tours. As to the flood of Somerset resignations predicted by some, the welcome news is that their 1987 membership shows an increase on the corresponding figure the same time a year ago.

What the purveyors of Botham 'hype' may not appreciate is that, while there are undoubtedly those, especially women, who lap up avidly anything relating to him, there are many sportsmen who find this Bothamania progressively more and more distasteful.

No sane cricket follower would question his immense batting talent, and the moral value to his side of the fear among the opposition (other than the West Indians) that he may be about to unleash a demoralizing assault. His quality as a swing bowler, which brought him such extraordinary success in his young days as a Test cricketer, is not, of course, what it was. He is, nevertheless, still an all-rounder in the Test sense, essentially a cricketer for the big occasion.

Allow these cricket gifts and discount much, apart from the irregularities he has admitted, of the stories of his private life, and one is left to deplore the figure that remains as an example to boys and young men. The great cricketers of history whom former generations set up as their heroes were, almost to a man, models of modesty and the highest standards of behaviour on the field. The household names were admired for what they stood for, as for what they did. Cricketers were rather special sorts of sportsmen. It is sad for the game at large, and principally for the sake of the young, that its most famous figure has such feet of clay.

THE CRICKETER
FEBRUARY 1987

Packer and Sponsorship

It cannot be inappropriate to open these monthly jottings with a quiet hallelujah of thanksgiving for the sudden news that Kerry Packer has sold the companies which by his deal with the Australian Cricket Board in 1979 acquired sole promoting rights in the game there for ten years. True, I write knowing nothing of the inclinations of the purchaser of Packer's interests, Alan Bond, the man who brought the America's Cup from New York to Perth. One's instinct is, though, that any change is better than none, the hope being that the ACB might be allowed to get back at least a measure of their former control of the game.

It is not for a mere Pom to interfere further than to wish the ACB well in any effort they make to re-establish the repute of orthodox inter-state cricket as the training and proving ground for future

Test sides. Cricketers who have been well grounded and of sound technique can make limited-over cricket, in moderation, a splendid attraction; but limited-over cricket itself does not *make* cricketers, and it never can do.

Sponsorship has been the name of the game from a decade before Packer and in England scarcely more so than now, what with the counties ever looking for more sources of revenue and on the national scene new names being sought to take over from the tobacco companies. It is, of course, the hopes of fat offers coming up that has caused players to delay signing county contracts. The generally unsettled scene is clearly one of great concern to the TCCB.

When Graham Dilley was dallying over a profusion of reputed offers, the distinguished Stock Exchange firm of Capel & Co. and Kent announced a two-year sponsorship renewal worth £100,000. This sort of patronage is mutually beneficial to the firm, to the county club and to its players. This is surely much more in the game's interests than a great splashing out on one star.

THE CRICKETER
MARCH 1987

Clouds Over the Caribbean

It has been an agreeable experience on my annual visit to this benign island [Barbados] – as readers will readily believe – to follow the last phase of England's highly successful tour of Australia, wherein, of course, the West Indies finished last of three. The local reaction, likewise not difficult to imagine, has been compounded about equally of surprise and deep concern. Success has been so taken for granted that any other outcome is seen as a slipping from grace by Vivian Richards's team rather than an exceptional effort by the opposition.

Pakistan nowadays is never an easy tour, and Abdul Qadir's great triumph with wrist-spin at Faisalabad, applauded by all right-thinking followers the world over, meant that the West Indies could do no better than emerge with a drawn series. In the Perth

Challenge it could be said that they started at a disadvantage against Australia and England in that their opponents had contested four matches of a Test series. There followed the World Series – so called, though with only three contesting countries the title is an obvious presumption – wherein Australia acquitted themselves much better than their dismal early-season form had suggested, while England continued to ride on the tide of success.

I have pointed out that to talk about a decline at a time when West Indies have not lost a Test series to England for eighteen years, to Australia for eleven, to New Zealand for seven, to India for eight and to Pakistan for twenty-eight seems premature. However, in this unique stronghold, at least, where every individual and collective shift of form is detected and analysed, they see the signs as being adverse. The famous fast attack has passed its peak, few fresh batsmen of quality have recently emerged, and – not least importantly – great cricketers do not necessarily make ideal captains. The fact is that while the foremost cricketers of all countries have been sapped of zest and freshness by the ridiculous merry-go-round which is Packer's legacy to cricket, the top West Indians are more jaded than most. I well recall a keen young enthusiast telling me of a talk he had during a Test match with Richards before his accession to the captaincy. One up in the series, it was a question whether West Indies could step up the pace to force another win; with a hard winter behind him and a full English summer ahead the great batsman finally smiled and said, 'You know, we're only going through the motions.' Body and spirit can take so much and no more.

On the technical side, by the way, I have a theory that the utter emphasis on speed in bowling has had an adverse effect on the quality of West Indian batting. Is it too much of an over-simplification to say that spending over after over fending the ball off from the ribs or higher is not the best situation for perfecting the cover drive or the square cut? Whether this theory is acceptable or not the fact is that this prime nursery of West Indian batting, Barbados, has not produced a top-line batsman since the emergence of Desmond Haynes ten years ago. Carlisle Best has been disappointing.

But while there can be two opinions about the value to the game generally of modern West Indian tactics and approach there should be no doubt as to the peculiar difficulties which face West Indian cricket authority in their administration at all levels.

The truth is that, although they are in duty bound to accept return visits by the other five countries, so giving their own folk the chance of seeing their heroes in Test match action, to have no home Test series is a financial blessing. For the limited capacity of all the Test grounds except Port of Spain, the relatively low gate charges which are all the various communities can pay, and the enormous cost of transporting visiting teams and putting them up in acceptable hotels in the high season combine to make heavy losses unavoidable. It is indeed doubtful whether any tour to the West Indies at any time has ever shown a profit.

In our February issue Tony Cozier reported that the loss on last year's England tour was £145,000. I am assured the figure was even higher, despite the Cable and Wireless sponsorship of £175,000. No cricket board can cover losses of such magnitude, the largest surely in Test history. This followed a loss on the 1981 England tour of £130,000, the particular reason on that occasion being a complete absence of revenue from the Georgetown Test from which England withdrew when the late and unlamented President of Guyana, Forbes Burnham, declared Robin Jackman *persona non grata*.

The immediate financial prospect for the WICBC suggests some recoupment, after what is bound to have been an unprofitable visit by New Zealand, from the World Cup in India and Pakistan in October–November, followed by a five-Test tour of India, but that again precedes a home visit by Pakistan in the spring of next year. Then comes – immediately – a full tour of England. It all adds up to a continued heavy strain on the top players, and with this current Shell Shield fixture-list cut in half on the dual grounds of expenses and the unavailability of the stars the opportunity of blooding fresh talent is limited indeed.

Whereas all countries rely greatly on sponsorship in various forms, WICBC are even more dependent than the others – on Shell, which has provided the financial backbone to their cricket since 1965, on Cable and Wireless, who reputedly were satisfied with their first investment, despite England's inability to put up a fight, and have an option on future series, and, not least, on the consistent goodwill throughout the Caribbean of Barclays Bank.

Looking at the general international picture it would seem that the ICC must address themselves promptly, among other serious matters, to the undue proliferation of tours and, especially, of one-day cricket, with special regard perhaps to the West Indies' position. The good health of their cricket and of that of the other major countries are inter-dependent. Their problems merit sympathetic consideration for the reasons I have tried to show. In response, however, I feel that the West Indies must toe the line both as regards over rates and the evil of intimidatory bowling, a subject on which I do not need to repeat myself.

THE CRICKETER
APRIL 1987

———————————— *Records at Lord's* ————————————

Sale of the century – or, to be accurate, of the bicentenary. Michael Sissons, my successor as chairman of the MCC Arts and Library Sub-committee, had the admirable idea of putting up to auction the quantity of cricketana of all sorts which the Club had no room to display in the pavilion or Memorial Gallery. What was the sense of their gathering dust in the basement? The sale, conducted by Christie's, took place in the Long Room, the first of the team of auctioneers being director and Arts and Library man Henry Wyndham, 6 ft 5 in, of mellow-voiced persuasion. There were 845 items and the proceedings lasted almost twelve uninterrupted hours. Seventy years after his death W.G. stole the show. A photogravure of Stuart Wortley's well-known picture of him standing at the wicket, signed by both subject and artist, the market price of which hitherto was around £200, went for £2000. Talk about his thousand in May – here he was chalking up four figures with almost every appearance. A George V £1 note signed by the 1926 Australians fetched £500. The final score came to £320,000, around three times the sum expected.

DIARY
13 APRIL 1987

MCC – a Celebration

There is no phrase more neatly expressive of the role of MCC in the evolution of the game than Sir Pelham Warner's well-worn description: a private club with a public function. It was 'Plum', too, who may well have coined the aphorism that 'MCC reigns but does not rule'. In common parlance, while it has been accepted as the final seat of authority it has not thrown its weight about. Pray notice the change of tense. We must write now in the past tense to the extent that though Marylebone Cricket Club remains the maker and custodian of the Laws, just as it has been since its formation just two hundred years ago, and although it still provides the ICC, according to custom, with its venue, its chairman and its secretariat, the Club has had since 1968 no more than a guiding voice in the governance of the English game in its various aspects both amateur and professional.

When at that time Mr James Callaghan's Labour administration agreed at last to make government grants available to sports and games, they could scarcely treat with a private institution, however venerable and respected. Hence, in consultation with the then newly created Minister of Sport, Mr Denis Howell, MCC made a voluntary devolution of its tacitly accepted though never explicit powers. The Test and County Cricket Board, formerly 'The Advisory', would in future manage and control the first-class game, and a new body, the National Cricket Association, would be answerable for all aspects of the amateur game, with special emphasis on the coaching of the young. Both these bodies, along with MCC, would contribute equal representation, a third each, to a court of appeal known as the Cricket Council. The gist of all this is no doubt apprehended more or less by the average devotee of *Wisden*; but it is an outline perhaps worth defining afresh in this celebratory bicentennial year.

The future of MCC will be what its successive Committees make of a wonderful heritage. Theirs is the ground, unique historically, perfectly placed geographically to remain, as it has always been, the natural headquarters of the game. When the spotlight turns on to Lord's this coming summer it will show an arena better equipped to accommodate members and public than ever before. The handsome new Mound Stand complements and follows the contours of the recently built Tavern Stand right up to the open decks of 'free seats' at the Nursery End. As the eye moves anti-clockwise the Grand and Warner Stands continue the line of the boundary round to the centrepiece of the pavilion, that four-square monument to Victorian self-assurance which seems likewise to be the very emblem of cricket's permanence as a national institution.

Behind the pavilion (which itself has been greatly modernized within and to which a library of fitting size and dignity has been appended), and contiguous with the real tennis and squash courts and the War Memorial Gallery opened in 1950, the TCCB and NCA are now comfortably and independently housed. So, alongside the Harris garden and in a separate building is the Middlesex CCC. Away on the Nursery ground stands the MCC Indoor School through which many thousand cricketers of all ages have passed since its opening ten years ago. Add to the picture the modern Tavern alongside the Grace Gates, and it strikes one afresh how greatly over the last two decades the face of Lord's has changed. What we must be truly thankful for is that the transitions have been wrought without loss of character. One cannot visualize any more significant building in the immediate future. In 1987 Lord's can face the years ahead confidently as it is. Thank Heaven it will always be a cricket ground – surely *the* cricket ground – never a stadium.

So much for 'the plant', but what of the men who have made MCC and Lord's what it is today? The gallery is a remarkable one, starting with Thomas Lord himself, whom that small band of noblemen commissioned to procure a ground for the club they were about to form. All that is known about Lord marks him as a man of quality. He had, say Lord Harris and F. S. Ashley-Cooper in *Lord's and the MCC*, a 'handsome presence and possessed a bonhomie that was almost irresistible'. Three grounds he had to find as London extended to the north, finally, in 1814, putting down his roots only just in time on the present site.

In those first days two men of a very different temper held the stage – the Rev. Lord Frederick Beauclerk, reputedly the best cricketer in England around the turn of the nineteenth century and the first Secretary of MCC, and Benjamin Aislabie, who doted on the game though much too fat to be any good at it. Thomas Hughes portrayed him affectionately on the occasion in *Tom Brown's Schooldays* when he brought the MCC team to Rugby. In the earliest pavilions (the first was burned down in 1825), Aislabie cast on the scene a benevolence which held the Club together, a necessary antidote, no doubt, to Beauclerk (descended from the union of Charles II and Nell Gwynne), who as a dictator of affairs on the field and off and a sharp betting man to boot, comes across almost as a villain of old-style melodrama.

Following Aislabie's death in office in 1842, the affairs of MCC declined to a point which brought press agitation for a cricket parliament to depose the Club from its position of authority. It was rescued from the hands of reactionaries such as Robert Grimston – who greeted with disgust the advent of the mowing machine – by a character ideally suited to the situation in R. A. Fitzgerald.

Bob Fitzgerald was clearly a popular personality and withal a lively one. 'Whether it was the magnificence of his swagger, the luxuriance of his beard, the fun that rolled out of him so easily, or the power of his swiping, I do not know, but as regards each he could not escape notice,' wrote Lord Harris, who, as to the fun, tells of Fitzgerald's favourite trick when a wicket fell of pretending to catch a mouse in the grass.

Fitzgerald reigned as Secretary of MCC from 1863 to 1876, having been the first salaried occupant. As an undergraduate, Harris was a member of the team which Fitzgerald in 1872 took on a successful pioneering tour of Canada and USA, the first ever under-taken by amateurs. He took sides to Paris and Dublin, and flew the flags of MCC and I Zingari in many unfrequented places. (The MCC colours of red and yellow date from his time.) He was both reformer and innovator. Alas, he perhaps drove himself too hard, for his health completely failed and he died young. A tangible memorial to him in the MCC Library is a collection of illustrated scrapbooks, donated by a grandson, T. G. Fitzgerald.

If young George Harris was on the threshold of a leading role in the rapid evolution of cricket, an even greater figure was another of Fitzgerald's North American party, W. G. Grace himself, already a rising star. The 1870s saw the dawn of county cricket wherein the Graces of Gloucestershire led the way. The game expanded mightily around the ample frame of W.G., who was, let it be said, ever a loyal MCC man. Middlesex began to play at Lord's in 1877, thus providing Londoners with a regular programme of first-class cricket. The following year came the event that popularized the game more than anything else, the first visit of the Colonials from Australia and their defeat of MCC in a single day.

Although for some years yet the financial prosperity of MCC continued to depend greatly on the three classic fixtures – Eton *v* Harrow, begun in 1805, Gentlemen *v* Players, from 1806, and the University Match, from 1827 – the frequent Australian visits along with the appeal of Middlesex brought an even wider public to Lord's.

No essay aiming to sketch the MCC story in its bicentenary year would omit mention of the longest-serving of all its officers, Sir Spencer Ponsonby-Fane, whose life was bound up with Lord's almost from his days as a Harrow boy in the mid 1830s until his death in 1915, aged ninety-one. For thirty-six years he served the Club as Treasurer, which was in his time and ever after the key post. Finding only two pictures in the place (admittedly Francis Haymans) he started the now incomparable Art Collection. Diplomat – he was secretary to Palmerston – and courtier, Ponsonby-Fane personified that close aristocratic involvement with MCC which was continuous from the foundation until after the Second World War.

On this point a word here in parenthesis. Although its beginnings and the close connections with Eton, Harrow, Winchester, the other major schools and the universities determined the style and pattern of its membership, MCC has not been, at least in living memory – and contrary to popular belief – a socially exclusive club. Granted a civilized standard of behaviour, good cricketers have always been welcome.

Next, chronologically, comes a very major figure in the story, Francis Lacey, a barrister by training, who took on the Secretaryship at the age of thirty-eight in 1898 and held it until 1926, when he was honoured with the first knighthood for cricket. Ignoring the advice of his predecessor, Henry Perkins, to 'take no notice of the damned Committee', Lacey put the Club on a sound administrative footing. Where MCC had been loath to involve themselves with the international and county scene Lacey had a keener eye for the game's welfare and the Club's responsibilities. The Board of Control for Test Matches and 'The Advisory' were formed early in his time, while in 1903 MCC (as the Melbourne CC had been urging them) undertook to choose and manage the tours to Australia.

Plum Warner led the first side out that winter and brought home the Ashes, and MCC has been a household name in cricket ever since. In due course, and over a span of seventy-odd years, the MCC colours were flown in South Africa, West Indies, New Zealand, India, Ceylon (now Sri Lanka) and Pakistan, as well as in many other countries not on the Test match circuit.

The post-First World War years saw the formidable Treasurer–Secretary partnership of Harris and Lacey, and it is fascinating, if profitless, to speculate whether if old Lord Harris had lived another year or so he might have scented the coming 'Bodyline' trouble in the late summer of 1932 and either scotched it at birth or at least apprehended the situation more swiftly when the first warning signals from Australia came wafting back.

The Bodyline message for cricket's rulers, so far as Test cricket was concerned, was to beware the sudden onset of unruly passions. There were storms to come, all right, but not yet. MCC were soon marking their 150th anniversary with three very successful matches and a celebratory dinner of many courses and toasts, of which the writer (recently elected) retains only a blurred memory.

Through the Second World War – as distinct from the complete 1914–18 shut-down – MCC kept the flag flying admirably with a regular programme of cricket each summer, culminating in the 'Victory Tests' between England and the Dominions. More people (413,856) watched cricket at Lord's in 1945 than in 1939 – an augury fulfilled by the vast crowds in the first post-war years of people anxious to dull the thought of past horrors and present shortages and discomforts.

MCC were more active than ever before in the period between the war's end and the transitions of 1968, presiding over ever more frequent Test exchanges, setting up enquiries at the behest of the counties – five of these, achieving much less than their labours deserved, sat within thirty years – and, especially, turning their attention to encouraging the young. The present comprehensive structure of School Associations Coaching and competitive cricket must be traced back to the foresight and energy in 1948 of G. O. (now Sir George) Allen and his subsequent partnership with H. S. Altham. (Their *MCC Cricket Coaching Book*, regularly updated, has sold 100,000 copies.)

Altham and Allen, successive Treasurers, apart from a single year, from 1950 to 1974, both steeped in all aspects of the game, have served MCC in the Harris tradition, if using a softer touch, in harness with three Secretaries of contrasting personality but equal dedication – Colonel R. S. Rait Kerr, R. Aird and S. C. Griffith.

An extension of the hierarchy must be mentioned here. The modern President is expected – indeed, obliged – to play a far more active role than ever before. What until the late 1940s was almost a sinecure has become a highly demanding post involving many hours a week, dealing with the complexities of both MCC itself and the ICC (of which the President of the day is the automatic chairman), and the evolving relationship with the new bodies.

Whereas in the forty years prior to the Second World War only eight Presidents had been first-class cricketers, over the last forty years the figure is twenty-eight. Most of these have brought to the job wide experience in cricket administration. When, however, a President has named as his successor a man of distinction outside the game – Lord Caccia, the late A. H. A. Dibbs, and the present chairman of finance, Sir Anthony Tuke, are recent examples – the Club has been invariably well served. It is easy to be too close to the game's problems and even to be insensitive to public opinion.

The most unfortunate instance of this was 'the D'Oliveira Affair' when the Committee had to withstand in the fateful year of 1968 a vote of no confidence – albeit fairly comfortably defeated – at a Special General Meeting. The Club, in the persons of the chairman of ICC and its representatives, had come much more favourably from the Throwing crisis of 1960. Harry Altham and Gubby Allen were chiefly involved here, ultimately with the decisive backing of Sir Donald Bradman.

When Kerry Packer's intrusion threatened to tear cricket apart in 1977 the ICC were lucky to find as their chairmen two patient negotiators prepared to travel the world in search of a settlement in D. G. Clark and C. H. Palmer. Who shall say that the business might not have been brought to a less damaging conclusion by them on behalf of ICC than the subservient long-term accommodation suddenly accepted by the Australian Board?

These are waters under the bridge, and the concluding question to be asked is how well equipped is the MCC of 1987 to fulfil its more limited but still crucial stewardship of the game in the future? Writing on the eve of the bicentenary, I take the mood to be of competence and self-confidence. The Club today is a unique sporting institution with a value and annual turnover measured in many millions, run by a President and Committee wherein cricket and business expertise are combined in a fairer mix of the generations than in some earlier days. It has 18,000 members and a waiting-list of embarrassing length. We are at the outset of a year marked by an ambitious series of large-scale events – a Ball, dinners at Lord's and the Guildhall, a luncheon on the site of the original ground at Dorset Square, and more besides. Much imagination has gone into the programme, and the news is that everything is over-subscribed.

There remains the culmination of the festivities, the match

between MCC, its team drawn from current county players regardless of nationality, and the Rest of the World. On this may Providence look kindly: fair weather, a good match worthy of the occasion, and – dare one hope? – something distinguished in the way of English participation.

WISDEN, APRIL 1987

The Blues' Innings Not Over Yet

Spring visits to the University Parks at Oxford and Fenner's Ground at Cambridge in their early freshness were always, for your cricket correspondent emeritus, a special blending of duty and pleasure. Likewise it has been a joy these last few days to revisit haunts of traditional peace and beauty and discover that things are distinctly *more* as they used to be than one had feared.

Both universities have been finding it difficult, if not at times impossible, to turn out sides worthy at least of giving the counties a worthwhile workout, and the first-class status of such matches has accordingly been queried in some quarters.

Today, in fact, happens to mark a distinct milestone in the history of University cricket in that for the first time it will be a combined team, drawn from Redbrick as well as Oxbridge, that contests the first round of the Benson and Hedges Cup. Oxford is the venue, Hampshire their opponents.

A trial was held last weekend at Fenner's. The batting was distinctly stronger than the bowling, Oxbridge beating Redbrick – theoretically there were fifty of them to choose from – by eight wickets with 2 overs to spare.

The ancient universities have co-operated amiably in this experiment with the enterprising cricket committee of the Universities Athletic Union. But to think of it as the thin end of the wedge is to ignore the practical impossibility of keeping together a mixed side from the length and breadth of Britain during the academic term, after which the best undergraduates of all shades, if they so wish, can earn good money on county staffs.

Two who will do so are John Stephenson, a batsman from

Felsted, with Essex, and Martin Speight, a nineteen-year-old wicket-keeper from Hurstpierpoint, with Sussex. Both are at Durham University, a focus for many young sportsmen, but one if not both would have been competing for Blues either dark or light if their promising credentials had been accepted.

Michael Atherton, a freshman from Manchester Grammar School, who has started his season at Fenner's spectacularly well, was luckier. It may or may not be a coincidence that he is up at Downing, of which the Master, Sir John Butterfield, is also president of the Cambridge University Cricket Club. To Downing also next year, fledged already as a Somerset cricketer, is due Jonathan Atkinson from Millfield with the game in the blood since his headmaster father was captain (now president) of Somerset.

Lord Blake, now alas in his last term as Provost of Queen's College, watching last week in The Parks, considered the turning-away of certain young men of admirable all-round credentials 'deplorable'. However, speaking as a former president of Oxford University Cricket Club, he thought there were signs, in some colleges at least, of a more balanced attitude to admissions. Dr Simon Porter, senior OUCC treasurer, thinks that the idea of 'a degree in life', as he termed it, might be gaining some acceptance.

This year's level-headed Oxford captain, Christopher Tooley of St Dunstan's and Magdalen, is adamant that Oxford games-players get rather better than average degrees: 'All recent cricket Blues have had very good seconds.' J. G. W. Davies, the prop and stay of Cambridge cricket as treasurer and fixture secretary for the last thirty years, tells me that E. J. Craig, a paragon who twice made 1000 runs for the University, got a *triple* First at the end of it and is now a don at Churchill, made a survey over a decade and proved that sportsmen emerged definitely above average in their final triposes.

So how does a benevolent observer of the scene see the future of University cricket? Well, if a TCCB directive were to ordain that Oxford and Cambridge matches against the counties were no longer to rate as first-class, the counties would scarcely go to the expense of playing them. Nor could the TCCB itself justify an annual subvention of £10,000 each, out of which the universities pay the coaches they use from the National Cricket Association.

Though they must allow pride of place over this last decade to the provincial universities as nurseries for the counties, Oxford and Cambridge have throughout history been the prime forcing grounds for county and Test cricketers. Though great players such as Chapman, Allen, Jardine, May, Cowdrey or Dexter do not at present roll off the production lines, the flow has certainly not dried up. Edmonds, Tavaré, Pringle, Marks, Ian Greig, and Paul Parker are six Oxbridge Test cricketers with their counties. There are other notable figures – Roebuck, for instance, Miller, Acfield and Boyd-Moss.

With cricket drying up in state schools, what greater necessity than to encourage and endeavour to increase *all* natural sources of players, first who may go on to teach the game and eventually also to govern it with wisdom?

Oxbridge today must help themselves as best they can. They have good coaches (at present Bob Carter and Graham Saville), good pitches to complement their lovely grounds, and, not least, captains of personality and humour.

Who can say that the all-round philosophy may not soon be revived among a few of those cloistered dons, or that some modern Cecil Rhodes may not appear with scholarships designed to foster the all-round ideal?

THE DAILY TELEGRAPH
2 MAY 1987

────────────── *MCC* en Fête ──────────────

The first of the two full-scale dinners to celebrate the MCC bicentenary was held in the Long Room, preceded by the opening by the Duke of Edinburgh of the new Mound Stand and of the adjacent gates presented by the Duke of Westminster in honour of his uncle, a former President and Treasurer, the one and only Charles Cobham, the 10th Viscount. The first course was a selection of smoked fish, the lemon with it encased in muslin – a touch of refinement not lost on John Warr, who started: 'Your Royal Highness, my Lords and Gentlemen, I knew this was going to be no ordinary dinner when I saw that they'd dressed the lemon up in a jockstrap.' Needless to say, after such an off-the-cuff start he never looked back.

What a contrast this relaxed evening was to the 150th dinner of my memory in starched shirts, with many courses and hours of stilted oratory. The Mound Stand and its architect, Michael Hopkins, have since come in for almost unqualified praise, with its ten white tent-like pinnacles standing clear on the skyline. High marks to David Male and his Estates Sub-committee.

DIARY
6 MAY 1987

Fond Memories of Frank Woolley

May 27, 1987 will mark the centenary of the birth of a tall, left-handed cricket legend called Frank Woolley. The event will no doubt evoke memories in print as well as in the hearts of the elderly. Let me confine myself here chiefly to personal recollections of my first hero, to whom all subsequent ones have always been subsidiary.

The first time I saw Woolley (F.E.) was at The Oval on Saturday, 13 August 1921 in the Fifth Test against Australia. Earlier in the summer at Lord's he had sustained the England batting almost single-handed against the awesome speed of Gregory and McDonald with the two innings, 95 and 93, which he always rated the best of his career. My father had just made me (aged fourteen) a schoolboy member of Surrey, so I watched from the privilege of the pavilion as Frank, batting 'beautifully', according to *Wisden*, collected 23 runs before allowing himself to be run out by Bardsley's strong flat throw from the neighbourhood of the scoreboard on the tram side of the ground. A tantalizing glimpse of the superlative.

My next sight of him was much more satisfying. The Oval pitches of 'Bosser' Martin's day suited Frank to a T, and he nearly always made runs for the Rest of England against the Champion County in the last match of the season there. In 1924 he and Percy Chapman took the Yorkshiremen apart (202 and 70* respectively), and at one point made 49 against Rhodes and Waddington in 3 overs. The ball kept flying over the crowd into the road beside the gasometers.

In, I think, 1926, armed with a note from a Kent and England cricketer, G.E.C. Wood, I went down to the Rectory Field, Blackheath, where Kent were playing the annual blood match against Surrey, in search of an interview for the defunct magazine,

All Sports. We sat on a seat in front of the pavilion, and I wish I could recall more than the quiet, civil reception of a teenager's presumptuous questioning.

Likewise this first article under my own name has disappeared without trace. Later that summer I saw him again in an Oval Test match make an abbreviated 20-odd, having come in on that still awkward pitch after Hobbs and Sutcliffe had gone most of the way to regaining the Ashes with the most celebrated of all their partnerships.

In 1930, now with the *Evening Standard*, I watched from the auxiliary press box below the Grandstand at Lord's the very perfection of batting on the first morning of the classic England–Australia Test. Without a hint of strain or effort Frank waved the ball away in that aloof, imperious way that was peculiarly his own, using height and reach either to get to the pitch or to go right back. He leaned on the first ball he received, sending it whistling past cover up the hill and into the crowd. One had visions of a hundred before lunch – by one o'clock even – when he cracked a shortish one mighty hard in the direction of Tim Wall, nominally in the gully but a good pitch's length back, and he somehow clung on to the ball down by his boots: 53–2–41 read the board, and the clock said quarter past twelve. Duleep – an admiring pupil of Frank's a few years earlier – came next to play, inspired by his mentor, the best innings of his brilliant, brief career.

In 1932, though he was forty-five and Jardine (appointed England captain the previous year) can hardly have considered taking him to Australia in the autumn, he sent him in first for the South against the North in a Trial Match at Old Trafford. Larwood and Voce in full spate had the new ball for the North, but there was precious little shine left by the time Woolley with that slightly stiff-legged gait walked back, having made 50 out of 72 in under the hour, caught in the deep off a full pitch. I expect I ventured a few purple patches in the recounting of that to our readership.

His final appearance in Gentlemen and Players, leading the latter in his retirement year, was unforgettable in several respects. On the first day he seemed almost unconcerned with the tactical situation in the enjoyment of watching the left-handed Hugh Bartlett, another of his pupils and a batsman after his own heart, demolish the professional bowling in an overwhelming innings of 175 not out. When the Players went in Kenneth Farnes, nettled at being dropped from the Test team, produced what *Wisden* described as 'the best fast bowling seen in this match since Arthur Fielder dismissed all the Gentlemen for 90 runs in 1906'. Farnes's fearsome speed was too much for all the professionals save for the youthful Len Hutton and his fifty-one-year-old captain, who made a model 41 before being applauded by an upstanding crowd all the way to the pavilion.

Though he took 2068 wickets (and made a record 1017 catches) he had done most of his bowling before my day. My memory seems concentrated on Frank's cavalier treatment of fast bowling. But in truth he never expressed a preference or otherwise for any one type or any individual bowler. Modest in private life, he was a disdainful antagonist, orthodox in his basic method, and with an armoury so complete that his 58,969 runs (an aggregate second only to Sir Jack Hobbs) were scored at an average rate, according to the historian R. L. Arrowsmith, 'exceeded only by Jessop and equalled by Trumper'. What a cricketer – what a hero!

THE CRICKETER
MAY 1987

A Woolley Pilgrimage

Frank Woolley was born 100 years ago today. In the previous eight years, following his death at ninety-one, old Martha Woolley has made the pilgrimage from Chester, Nova Scotia, to attend the eight o'clock Communion at the cathedral at which he is annually remembered, then to place flowers in front of the stand on the ground which bears his name. This time her doctor forbade her to travel, and I therefore took her place, as I have continued to do since.

Frank's last years were enriched, as hers have been, by his chance meeting in South Africa with an American widow, Martha Wilson Morse, previously married to an English cavalry officer. Frank, shortly after the death of his first wife, was at the Cape on a visit to a daughter, she to present to Capetown University a copy of her book, Before Apartheid – Memoirs of South Africa.

Frank went back to her home at Chester, Nova Scotia, and they came annually to England and to Canterbury Week. There, spare and upright, as he walked across the field he had the look of a bishop in mufti. Martha

Woolley did everything to preserve his reputation, including the com-missioning of a bronze head by Willi Soukop, RA, now to be seen in the Writing Room at Lord's.

At his death this redoubtable old lady pressed for a Memorial Service in Canterbury Cathedral. The Dean and Chapter agreed. But how many would come on a Saturday in November forty years after he had played his last innings for Kent? How many had survived who saw him play? Would 150 turn up – or 300? The answer was 600, the full capacity of the Choir – which testified both to the love of cricket in Kent and to the unique appeal of the county's greatest cricketer.

DIARY
27 MAY 1987

MCC as Lewis Sees It

Tony Lewis faced a testing challenge when he was given the first option of writing the definitive book to mark the bicentenary of the MCC. So many gifted pens had covered all or most of the ground before him: notably Altham, Harris, Ashley-Cooper, Warner, Peebles, Diana Rait Kerr and Moorhouse.

Something of authority, yet distinctive, was called for, a book of quality with no hint of stuffiness. One is indeed reassured at once on this point by Paul Cox's colourful, almost H. M. Bateman-ish jacket and endpaper of *Double Century* (Hodder & Stoughton, £14.95). They enclose a handsome production, admirably illustrated.

In his preface the author makes clear that he has not attempted, for reasons of time and space, a formal history of MCC and cricket but has rather sought continuous themes over the 200 years and 'plaited them into a narrative'. He has attempted, and brought off brilliantly, the picture of cricket down the ages on a broad canvas, showing the game and players in the social context of the time.

He quotes G. M. Trevelyan telling how Lord John Sackville was happy to play under the captaincy of his gardener at Knole, adding his well-known aphorism that, 'if the French noblesse had been capable of playing cricket with their peasants, their châteaux would never have been burned down'.

The respective attitudes of Gentlemen and Players, their relationships with one another and their particular contributions to the growing game are dominant themes through all but the last quarter of a century.

Occasionally Mr Lewis's judgement is arguable, as when he talks of MCC, in the celebrated Brian Close case, 'demanding leadership that observed exclusively the *amateur* ethics of behaviour and fair play'. In my experience the professionals were no whit less jealous than the amateurs to preserve the true spirit of cricket. Close was unanimously found guilty of gross time-wasting, which cost Warwickshire victory over Yorkshire.

Though appreciative of the vast unpaid labours of generations of men who have undertaken the governance of cricket, there are enough other instances where Mr Lewis is critical of the establishment stance to underline the wisdom behind MCC's choice of author. For the boy from the valleys who played the violin in the Welsh Youth Orchestra before winning his way to Cambridge from Neath Grammar School is by background and temperament very much his own man.

This is no bland history but an almost quizzical personal impression informed by wide reading. He has a quick eye for character, from Beauclerk and Aislabie through MacLaren and Barnes to Allen and Dexter. Naturally he is specially at home in his own era, writing with the experience not only of leading university, county and country but of playing under the MCC flag in various outposts of Asia and South America.

Those loyal MCC members mystified by the reported goings-on at the recent AGM may be fortified to know that the author sees the prospect of a vital further service that the Club might render in the years ahead. 'Now that MCC is freed from running English cricket, it has the experience to offer to become a world unifying force . . . it could run the world's cricket', through a revised and strengthened International Cricket Conference.

THE DAILY TELEGRAPH
29 MAY 1987

——— *Positively Last Performance* ———

This was the last of several matches between my Arabs and W. F. Sale's XI at Wellesley House, Broadstairs: the idea to show the boys of this splendid school some allegedly decent cricket. I was reminded of my positively last ignominious appearance on the cricket field, playing (aetat. 64) in the Fathers' Match at Wellesley, under dubious colours at that, being step grandfather to young George. I managed a few creaky overs and finally, batting number eleven and with a handful to win, ooh! there goes the knee, a hobble to safety, runner called for and the game tamely drawn.

DIARY
14 JUNE 1987

——— *Whisky Galore* ———

At their annual pre-Test dinner the Lord's Taverners had the typically thoughtful idea of making presentations to five octogenarians. So each of the following in turn received from the chairman, Ronnie Corbett, a pewter and glass decanter the shape and size of a dimple Haig bottle, with precious fluid to fill: Bob Wyatt (86), Gubby Allen (84), Alec Home of the Hirsel (83), Les Ames (81), and a much-flattered me. At Ronnie Corbett's table the little man cracked spontaneously away as though the television cameras might be rolling with Ronnie Barker appearing at any moment. For me the pair of them are in a class of their own, inimitable.

DIARY
17 JUNE 1987

——— *Wimbledon in Style* ———

Seats in the Royal Box at Wimbledon, a lovely eightieth birthday present from the All-England Club chairman, Buzzer Hadingham. We were unlucky with spitting rain, just enough to blot out most of the programme, but had the great bonus of meeting our number one Arab lady, the Duchess of Kent, who used to score at Hovingham when we played her father's team on the Northern Tour. Sir William Worsley would umpire, with Maurice Leyland one year at the other end, the latter in the earlier stages of the dreaded Parkinson's disease which caused him to keep the affected hand in the pocket of his white coat.

It was only my second visit to Wimbledon, the first being pre-war when I

*was playing cricket across the road. After getting out I sauntered over in
flannels and blazer to have a look. When a few autograph books were thrust
in my direction I graciously signed them.*

DIARY
23 JUNE 1987

───────── *The Perennial Johnners* ─────────

*A grand BBC dinner to celebrate Brian Johnston's seventy-fifth birthday.
When these denizens of the Beeb let their hair down the result is an
exceedingly rich dose of bonhomie and goodwill. And could there be a more
fitting occasion than this? The perennial Johnners first signed up for the
BBC in January 1946, so, birthday apart, they were honouring almost the
oldest inhabitant, Alston excepted.*

*When in the 1930s I used to begin my personal cricket season in late
April, playing for the Cryptics at Oxford, I became aware of a ridiculously
long beak hovering over the stumps on the New College ground. It
belonged to a cheerful, gregarious, conversational undergraduate by the
name of Johnston.*

*Brian, albeit he had not made the Eton XI, was a better than average club
wicket-keeper, good enough to have been elected to that reservoir of talent
beneath the University XI known as the OU Authentics. From the first he
was something of a character, who stood out as such even among Etonians,
that distinctively individual breed.*

*In his Oxford days and for many years afterwards an assemblage of
otherwise respectable cricketers used to converge on the 'free seats' of F and
G block at the Nursery End of Lord's during the Eton and Harrow, there to
trade amiable badinage and outrageous insult with the enemy. The focal
point was Brian, whose first essays into ad-lib running commentary on one
such occasion brought a rebuke from the office of the Secretary of MCC.*

*As a mild response to all the terrible tales he has invented about me over
many years I am pleased to perpetuate the strong rumour that as a result of
giving a hard time − in the friendliest possible way, of course − to the
long-on fielder (Tony Allen, afterwards of Cambridge and Northamptonshire), Brian's election to MCC was put back a year at the instigation of the
Secretary, Billy Findlay. If it wasn't, it might well have been.*

*Brian's success as a broadcaster owes something to the comedian strain in
his character. He is naturally funny, and as a humourist his Mr Punch-like
profile gets him off to a good start. He is also a life-long lover of cricket and
friend to cricketers of every sort and generation. The prime key, however, to*

his appeal, both in and beyond the field of sport, as he has come across to listeners in a variety of programmes and notably in 'Down Your Way', is an unquenchable natural benevolence. He sees the best in mankind and brings out the best in consequence. The atmosphere of the 'Test Match Special' team of commentators reflects his good nature. Thanks not a little to the lead he gives, Test cricket comes across as – despite all contrary evidence – a civilized game played, for the most part, in a sporting spirit.

This is why, though he has long passed the normal retirement age, and despite those brazen hints about chocolate cake and those awful puns, I hope he prattles on for a few more summers yet.

DIARY
26 JUNE 1987

A Plague on Heavy Bats

When I heard the sad news from Charles Churchill, master-in-charge of cricket at Summerfields, that boys were coming back to school with such heavy bats that he had forbidden their use, I sought the views of Gordon Jenkins, manager of the MCC Indoor School, who probably has more boys passing through his hands than anyone.

Mr Jenkins had a sorry story to tell:

> I am in complete agreement with your comments regarding the weight of bats. A lot of first-class players could struggle on the uncovered wickets with the bludgeons they now use. The problem in the Indoor School shop is two-fold: the young boy who will only have a specific manufacturer's bat, irrespective of how heavy it is; and parents who insist the boy must have a bat which will last for two or three seasons. Therefore, initially, it is too big for him. The damage to his basic technique is almost beyond repair.

One can understand parents not themselves cricketers seeking to save a little by choosing a bat that their young hopeful will 'grow into', but, as the manager says, it is an expensive economy. The master hand in the pick-up should be the left as the wrists gradually cock so that the maker's name is shown to point. If the bat is too heavy it will be levered up by the right hand, almost inevitably with the face shut and the stroke made across the line. Talking of maker's names, the manager tells me he refuses to stock a certain popular maker, all of whose boys' bats are too heavy.

Professor Alfred Gover, whose cricket school at Wandsworth continues to flourish and who still (aged seventy-nine) can turn his arm over for an hour or two in an emergency, warmly agrees, and on being pressed gave the names of at least three makers who do produce bats of the proper weight for boys – Gray-Nicolls, Slazenger and County Sports. To these three Mr Jenkins adds the favourite bat of one's youth, Gunn & Moore.

This matter of weight is another example of a dangerous habit by top players filtering down. The fact that some strong men prefer to wield a 3 lb cudgel need not concern anyone else. No modern player hits the ball harder than Walter Hammond, whose bats weighed around 2 lb 4 oz.

The MCC Indoor School manager even proposes a radical solution which I notice Peter Roebuck also made in our last issue – in the course of some thoroughly unsound (to my mind) remarks on uncovering. If the law lays down a maximum weight for the ball, why not also for the bat? That is a prospect which would set the makers chuntering. Roebuck proposes a maximum of 2 lb 10 oz.

THE CRICKETER
JULY 1987

Gents and Players:
A Story of Mutual Respect

It is just a quarter of a century since Gentlemen and Players faced one another for the last time, and the annual match at Lord's maintained its appeal, despite or possibly enhanced by the anachronism of the ancient title, right to the end.

The generations since them have been likewise intrigued by the former relationship between the paid and the unpaid.

In his book *Gentlemen and Players* just published (Grafton,

£14.95), the MP for Arundel, Michael Marshall, has achieved two things. First, by giving the full scores of all matches between 1919 and 1962 he has filled in a historical gap since Sir Pelham Warner's *Gentlemen* v *Players 1806–1949* ended with the series still going strong. Further, he has pursued the theme of amateur-professional relationships in quoted conversations conducted over several years with a wide age range from Frank Woolley and Bob Wyatt to Tony Lewis and Fred Titmus.

How appropriate it was, as Mr Marshall brings out, that the last captains chanced to be so completely representative of the traditional upbringing of amateur and professional, the attacking batting of one, the explosive fast bowling of the other, of the ancient rivalry between north and south.

With Dexter as captain and the Duke of Norfolk as manager of MCC's side to Australia of 1962–3, the old régime went out in style. One recalls the Australians standing in unnecessary awe of the Earl Marshal of England at Kalgoorlie where we had to form a queue for the shaving mirror:

'After you, your Grice [sic].'

'No, no, you were here before me.'

As Dexter remarks, everyone knew where they stood with the Duke: 'I remember early in the tour when he was changing with us in our dressing rooms, he said, "You should call me Duke or Sir in public, but you may call me Bernard in the bath."'

Titmus, by the way, confirmed the story of the announcement over the Lord's public-address system in the days when status was shown by the position of the initials: 'Ladies and Gentlemen, there is a correction to your scorecards. For F. J. Titmus, read Titmus, F. J.'

Despite pinpricks, the attitudes of a few, and the favouring of the amateur in selection (sometimes a matter of cash), in umpiring decisions and (strange but true) in the press, the attitude which comes through strongly in the book is the respect that each element has had for the other.

One was reminded of the *Talks with Old English Cricketers*, which had a success at the turn of the century, written by 'Old Ebor', who was A. W. Pullin, doyen of the Yorkshire press.

The true loss to the game in 1962 was that of the amateur's independence, a point made by Fred Trueman, who led the professionals in the last of the classics against the amateurs of Ted Dexter:

. . . I never complained about the inclusion of an amateur – if he was good enough. When it came to captaincy there was no question in my mind that the independence of the amateur who was willing to speak up for his team and if necessary to take on the county committee was the best combination we ever had.

THE DAILY TELEGRAPH
21 JULY 1987

MCC's Unwelcome Fixture

Since Alan Gibson drew the attention of *Spectator* readers some weeks ago to certain discordant noises emanating from a section of MCC members, the President and Committee have decided to bring the matter to the test once and for all. Having called a Special General Meeting at the Central Hall, Westminster, on Thursday next, 30 July, in order to pass the report and accounts which had been rejected on a show of hands and after much emotive oratory at the AGM at Lord's in May, it has now sent to all 18,000 members a lengthy memorandum on the subject which has been built up by some into a burning issue – the relationship between MCC and the Test and County Cricket Board.

This was the body which the Club itself set up, back in 1968, in order to run the first-class game. When MCC, the private club with a public function, at that time decided to devolve into a democratic form, its traditional paternalistic role, its future contribution to the game that it had guided and nourished for all but two centuries seemed evident enough. It would give all encouragement and practical help, consistent with the interests of its membership, to the new bodies it had formed – there were also the Cricket Council to act as a sort of Upper House, and the National Cricket Association which was to run the recreational (amateur) game.

The Club would continue (with the co-operation of the various international bodies) to frame the Laws of the game, as it had done since its first Code of 1788. It would continue to supply, as it had always done, in its current President, the chairman of the International Cricket Conference and also the secretariat. As the owner of Lord's Ground, the incomparable headquarters of cricket, on which the TCCB would rely for a large part of its revenue, Marylebone Cricket Club could afford to regard the scene with, shall we say, a wary benevolence, looking after its great inheritance and, incidentally, continuing to send 200-odd of its teams to play against opponents the length and breadth of the UK and on missionary tours overseas.

For a while this was the sort of pattern that emerged. But discord soon followed J. A. Bailey's appointment as MCC Secretary following S. C. Griffith's retirement. Mr Bailey fastened upon what he took to be an erosion of MCC's authority, and the TCCB found him increasingly intractable. As a member of the MCC Committee for the ten years following the Secretary taking office in 1974, one lost count of the number of weary hours taken up with semantic points that could have been painlessly determined, granted a degree of flexibility and mutual goodwill. Much centred on just what comprised the 'ultimate responsibility' for major matches. This authority the TCCB assumed in its original constitution, which MCC itself wrote and to which, as a constituent member of the Board along with the counties, it was both loyally and legally bound.

The five county-owning Test grounds accepted the 'ultimate responsibility' proviso without demur, and since MCC and these counties continue to undertake the administration of big occasions it is hard to envisage in practical working any profound difficulties. It was sad to see a man of Mr Bailey's obvious qualities taking such an uncompromising stance, even, according to the MCC memorandum, to the point along with the Treasurer, of thrice consulting counsel without the knowledge of the Committee and without disclosing to them the advice given.

The TCCB at certain times reacted in kind to the posture of the MCC Secretary. The uneasy tension lasted for a decade, during which successive committees might be censured for not effectively ensuring that he reflected its own general policy. President after President, annually appointed but limited to a few months of effective power, came near to initiating a termination of employment. When, finally, Colin Cowdrey, most reasonable and peaceful of men, decided that enough was enough, the Committee decision to offer Mr Bailey early retirement was unanimous apart from the abstention of the Treasurer, D. G. Clark. He took his lone support to the point of resignation, and it was the double departure which set alarm bells ringing.

The cry that 'we're being robbed of our rights' is always likely to have its appeal, and it is that which the memorandum seeks to refute. If anyone doubts, as they well may, that such a lengthy and detailed 16-page catalogue was necessary they may care to know that an inflammatory round-robin demanding 'full and frank disclosure' of the whole sorry saga has been circulated, by one individual representing a dissident group, to hundreds – maybe thousands – of members, some of whom have riposted to the intrusion with sadly rude replies. It seems that 200 signatures have been collected.

What sort of people, it may well be asked, run the TCCB? The answer is that, far from being a radical crew bent on putting the old Club in its place, they are chiefly men who have played with distinction for England and proudly worn MCC's colours on overseas tours. Their successive chairmen have been Douglas Insole, George Mann, Charles Palmer and now Raman Subba Row. Donald Carr, until recently secretary, has been succeeded by Alan Smith as chief executive. These are men of integrity well able to absorb any conflict of interest within what – however cynics may sniff – I would still call the fellowship of cricket.

With the game in a bad way economically in the 1960s the TCCB saw a primary duty as exploring fully the avenues of commercial patronage which, in cricket as in other sports, were just opening up. The following figures from the MCC memorandum indicate the measure of their success. The distributable surplus over fifteen years rose as follows:

1970	1975	1980	1985
£64,807	£308,088	£1,496,105	£3,336,047

MCC's share of the take rose proportionately from £5319 in 1970 to £243,602 in 1985. In addition, MCC's revenue from the major matches' peripheral income (boxes, advertising, parking, catering, etc.) in 1985 added up to £472,700.

The fact is that the TCCB have capitalized for the good of all cricket the various sources of sponsorship, television fees and so on to a degree which MCC alone could not have matched. These funds also support the Minor Counties and a thriving national coaching scheme as well as the Test ground owners and the other twelve major counties in due proportion. On the face of it the TCCB has done, and is doing, a pretty good job.

Colin Cowdrey's letter, requesting from the members the two-thirds majority required according to rule for a postal vote, says: 'I am pleased to say that a much improved working relationship now exists between MCC and TCCB, and I can assure members that our traditional rights and privileges will be fully protected.'

My conclusion is that, though it has been represented otherwise, this cloud over MCC's bicentenary year is much more a matter of personalities than of policies. It is inconceivable that the membership will not agree the passing of the report and accounts and so give the Committee the vote of confidence it needs before the culminating events of the bicentenary, the great match between MCC and the Rest of the World (tickets for which are almost sold out) and the Guildhall dinner preceding it.

Unhappily, however, they will not be presided over by Mr Cowdrey. He will be in the hands of surgeons for a serious operation, which may well be thought to have psychosomatic roots. What an uncomfortable thought to end on!

THE SPECTATOR
24 JULY 1987

———————— *Cricket in Perfection* ————————

The MCC bicentenary season, marked at its beginning by an angry and thoroughly unworthy AGM, ended with a match which, on an excellent pitch, touched perfection as an illustration of the arts of cricket and the spirit in which it was played. Enjoyment was the keynote, beginning with the players and reflecting, as always, on the crowd. The game was played hard enough but without, of course, that antagonistic, nationalistic edge which too often degenerates into more or less acrimonious dispute. It was sad that rain obliterated the last day when both sides stood with a chance of winning, but we had had enough and to spare for which to be thankful. Of four admirable hundreds I gave the palm to Gavaskar's. For the record the scores were:

   MCC: 455 for 5 dec. (Gooch 117, Gatting 179) and 310 for 6 dec.
    (Greenidge 122)
   Rest of the World: 421 for 7 dec. (Gavaskar 188) and 13 for 1.

On the Saturday afternoon the 'Test Match Special' commentary team kindly stood aside for a time while Alston, Arlott and Swanton, who had operated together forty years before, did their stuff – without, it was thought, altogether disgracing themselves.

DIARY
25 AUGUST 1987

Return to Arcadia

Why does my pen speed lightly over the paper this morning? Why (borrowing for a moment the simplistic language of the *Sunday Express* leader-page) did the members smile at one another as they left the ground and say they wouldn't have missed it? Here are a few clues. There was no intimidating bowling or fielding, no 'sledging' of batsmen. There was not a helmet in sight. No one kissed anyone. No twelfth or thirteenth or fourteenth man trailed on and off the field substituting for cricketers with piffling or non-existent ailments. A leg-spinner had a good bowl and was countered by quick footwork. The turn-out was perfect. One team all wore caps. They dressed in blazers for lunch and tea. When the umpires went out the fielders and batsmen followed them as though they could not wait to start. There was no press conference at the end with one-sided, ungenerous versions of the day's play.

Yes, madam reader, you are right. I was watching England play Australia – and, incidentally, beating them in an exciting finish – in the women's one-day International in the ancient setting of the St Lawrence Ground at Canterbury. From their celestial height Lord Harris and Frank Woolley must have approved – and for once fully understood – what was going on.

The game itself will be very old hat by the time these words see the light of day, though they will appear at least before the last fixture of the Australians' tour, the four-day 'Test' at Hove beginning on 29 August which I warmly recommend to the cricket world of both sexes in Sussex. Meanwhile, a few bouquets. Lindsay Reeler's 60 for Australia was a cultured innings, her opening partner in a stand of 54 being a young lady assured of a warm welcome in Kent, Denise Emerson, sister of Terry Alderman. The quickish left-arm over the wicket of England's star all-rounder, Sarah Potter, might have made its mark, one thought, in masculine circles.

When England went in to chase 178 in 53 overs a bright stand by Jan Brittin and Carole Hodges, the captain, was first slowed and then broken by the leg-breaks of the latter's opposite number, Lyn Larsen. Against admirable Australian fielding England could not push along quite fast enough until Jo Chamberlain, a tall left-handed teenager from Leicester, joined Jackie Court, England's most tried and trusted cricketer, and together youth and experience brought their side home. Seven true fours the youngster hit, and if six wickets and 3½ overs seems a lot it was only easy at the end.

This is the Golden Jubilee visit of the Australians to England and it is a little puzzling that women's cricket in England has not quite taken off, as it were, in the intervening half century. There were perhaps around sixty clubs then and only that now – about the same, so Miss Cathy Mowat, the WCA chairman, remarked, as there are in Melbourne alone.

Is cricket thought not a graceful game for women? As played by the best I would not subscribe to that at all. I suppose that at girls' schools lawn tennis takes up less space and is more easily organized and taught. Perhaps the grounds of mixed preparatory schools, idle after mid-July, might be made available, following the example of the Elms at Colwall where, thanks to the Singleton family, the annual women's Cricket Week is a time-honoured tradition.

Realistically, it seems to me that women's cricket in England would be given a notable boost under the long-term patronage of a good sponsor. Funds are so short (following a less than successful tour by the Indian women last year) that the top England players, half of whom come from Yorkshire and Lancashire, had to pay their own expenses down to Kent. It has always been a job to make ends meet.

Is there not some fitting product or business organization that would profit from being associated with a civilized, admirable body such as the WCA?

THE CRICKETER
SEPTEMBER 1987

Introduction to
The Men in White Coats

The quantity and variety of cricket books may well be a recurring source of wonder, but there is little, as a rule, that is surprising about each individual writer or subject. This one, however, is undeniably different, an attempt at a history of umpires – a novel theme attempted by a highly improbable author. Let me introduce her, though I fear she will not thank me for doing so.

One evening in the middle 1970s, after talking to the Cambridge University Cricket Society, I met Teresa McLean, who had been one of the audience and about whose background I already knew a little. She had read history at Lady Margaret Hall and been viva'd for a First. She had played cricket for Oxford against Cambridge and in her first year taken 8 for 45 – perhaps the proudest achievement of her life. She had taken herself off to India to work for Mother Teresa's Sisters of Charity in Bombay. In six months there she developed a species of diabetes so debilitating that she lost 3 stone and on her return was unrecognized by her mother.

Some years later she went up to Trinity, Cambridge, to research for a thesis on the medieval monastery at Ely. Thus we met. She knew by now that 'the beast' would always be close behind her, that highly virulent form of diabetes which involves the utter prostration known as hypoglycaemia. Her life then is a triumph over a handicap almost unimaginable. For the benefit of other sufferers she has described her own case in a highly acclaimed autobiography called *Metal Jam*, so named by reason of the aftertaste left by artificial sweeteners. This she added to two previous books, *Medieval English Gardens* and *The English at Play*. She has more than dabbled in journalism, and contributed theological articles in the religious columns of *The Times*.

Married now and with an infant son to look after as well as a husband who is a Cambridge history don, she has tackled a subject on which, so far as I know, no previous book has been published. Scholars and artists in many fields far removed from cricket have been magnetized by the game, but in few can its love have survived in more extraordinary circumstances than those of Mrs Martin Brett (née McLean), who can write:

As it happened I was the first person to get a Blue both for Oxford and for Cambridge, which is a lightweight achievement; the standard was low. But I regard even the smallest cricket honour as priceless and I am thrilled with mine.

Teresa writes as a cricketer, and she also writes as an umpire: not any old ump, need I say, pressed haphazardly into service and white coat, but one who has tackled and passed (the only woman on the course) the written part of the advanced examination of the Association of Cricket Umpires. While this book is in the hands of the printer she looks for a summer's cricket divided between playing and umpiring women's games, and also making a second attempt at standing for men's clubs in East Anglia. Her first experience in this direction, as described in the Author's Preface, strikes the most depressing note in the book. A wrily humorous comment in the last chapter was clearly written from first-hand experience. Men, she says, are particularly bad at accepting an unfavourable decision from a member of the opposite sex, 'especially small men with moustaches'.

Well, it seems that the club cricketers of East Anglia are going to be given a chance to redeem themselves. So be it, and if they do not give my friend better satisfaction I shall have to indulge in some investigative journalism at their expense. They have been warned.

After all of which, you will ask, what has the author made of her novel assignment? As a scholar and a sociologist she has researched widely, well beyond the confines of cricket literature. Having absorbed a formidable list of established authorities – of whom Ashley-Cooper, Haygarth, Nyren, Pycroft, Buckley, Altham and R. S. Rait Kerr are but a few – she has delved into archival material, especially those of the Wealden counties but also, as the game climbed up north, the strongholds of Nottingham and Sheffield, and on into the homes of the Yorkshire and Lancashire leagues.

The early years she covers with a racy pen and a highly critical eye for the social implications of a game promoted by rich and noble patrons wherein high stakes and liquor frequently combined to spark off dispute and disorder. Those whose familiarity with the game on either side of the turn of the eighteenth century derives from *The Hambledon Men* and Mary Russell Mitford's *Our Village* must prepare themselves for a distinctly less romantic picture, a debunking almost. Where so much money hung on the result – a good deal more than depends today when one considers what is the present equivalent of 500 guineas – the pressures on umpires, who in many cases were in the employ of the patrons, are obvious enough. (Such of the staff as gardeners, gamekeepers, bailiffs were old cricketers hired originally for their playing skill.) In lesser matches at least 'sides combined to walk off and sit down in protest with monotonous regularity'. Medieval cricket had its rough and ready side after the habit of the times, but at least after 1787 there existed in MCC a body which was both the law-maker and appeal court in one – not that the early days on Lord's grounds were free from strife and malpractice.

The author gives a highly plausible explanation of the everlasting association between cricket and pubs. Publicans were the match-makers since beer for cricket matches (and horse-races) could be brewed free of excise duty. In the pub after the game the classes mingled whether to celebrate or console. 'The events were well attended and well-oiled.'

Who was the first named umpire? The answer is amusing enough, for it was the immortal butterfingers Thomas Waymark who, at the climax of the famous match of 1744 between England and Kent (the very first of which the full score is preserved), when the last pair were together needing 3 runs to win, was confronted by a skier, whereupon, according to James Love's poem:

> The erring ball, amazing to be told!
> Slipp'd through his outstretch'd hand and mock'd his hold.
> And now the sons of Kent compleat the Game
> And firmly fix their everlasting Fame.

Poor Waymark, a sickly fellow, Miss McLean tells us, who after-wards took to umpiring – no Chester or Bird, we may be sure. We should have more confidence, perhaps, in a contemporary of Waymark's, 'Mr William Austen, of The Lady and Cat in Barnaby Street, who gave his judgement with the greatest impartiality, and received the thanks of the whole body, who afterwards had an elegant entertainment at his house.'

I must resist the temptation to linger longer in the pre-Marylebone days and salute the arrival on the Lord's scene of 'Honest Will' Caldecourt. A ground-boy at the age of nine, ground bowler at fifteen, and later an all-rounder for Hampshire and the Players, he came to distinction as a bold and popular umpire, and in particular a rigid upholder of the bowling law, the Sid Buller of his day.

Caldecourt officiated in the mid-nineteenth century 'in a Napoleonic pose, wearing a tricorn hat', but the white coat soon became normal wear at least in the great matches, and with a uniform came a gradual rise in status if not for many years in financial security.

Caldecourt was followed by another famous figure, 'Bob' Thoms, 1826–1903, a man of shining character and the friend of cricketers of every degree. Thoms officiated throughout the prime of W. G. Grace, and mention of the greatest of all cricketers bids me make a reluctant but emphatic disclaimer of the picture the author draws of him as being prone to all sorts of sharp practice and 'overwhelming players and umpires alike'. Thoms was not a man to be put upon, let alone overwhelmed, and in his *Wisden* obituary Sydney Pardon goes out of his way to say that 'The Graces, as cricketers, had no more fervent admirer than Thoms.' Though W.G. sometimes overstepped the mark in minor matches, I know of no contemporary assessment of his nature that does not breathe affection and respect. Doubters are advised to find a copy of Bernard Darwin's inimitable biography in Duckworth's 'Great Lives' series wherein that hint of boyish rascality is shown in due perspective.

In earliest days umpires were inclined to be ignorant and social stresses often made impartiality difficult for them. As the game evolved, knowledge as well as respect for the Laws increased, and first-class cricket came to be directed ably and impartially by retired players just as it is today. The one rider to this tribute which has *always* applied is the extreme reluctance of even the best umpires to make a moral judgement in respect of unfair play. Whether it be throwing or intimidation or the niggling gamesmanship that is so irritating today, umpires are seldom prepared to apply Laws which would land fellow professionals into serious trouble, deprive them even of their livelihood. Even Thoms said in respect of throwing that if they wanted the Law obeyed 'you gentlemen' will have to look to it. His successors have uttered or implied the same sentiments.

The author has lightened her tale with curiosities and farcical interpretations in the humbler regions such as are to be found among the illustrations. We read of the village umpire who, while giving general satisfaction, was regarded 'as a little too fair for such important competitions as the Derbyshire Wake Cups' – 'taking into consideration the peculiarities of other umpires'. The partiality of village umpires has been an everlasting joke. In extreme form it is scarcely, I suppose, comical – as, for instance, for opponents of the club whose combination of the vicar bowling and his sexton umpiring was said to be unbeatable.

The umpires of today and yesterday are the heroes of this book. Alex Skelding, the inimitable humourist, earns appreciative mention, including as a sample the opening sentence of his report on his benefit: 'Play began in a biting wind before a sparse crowd.' Delicacy no doubt prevented the telling of Bill Reeves's remark when Walter Robins told him what to do with his Middlesex sweater and its badge of scimitars. Buller naturally was a prime favourite. The author underlines the unique influence on his calling of Frank Chester who, between the wars, having lost an arm at Salonika, joined the first-class list as a young man of twenty-six and retained his pre-eminence for thirty years. In her last chapter on the modern game she has wisely steered clear of the threat of the instant replay, but has clearly profited from talks with 'Dicky' Bird and David Constant. She still nurses the impossible dream of umpiring a Test match!

THE MEN IN WHITE COATS, BY TERESA MCLEAN
OCTOBER 1987

Benevolence Regained

Writing soon after the bicentenary match at Lord's, one's prevailing feeling is one of great thankfulness that the whole affair was such a total success – that and also gratification that the public repute of MCC in the course of a month has undergone such a transformation. For loyal members of the Club, as for the wide world of cricket at large, the face of Lord's was clouded from May onwards by the disruption at the Annual Meeting, the dark rumours following it of internal strife, and the prospect of a Special General Meeting at which further blood would be spilt. The energies of the high officers of the

Club were being diverted and their self-confidence sorely tested at the most inappropriate time.

The proceedings at the SGM at Central Hall on 30 July proved by an emphatic vindication of the establishment to be the first of three phases in the restoration of the Club's esteem. Then came the Eve of Match dinner in the Guildhall and finally, and more importantly, the match itself.

Let me return later to the SGM. As to the dinner, when one considers the guest-list of 200 – leading dignitaries from all the ICC countries, the MCC and Rest of the World teams, something over fifty other Test cricketers of earlier times, including former England and overseas captains and the Honorary Cricket Members of MCC, the leading cricket writers, and men with special Lord's connections – one can only conclude that there was never a more representative cricket company dining under the same roof. The 500 MCC members who had been successful in the ballot brought the total to the Guildhall's capacity of 700. The setting, the speeches and the prevailing spirit combined in perfect harmony to make an unforgettable evening.

Now for the melancholy prelude. When a newspaper of such repute as *The Sunday Telegraph* prints no fewer than three jaundiced articles hinting at a TCCB take-over of the Club and dark deeds in the enforced early retirement of the Secretary, who with the aid of the Treasurer had apparently fought so valiantly to avoid it, a general state of alarm was not to be wondered at. Complementing this campaign was a circular letter from a member to hundreds of others, accompanied by stamped envelope, soliciting signatures in favour of 'full and frank disclosure' of every relevant document in the Club's possession, and demanding a further SGM if full satisfaction were not obtained at the one which had been announced already. The 200 signatures having been produced (in addition to some sadly impolite comments from some to whom and by whom the writer was quite unknown), the MCC Committee decided to offer two full-length speeches at the Central Hall SGM, one at the beginning and one at the end of the debate, to men of the dissidents' choice. This was in addition, of course, to those of any others who caught the Chairman's eye.

I never thought that the Committee were in danger of attracting less than the two-thirds majority needed to pass the once-rejected report and accounts after they decided, as they were bound to do, that on so crucial an issue members unable to be present in person might vote by proxy. (In the event, as reported in the last issue, they won overwhelmingly by 88 per cent; 7138 for, 981 against.) What was even more reassuring was that among the 2000 or so in the hall the proportions in favour among those who had not already voted by post was 80 per cent, 636 against 163. The assumption could only be, considering that the opposition was London-based, that many came to the meeting with their minds not fully made up. Any such must have voted, on the evidence of the debate, in favour of the Committee.

When it came to the crunch the case against them was seen to be flimsy to a degree. The Treasurer, Hubert Doggart, whose tactful handling of the meeting was universally admired, gave everyone a chance to speak in the 2½ hours of debate. Yet against the Committee's case, put fairly and objectively at the start by Michael Sissons, no answer of any substance emerged. Members had been kept in the dark over the years, it was said, about differences with the TCCB. But how could the Committee comment in print thereon when these differences revolved round the attitudes of their Secretary and Treasurer, whom they were endeavouring, up to the last, to change their course? The signature-collecting member, no doubt wisely, uttered no word. The one valid charge – and it came from defenders and detractors alike – was that MCC needed to look really seriously at its public relations. That point has been clearly received and understood.

When it was all over one of the most prominent dissidents had the grace to congratulate John Warr, the President designate. He said, 'You have bowled us middle stump. So far as I am concerned the thing is over.' So be it. The mood of Mr Warr and his Committee as they embark on the Club's 201st year I judge to be positive and forward-looking. They are in no doubt about MCC's role in its third century – benevolent, constructive, ever servants of the game.

THE CRICKETER
OCTOBER 1987

————— *Errol Barrow Passes On* —————

Yet another Barbados service in the Abbey, this time for Errol Barrow, who led Barbados into Independence and was Prime Minister for the third time at his death. Errol was both a proud West Indian and a warm-hearted Anglophile, who, coming to England to continue his education at the London School of Economics, joined up in the RAF, aged twenty, and served for seven years, flying forty-nine operational sorties and ending as navigation officer to the commander-in-chief BAOR. With an economics degree and having been called to the Bar, he pursued the law and politics on his return to Barbados. By the time of his death the island enjoyed a reputation within the Commonwealth and beyond out of all proportion to its size.

Fond of cricket, he was reputedly a somewhat defensive bat whom they nicknamed Dipper after that sticky Gloucestershire batsman. Like Bob Menzies he tended to slip up to Lord's at the time of Prime Ministers' Conferences.

When, after nine years, we sold the house we had built in Barbados he very kindly lent us his on Paradise Beach one year. My stepson Eddie Carbutt being there alone one afternoon had no reason to recognize the black man coming on to the patio with a sack over his shoulder. Happily the penny soon dropped. Errol had been out for a sail and brought us some flying fish.

DIARY
13 NOVEMBER 1987

Landmarks Passed from Sight

One does not have to have one foot in the grave to remember when a number of traditional landmarks signalled the way along the sweet procession of the English season. One by one, and in several cases for no good reason discernible to pre-computer man, the annual fixture dates have been obliterated. The very last faded from sight only this summer – the annual spring and August bank holiday meetings between Yorkshire and Lancashire and between Middlesex and Sussex.

Ever since I began to sit up and take notice of county cricket directly after the First World War these were fixed points in the calendar, looked forward to with utmost eagerness by supporters, many of whom arranged their affairs in order not to miss these battles with a special flavour, at Bramall Lane, Headingley, Park Avenue and Old Trafford, Lord's and Hove.

There were other confrontations each fixed immutably at given times. People arranged their holidays around them, not least expatriate Yorkshiremen who knew that their beloved heroes could be seen at Lord's over the second weekend of June and likewise at The Oval the last of July. The following weekend at The Oval it was always Surrey *v* Nottinghamshire, the return of the Whitsuntide match at Trent Bridge. The custom meant that home supporters identified not only with their own favourites but with old familiars in the opposition. The Gunns and the Hardstaffs were respected in Kennington, just as the Surreyites were around Nottingham.

The first of the season's fixed points was, of course, the tourists' introduction to the county circuit below the cathedral at Worcester – a peculiarly appropriate beginning for them: a lovely setting and a perfect wicket in the heart of England, against opposition not too demanding. With luck they would see the first of the fruit blossom on the way.

Myself I generally patronized either Lord's or the Roses' Match over Whitsun, by which time I had inspected Oxford in The Parks and Cambridge at Fenner's (treating myself, by kind permission, to a net in each). As the youngest county, by the way, and among the least financially secure, Glamorgan at one time were accorded two matches against the tourists, one each over the bank holidays, and notable events they were in the rugger strongholds of Cardiff and Swansea.

I must not forget local Derbys such as Kent *v* Surrey at the Rectory Field, Blackheath – for years Surrey's graveyard – and the visit of Yorkshire across the border to Chesterfield. In the same category, too, came those rare dog-fights between Gloucestershire and Somerset at Bristol and Taunton. Most famous of all, hard fought in its own right and more so when Championship hopes were involved, was Middlesex *v* Surrey, which brought to a close the county season at Lord's.

Of course, you may be thinking the increased number of Tests and the proliferation of one-day cricket put the whole county programme into the melting-pot, and to some extent this is true. Yet the disruption of the traditional pattern cannot be thus excused because this had largely happened before 1968 when the John Player League became the second of the one-day competitions and the Championship was reduced from twenty-eight matches to twenty-four. The rot started earlier when some of the lesser counties complained that too many of the plum dates were denied them by the top six, Yorkshire, Lancashire, Surrey, Middlesex, Nottinghamshire and Kent. Perhaps in those days these six were too polite to point out that it was they whose gates and whose Test cricketers did most to keep the game viable. The egalitarian tendency, on being introduced today into the computer, can come up with such manifest absurdities as in 1987 when Middlesex played Yorkshire only once in the Championship – at Lord's in April.

It is no good crying over spilt milk, to coin a phrase: what has been scrambled cannot be unscrambled, to coin another. The weakening of the county spirit by these things is rather less important anyway than that occasioned by the increase in the number of player-transfers from one county to another. There is, however, one more possible inroad that some counties must be wary about. The six four-day county matches due to be introduced from 1988 to 1990 inclusive are to be played three at the start of the season and three at the end. County weeks are not, therefore, directly affected. But Essex, Gloucestershire, Hampshire, Kent, Somerset and Sussex must watch out – especially Kent. To interfere with Canterbury Week would be the ultimate sacrilege.

CRICKET SOCIETY JOURNAL
DECEMBER 1987

Umpires Must be Obeyed

If there was ever a more dispiriting, disgraceful Test match than the one which ended in England's wholesale defeat at Lahore last weekend, I cannot recall it. The omens for this utterly superfluous Test series were always adverse, and the reality of the anti-climax has been even worse than expectation.

There are pictures that only time will blur, starting with England's captain on the first morning remaining on his knees, having been given out lbw second ball, sweeping at a leg-break, pitching clear of the off stump: a ridiculous stroke and a bad decision, ill-received.

In England's second innings, who can forget Chris Broad simply standing his ground for an age after being caught at the wicket? I put it thus because he was given out, and therefore he was out. There is no other way of playing than to obey the umpire – the first and basic lesson of cricket.

That evening Peter Lush, the manager, having announced that Broad had been reprimanded but not fined, went on to make serious insinuations about the umpiring. Dedicated a cricketer as he is, Broad's prolonged dissent richly deserved a fine, which would have illustrated England's respect for the rule of law and at the same time sent a clear signal to young cricketers everywhere, who, of course, take their cue from their heroes. This aspect of the situation is the most depressing of all.

Finally, after the match was over, Mike Gatting apparently talked to the press for 15 minutes, reiterating with regard to the umpires the dangerous word 'blatant', but giving no credit to his opponents or to Abdul Qadir for his outstanding bowling performance.

Within four days, in fact, the England party allowed themselves to be provoked into a moral position from which they can scarcely escape. Indeed, if one of the next Test umpires performs according to reputation, worse tribulation could be in store before the remaining two Tests are completed.

It goes without saying that Gatting and his team have a grievance. Pakistan have not, so far, named any of their three umpires who apparently gave satisfaction in the World Cup. They have ignored the custom of seeking the prior agreement of the visiting side to their choices before making them public.

This is in retaliation for the TCCB's rejection of their complaints against the appointment of David Constant in England by their manager, the egregious Haseeb Ahsan – he who never stopped talking all the summer and among his choicest remarks maintained that nowadays in international cricket cheating was 'necessary'. What hope for the civilities of cricket while such a man remains his country's mouthpiece?

All the clearer reason, following a defeat by an innings and 87 runs, for a manager and captain to keep quiet until the series is over. Among those who have now intimated this in no uncertain way, I

am pleased to see, is David Gower. Surely his friends and contemporaries will listen to him.

The one good that must come out of these sad happenings is a
re-examination by the International Cricket Conference of the
advantages of neutral umpires. To their credit Pakistan have themselves urged this, and the merits of the case have been underlined by
the orderly conduct under neutral umpires of the World Cup.

To be acceptable to the TCCB and the English public any such
scheme would need to ensure that English umpires stood in Tests in
this country as members of a panel who would also include men
from overseas. English umpires are rated the best in the world, as
they should be because they have the experience of so much more
cricket. To offer summers here to the best overseas umpires should
widen their experience to good effect. Likewise all parties should
gain from some Englishmen officiating abroad in the winter.

No such scheme, however, would be of benefit unless all con-
trolling bodies adhered to an agreed code of conduct and penalties.
Yes, this is what cricket has come to, in this over-commercialized
and ultra-nationalistic age.

THE DAILY TELEGRAPH
13 DECEMBER 1987

Gatting Discredited

A week ago I wrote in these pages that if there had ever been a more
dispiriting, disgraceful Test than that at Lahore I could not recall it,
and I added that with Shakoor Rana due to umpire at Faisalabad
even worse tribulation could be in store.

In truth it was too much to expect that in an atmosphere of such
general hostility the remainder of this tour could be continued on a
chivalrous note. Even so, the present impasse exceeds one's worst
dreams.

It seemed, indeed, not so much a dream as a nightmare to see on
television the England captain and the umpire nose to nose, locked
in an abusive exchange that looked almost on the point of coming to
blows. Whatever the provocation, and he and his team have

endured plenty, Mike Gatting has rendered English cricket a grave disservice.

As to the incident itself I understand that the batsman concerned, Salim Malik, confirms Gatting's claim that he did advise him before Hemmings began his run-up that he was moving his long leg closer. Otherwise Gatting would have been guilty of transgressing traditional custom and be taking an unfair advantage.

If Shakoor Rana, standing at square leg and noticing Gatting's gesture to his fielder, had not heard his warning he was nevertheless following the Law in calling dead ball.

The factor that increases the likelihood of the tour being terminated is the apparently complete lack of rapport between the English management and the Pakistan Board.

Interviewed on BBC radio, Lt Gen. Safdar Butt, the Board president, sounded almost as indignant as the umpire, while Ijaz Butt, the secretary, is equally uncompromising. It is a sick joke, perhaps close to the truth, to say that the tour is all Butt over.

I suppose Raman Subba Row, the TCCB chairman who has a deserved reputation as a conciliator, might succeed in a last-minute effort, if the Cricket Council or his Board, who meet today, require him to do so. But the events at Lahore and Faisalabad have given him a sadly weak hand to play. A strict code of discipline and some scheme of umpire exchange between countries must all be worked out. But they cannot happen overnight.

THE DAILY TELEGRAPH
20 DECEMBER 1987

1988

TO FIND A CAPTAIN

New Year Blighted

It behoves us, no doubt, to approach the New Year with hope, but how can a cricket lover do so without equal apprehension?

Close behind us lies the sinister cloud of the Pakistan tour. In India, Vivian Richards, the West Indies captain, has been indulging in yet another of his gesticulating and apparently abusive tangles with umpires.

Next summer the West Indies are due in England for a full tour of five Tests with the prospect of much fast bowling, which nowadays is almost always a source of tension, and with the probability of opposing captains who have been guilty of conduct towards umpires which in any other era would have been unthinkable. No doubt Mike Gatting was sorely provoked in Pakistan, but to greet him on his return as a hero is to turn upside down the only code of behaviour that makes the game's continuance possible.

It was a relief to read the *Daily Telegraph* leader and Peter Deeley's article just before Christmas which underlined traditional sporting concepts and put the Gatting matter into perspective.

Then has come the unequivocal supporting letter (29 December) of R. E. S. Wyatt, England's senior living Test captain, quoting a decision that cost a Test match in Trinidad in 1934–5 which was even more gross than anything our side had to put up with in Pakistan. He described how Maurice Leyland's only comment on returning to the dressing room was, 'Has't seen owt like it?', or words to that effect.

I had heard an extended version of the story which Bob Wyatt tells me on the telephone he had forgotten, but is true. As all the players trooped off after the Test had been lost and won by Leyland being adjudged lbw to a ball which hit him high in the ribs from Constantine bowling round the wicket, he was seen to be saying something to an excitable fellow who had led the chorus of appeals from short leg. Pressed on his return to the dressing room to tell the others what transpired, that great Yorkshireman replied, 'Ah only said, "and tha' were at Cambridge!"' ' The A was pronounced very long. Incidentally – but not without significance – foul language on the field was unknown to that generation and for many years following.

At the end of his career, I asked Don Bradman (shortly to be knighted) whether he would agree that touring sides usually thought they had had the worst of it as regards umpiring. 'No, not usually,' was the reply, 'always!' Feelings on the field, however, were contained, poor though the standard sometimes was, in South Africa especially.

Bradman thought Frank Chester the best. Yet I saw the latter give R. T. Simpson in during the Headingley Test of 1953 when he was out by upwards of a yard.

Now neutral umpires are being called for from all sides, and the Test and County Cricket Board have committed themselves to prompt enquiry, though whether in time for next summer is uncertain.

My feeling on this is that the International Cricket Conference must be spurred, if necessary, into action to select an international panel of the best. The system that emerges, however, should not preclude some umpires standing in their own countries, along with others engaged for the season from overseas.

Whatever the answer, the game would be improved and the umpire's job made easier if steps were taken about intimidation around the bat.

I would lay down a no-go line for fielders at a fixed distance, and deny them the use of helmets. I still favour, as also do Sir Donald Bradman and Mr Wyatt, a line across the pitch to penalize intimidatory bowling.

THE DAILY TELEGRAPH
1 JANUARY 1988

Let Sydney Revive Our Pride

In Australia's year of celebration there had to be a focus on cricket, and it is only proper that the occasion should be at Sydney, the scene of the first settlement 200 years ago and of the first rudimentary games involving 'free' settlers, resident soldiers and ships' companies.

By 1803, on Hyde Park (which is as central to Sydney as its counterpart is in London), batsmen were stinging their fingers using bats fashioned from cedar and iron-bark to hit primitive leather balls stitched around cork by shoemakers. Scorers still registered runs as notches marked on their sticks.

It was half a century later that Sydneyites answered a challenge from Melbourne Cricket Club, which soon became the de facto equivalent of the English MCC. Hence it was on 'the paddock that grew', in Keith Dunstan's happy phrase for the vast bowl of Melbourne, that the Centenary Test between Australia and England was played before enraptured crowds in 1977. Australia won then by 45 runs, precisely the margin by which the raw colonials had beaten the mother country a century before.

Incidentally, though domination has naturally ebbed and flowed, after 257 Tests the margin of wins between them is ten – eighty-six to England, ninety-six to Australia, with seventy-five matches drawn. England were ahead until after the First World War when eight victories in a row gave Australia a lead they have not since lost.

That centenary match, with its shifts of fortune, the marvellous bowling of Lillee, the heroic 174 of Randall, but above all its spirit, found a parallel in the bicentenary match between MCC and the Rest of the World at Lord's last August. May these two occasions serve as patterns to be followed when the two countries meet at Sydney Cricket Ground on Friday. For if ever all who profess and call themselves cricketers need to be reminded how Test matches between the best can and must in all respects set standards, the time is now.

This is not a vintage era either for England or Australia. Indeed, it could be argued that if the seven Test countries were to be ranked on recent form, they would be incontestably superior only to Sri

Lanka. Nevertheless, there should surely be the talent to make a worthy match and I take it as a good omen that nowhere nowadays, outside India, is so much spin-bowling seen in Test matches as Sydney, and nowhere over the last seven years has it been as successful. So says a survey in the new *Cricketer* magazine. Thank goodness for those two altogether admirable cricketers, Emburey and Hemmings.

Before the marketing men disfigured it, I always rated Sydney as (Lord's apart) the perfect Test ground, with the clearest of light, comfortable stands with their Edwardian wrought-iron trimmings.

This is a moment to reflect how much the evolution of the game has depended down the last century, and more, upon those great series between England and Australia. For nearly all that time, these have been the Tests compared to – and all others have been of lesser degree.

The top brass of English cricket will, of course, be at Sydney for the match, and will take the happy chance of talking informally to the Australian Cricket Board on the pressing problems that face them all and the game at large.

THE DAILY TELEGRAPH
26 JANUARY 1988

Octogenarian With a Difference

As I was remarking last month, there is no shortage nowadays of distinguished cricketers who have passed the milestone of eighty. As this issue of *The Cricketer* appears Alfred Richard Gover is due to join their number, though in his case with the 365 to 1 difference that on 29 February, this being leap year, he will be celebrating only his twentieth birthday. Come to think of it. Alfred is a not inappropriate bearer of the distinction for in his fast bowling days that unusual arm-pump action in the run-up culminated, immediately before an orthodox sideways on, high-arm delivery, in a distinctive and rather menacing leap. What is more relevant today is that, metaphorically speaking at least, he's still leaping to it. 'If I can get away from the office,' he says, 'I still like to spend an hour in the nets, coaching *and bowling.*' When the school is busy it's sometimes a good deal more than an hour.

This, of course, is in his indoor school at Wandsworth which, with its four nets and despite the counter-attraction of more modern schools, is still going strong after sixty years. When it was started in 1928 by those two other great Surrey cricketers, Andrew Sandham and Herbert Strudwick, there was only one other indoor cricket school in London, the famous one started by the legendary South African, Aubrey Faulkner, at Hammersmith. Soon after he stopped playing Gover assumed financial control and the Sandham-Strudwick became the Gover Cricket School.

Alfred Gover's service to cricket has not been confined to his school, for he has been a foremost figure with Surrey and the Lord's Taverners and is a past president of both. Furthermore, for thirty full years he has contributed his tuition notes for the benefit of countless cricketers, young and old, to *The Cricketer.*

It happened that his career coincided with my earlier years as a cricket writer, and so my recollections of his toiling manfully away on those flawless Oval pitches of 'Bosser' Martin's making are vivid still. No help assuredly was there from the pitch, and nothing very distinguished was forthcoming at the other end. These factors notwithstanding, Gover (A. R.) in both 1936 and 1937 took 200 wickets, the first English fast bowler to do so since Tom Richardson, also of Surrey, in 1897. When it came to picking the MCC side for Australia the winter of 1936–7 Bill Copson was chosen to the exclusion of Gover, according to the captain, Sir George Allen, because the ball would lose its shine very quickly out there and Copson's movement off the pitch was therefore preferred to Gover's out-swing. Personally, I favoured the lively, Tate-ish J. W. A. Stephenson to augment the attack of Allen, Voce and Farnes; but on the face of it Gover was the unlucky man out.

Like many another, Gover spent much of his prime years in the Services – which makes it the more noteworthy that Richardson (with 2105) is the only Surrey fast bowler to have taken more than his 1555 wickets. Alec Bedser (also frustrated by the war) had 1924 and George Lohmann 1805, two undeniable greats, but the 'keeper stood up to them. The nearest Surrey approaches among those of genuine speed are Lockwood and Loader, each with 1300-odd.

Alfred came back to The Oval for two more summers after the

war, and picked up 119 and 121 wickets respectively. He even collected his fourth and last Test cap. Errol Holmes, his captain, wanted him to carry on beyond his fortieth birthday but readily agreed he was right to retire when told the reason. Towards the end of the long, hot summer of 1947 he said that for the first and last time in his life he didn't enjoy his cricket anymore.

He had always very obviously enjoyed bowling, and now he did not – apart, of course, from the nets, around which his life was to centre for the next forty years. It was not a matter of fitness for Alf had always been conspicuously fit and is proud of having gone through the 1930s without missing a match through injury. 'If I had a strain I used to strap it up and carry on.'

I had to remind him, though, of the occasion made famous by Ian Peebles of how on Lord Tennyson's team's tour of India a Maharajah's curry had once caused a certain disruption, making it impossible to get a fit team on to the field. Perhaps Ian's description in his autobiography *Spinner's Yarn* may bring this small tribute to a cheerful end:

> Alf Gover heroically rose from a bed of sickness to lead the attack. He did not lead it very far. We lost the toss, and Alf started off at a very respectable pace. About his third over a desperate expression compressed his features, and his run-up developed into a wild gallop. He shot past the umpire, the crease, the batsmen, and fairly flew up the pavilion steps in a cloud of dust and gravel. We all hoped he made it, and were soon reassured by sounds of primitive plumbing.

'Ah, yes,' said the victim, 'that was against Rajputana at Ajmer.' It was the nearest our conversation got to Pakistan.

THE CRICKETER
MARCH 1988

—————— *'Hal' and 'The Hewitt'* ——————

The Halford-Hewitt here again; with sixty-four schools fielding five foursomes each, 640 golfers in all, it is the world's biggest. Cranleigh lose in the third round to Edinburgh Academy by the odd match. We are pleased enough, but still remember with anguish the moment at Deal twenty years ago when John Davies's partner 'had only'(!) to get down in two from below the little bank giving on to the 18th green to beat Eton in the final. But alas . . . ! On the 20th a long pitch from the rough by the enemy after they had missed their drive finished inches from the pin for a monstrous three, and that was heart-breakingly that. A less inglorious failure, though, than the one when a mustachioed colonel, hero maybe of many a feat of arms, 'had only' to propel his ball forward with his putter on the 19th green to win the Cup for his school. Having studied the line with care, he passed his club over the ball, waggled, wiggled, waggled again and knocked it backwards into the stream.

The genesis of the competition, according to Longhurst, was on this wise. One day in the early 1920s John Beck was discussing the idea with one G. L. ('Susie') Mellin after lunch at Addington. Beck said, 'All we need is some bloody fool to give the Cup', when lo! Halford-Hewitt walked through the door. Thus, no doubt over a glass of Kümmel, he was immortalized. 'Hal' was benevolent, generous, rich and very deaf. His affliction encouraged his team, Charterhouse, 'who treated him', wrote Bernard Darwin, 'with an affectionate lack of respect', to perpetrate various ridiculous practical jokes. At one final's lunch, the founder presiding, Peter Ryde, author of the history of the event, tells us, 'John Beck, as Carthusian captain, went through the motions of making a speech but without a sound escaping his moving lips. Those present had been well briefed, and at intervals looked towards Hal and applauded. He sat there beaming and imagining all the nice things John must be saying about him. It was some time before he realized what was going on.'

Were we all more easily amused in those happy, carefree days? I expect so.

DIARY
9 APRIL 1988

──────────── *A Day of Contrast* ────────────

A day to remember in two parts. First was the Service of Dedication for members of the Most Excellent Order of the British Empire in St Paul's. Thousands came to the cathedral by bus, tube and taxi, having converged on London from all over the country to see again and worship with the sovereign who has rewarded them, for acts or accomplishments of many kinds, with one or other classes of the order. We are the lucky few, recognized where many equally deserving were passed by, admitted to an order of chivalry instituted when half the map was coloured red. Today we dedicate ourselves to 'the service of God and the Commonwealth and all mankind'.

From the procession of the highest ranks of the order, the Knights and

Dames Grand Cross, up the aisle from the West Door as the Grenadier Guards band renders Bach and Elgar, to the moment when the Bishop of London and the Dean and Chapter conduct the Queen and the Duke of Edinburgh out again, the service follows a rhythmic, ceremonious pattern. Glitter, yes, but a sense of fellowship and devotion, too.

We remove our medals and insignia as we stream down Ludgate Hill, I to be picked up at the old Daily Telegraph *building, now a lifeless shell, and transported to the new one. What a metamorphosis from the intimacy of Fleet Street to the open-plan and wide vistas of the Isle of Dogs! No doubt there are disadvantages in the new computer-age environment apart from those of longer travelling time. What strikes an old outside man looking in is the greater convenience of communication. Here is the Peterborough desk; sport is over there; obits and copy-takers not far away. Only Editor and Executive Editor enjoy the relative privacy of separate glassed-in quarters. Such detail aside, all may surely rejoice that, thanks originally to Eddie Shah, the old tyranny of the print unions is merely a bad dream. The journalist at last has come into his own. Those at any rate were my thoughts as, in one of the two motor launches ('Max' for Hastings, 'Perry' for Worsthorne), I was hustled back up-river to Charing Cross pier.*

DIARY
17 MAY 1988

Layman's Sketch

My first, and probably last, publishing venture outside the areas of games and autobiography. The Anglican Church: From Its Origins to the Present *is described on the front as a 'Layman's Sketch', and it is graced by a foreword from Archbishop Runcie. The diocese of Canterbury printed 1000 copies of the 32-page pamphlet. Parishes ordered copies on the understanding that they should be sold for £1 and all proceeds directed to the Church Urban Fund. I am glad to say they were all acquired quite quickly, so a good cause was £1000 the richer. The essay is divided into seven chapters, each having appeared originally in the parish magazine of St Clement's, Sandwich. The object was to remind Anglicans of their histori-*

cal heritage in the year of the Lambeth Conference. I enjoyed the limited research involved and wished I had broadened my knowledge earlier in life.

DIARY
29 MAY 1988

Ill-judged Return
to Full Covering

In this corresponding issue a year ago I was expressing a modified degree of satisfaction because, after seven summers of total pitch covering in County Championship cricket, in 1987 the business part of the pitch, though neither the creases nor the bowler's run-ups, were to be left open to the weather. Now after just one year of this compromise the TCCB have ordained that the pitches go completely under wraps again, as they were between 1980 and 1986 inclusive.

So much the worse for cricket, I expect runs to continue to be as cheap as ever in history and bowlers of aggressive intent as rare. Does it not occur to the TCCB and county cricket committees that the lack of English bowlers of distinction is related to *two* factors: one is the concentration on one-day cricket when the object is to contain rather than take wickets; the other is the dull uniformity of the pitches of the 1980s, all too often lifeless, deprived stretches which likewise have given the bowler no incentive to attack?

Captains disliked the 1987 compromise chiefly, they said, because covered run-ups enabled them to use their faster bowlers after rain rather than the spinners, who in any case were mostly a sparse, dispirited lot, accustomed, if used at all, to pursuing an economical line and trajectory – the defensive stuff called for in one-day cricket. The captains had an argument, certainly, but I suspect they called loudly for covering because that produces the pattern of 1980s cricket they have been used to. Similarly, most of them approve the experiment with four-day cricket because a similar pattern will ensue over more hours without nearly so much recourse to last-day run chases. Again, they have a point.

The issues, however, are larger than can best be judged either by contemporary captains or (apparently) by the cricket brains of the county clubs. The basic fact is that every great English batsman and every great English bowler throughout history, fast, medium or slow, has learned the game and refined his art on pitches left open to nature. Sun and rain maintained the vitality of the turf, which the groundsman nourished with a judicious use of fertilizer. His skill and experience regulated the amount of cutting and rolling. Morning and evening, the dew was his friend.

The cricket played on every pitch reflects the response of batsman and bowler to its character and that character has always varied, both before the match and during it, according to the weather. And variety is the breath of cricket. We need it in all directions and especially in bowling types.

The subject has many facets, but I would add now only two points. First, I am referring only to the English game. Covering is a requisite in tropical and sub-tropical countries where heavy rain on hard pitches can produce conditions that are a lottery and a dangerous one at that. Also, if pre-match weather has been unduly wet, groundsmen should be allowed to use their discretion as regards prior covering of the whole pitch as well as the creases, which should be protected against rain at all times. All this, in fact, has been allowable since 1924.

THE CRICKETER
JUNE 1988

Hugh Bartlett

Hugh Bartlett, who has died aged seventy-three, was one of the most exciting young cricketers of the 1930s. He belonged to the generation whose promise was cut short by the 1939–45 war, during which – like Billy Griffith, his great friend and contemporary at Dulwich, Cambridge and Sussex – he won the DFC at Arnhem as a glider pilot. Both reached the rank of lieutenant colonel in the Airborne Division.

Bartlett commanded 'A' Squadron and took part in three vital operations: the hazardous assault in Normandy in advance of the landing troops on D-Day, when they encountered formidable German opposition; the Arnhem operations the following September, in which Bartlett carried Lt Gen. 'Boy' Browning's HQ to Nijmegen; and the Rhine Crossing in March 1945, when Bartlett flew Maj. Gen. Eric Bols, the divisional commander.

Hugh Tryon Bartlett was born in India in 1914 and had the highly unusual schoolboy distinction of playing six summers in the Dulwich XI and captaining it for three. He scored two double-hundreds for the school, ending his career by making a top score of 87 and leading the Public Schools to a then unprecedented victory over the Combined Services at Lord's.

At Cambridge he achieved the unique honour of being awarded his Blue as a freshman after the first match of the season. He led his side to an easy victory in the University Match of 1936.

He averaged 51 with MCC in South Africa in 1938–9, but was not needed in the Tests, such was the galaxy at W. R. Hammond's disposal. After the war he was never the same player, but served Sussex well as their captain in the years 1947 to 1949. In his career he made 10,098 runs, averaging 31 and with sixteen hundreds.

Bartlett was a youthful phenomenon, a tall left-handed hitter of remarkable power, a somewhat nervous starter who, when his eye was in, was capable of cutting the best bowling to ribbons.

As captain of the Players at Lord's in 1938 the great Frank Woolley – who with the master-in-charge of Dulwich cricket, C. S. Marriott, was his mentor – saw Bartlett make 175 for the Gentlemen out of 256 in 2¾ hours, a score only once exceeded in the history of the match. His four sixes included one that hit the highest part of the turret at the end of the Grandstand.

A few weeks later he made a devastating 157 against the Australians at Hove, reaching the fastest hundred of the season in 57 minutes.

He spent his working life on the Stock Exchange, and leaves a widow and two sons.

THE DAILY TELEGRAPH
I JULY 1988

Bishop–Ferrying

I enjoy a little taxi-work ferrying overseas bishops and wives arriving for the Lambeth Conference, from Canterbury East station to their rooms in college in the University of Kent. They are put up in undergraduate quarters, clean, Spartan, spare. Some Americans in mufti looking not at all episcopal. About 120 bishops came from the Episcopal Church of USA. In cold figures their voting strength was 25 per cent of the whole of the Conference, whereas their church membership was only 2.5 per cent of the Anglican Communion – and, since their ordination of women, shrinking steadily. A delightful Australian from Grafton, NSW.

By all accounts our Archbishop throughout the Conference won all but universal admiration. The final cathedral service was shown on ITV not BBC. As Dr Runcie processed out last he was applauded from St Augustine's Chair all the way to the West Door by his five hundred fellow bishops. Sadly the programme was cut immediately after the Blessing, and so the watching millions missed the spontaneous tribute. It might have given pause to some critics of one the latchet of whose shoe they are not worthy to unloose.

The Lambeth Conference of 1998 is perhaps unlikely to concern me closely. In any case I think I would not take the risk of transporting a woman 'bishop' of whatever colour, whether or not a divorcée and irrespective of her having received theological training or otherwise.

DIARY
16 JULY 1988

Champion Eaters

Gerald Pawle, I see, in the spring issue of the admirable *Cricket Society Journal* (from 26 Thirlmere Rise, London Road, Bromley BR1 4HY for £3.00) has provided a touching pen-picture of that highly likeable, uniquely solitary cricketer, P. A. Gibb, who was among other things a redoutable eater. He tells how Paul, noticing a bowl of strawberries doing nothing at Sir Julien Cahn's lavish board at Stanford Hall, demolished the lot apparently oblivious of the fact that he had poured out of the wrong jug, covering them with mayonnaise instead of cream.

That recalled to me a visit to Fenner's in the 1930s by Somerset, who claimed that they had a chap of equal capacity whom, since he is still alive, I will not embarrass by naming. Opposite to one another but both unaware of the previous talk the pair set to on one of Mrs Coote's ample luncheons. We watched in fascination, unobtrusively pushing along dishes to sustain the intake. But after 40 minutes, the umpires began to move out, and while Somerset's man carried on, Paul picked up his wicket-keeping gloves from under his chair and followed his captain briskly out. So a draw it had to be. I say briskly because, despite his appetite, he never carried a spare ounce of flesh.

Ian Peebles used to maintain that once on board ship Gibb, recumbent in a deck-chair, consumed such an enormous quantity of ice-cream that he froze himself solid and had to be lifed bodily to the perpendicular. That might have been stretching the facts a bit, but it became a popular addition to the Gibb saga. He was a gritty cricketer in the true Yorkshire tradition, whose love of the game drew him on retirement to the first-class umpires' panel and life in the summer in a caravan which he drove from ground to ground. He ended his life as a bus driver.

THE CRICKETER
JULY 1988

Blowers' Way

We old fellows of the Reith era could never have competed, surely, with the modern commentators' range of vocabulary. Within a few minutes at Headingley during the one-day International there the inimitable Henry Blofeld had Emburey moving in to field the ball 'in scholarly fashion', and an itinerant crow 'hugging the Kirkstall Lane chimneys'. Then a batsman sent the ball 'bubbling away for four'. How's that for an Eton education?

THE CRICKETER
JULY 1988

————— Cricket and J. Paul Getty —————

If one had to witness a Kent defeat at Lord's in the Nat West quarter-final, to be a guest of Paul Getty was much the least painful way of doing so. His box in the Mound Stand (which bears the names of J. Paul Getty, KBE, and Sir George Allen, CBE) has become a focus for invited friends, both the exalted and the humble of the wide world of cricket, who share the hosts' love of the game.

If Paul is by nationality and upbringing one of the least likely of devotees, his commitment is as total as anyone's. He has not only a select library but probably the most complete collection of cricket videos. A smiling photograph of W.G. is the first thing to strike one on entering his flat. A screen is decorated with a montage of the Vanity Fair *cricketer cartoons. Cricketana is everywhere. A close friendship of several years' standing with Gubby, bonded by cricket, has cheered the lives of both. Paul Getty's patronage of cricket, as of many other causes, has been munificent to a degree, yet in the current jargon extremely low-key, for he is a retiring person who hates the limelight.*

DIARY
27 JULY 1988

————— Oundle *Win* The Cricketer *Cup* —————

Having been raised to the honorific heights of president of The Cricketer *and of* The Cricketer Cup, *I was selected to make the presentations at the Final at Vincent Square, standing in for the MCC President, John Warr. We had a lovely day, an excellent pitch, and a fine match which ended in a narrow win for Oundle Rovers over Shrewsbury Saracens: 421 runs in 110 of the keenest overs imaginable. There was a proper hero in Andrew Townsend, aged twenty-two, who made the first hundred ever in the twenty-three years of the Final, this to the vast delight of Alan Watkins, whose excellence as Oundle's coach is a byword. Two sixes over long-off in the last overs smacked of the highest quality.*

One's mind went back to the concept of a Cup for old boys of a limited number of schools. To Antony Winlaw and Henry Lewis goes the credit for pushing the idea. The Cricketer *took up the running of the competition in 1967, originally for sixteen clubs, extended after two years to thirty-two. To those clubs who narrowly missed selection among the second sixteen I can only say the list was not completed without the most earnest, not to say agonizing, consideration by the committee.*

The Cup caught on from the first, everyone as keen to compete as the soccer players in the Arthur Dunn Cup and the golfers in the Halford-Hewitt. Nineteen Test cricketers have played for their schools; more than a hundred so far have been county cricketers. What was not predictable – nor, I think, desirable when carried to its present pitch – is how within a few years of our beginning, resident club cricket in the south forthwith organized itself into cups and leagues to the virtual exclusion of all else. Outside the wandering clubs all of them almost all the time go into the field to deny the other side runs rather than bowl them out. The altered objective is, of course, fundamental. Limited-over cricket is certainly sharper, but whether it is better cricket and as enjoyable to play is debatable – a matter to some extent, no doubt, of individual temperament. Some sort of transformation must have happened one day, so strong was the competitive urge, but I fear it was the founders of The Cricketer *Cup who unwittingly set the trend.*

This Cup of 1988 is the last of many played under the generous patronage of Moët et Chandon. It sees the last, therefore, of those halcyon visits of the winners and their ladies to the Château Saran at Epernay. Which reminds me of the marvellous gaffe that has gone down in the annals. Pre-Moët the sponsors were Pol Roger and the Cup was presented one year by Mme Pol Roger. She was introduced by Lord Nugent, most urbane and well-practised a hand. Having said all the right things he added, with a courtly bow to the lady, that he would now hand over to Mme Bollinger.

DIARY
7 AUGUST 1988

Brightly Flows The Don

Yes, there's no doubt about it, eightieth birthdays are apt to bring forth kind tributes from friends of the survivor, and in Sir Donald Bradman's case that should mean the whole world of cricket. For millions have enjoyed seeing his supreme artistry in the flesh, while the game in general has been the richer for the stimulus he gave it during his playing life, and also for his wise guidance of it since his retirement forty years ago.

Let me complement Kenneth Gregory's original and characteristic researches with a few recollections. I suppose I saw him make as many runs as most, from his first innings at Worcester in the spring of 1930 to the last at Lord's eighteen years later; and since I was not in Australia in 1932-3 the picture is of a scarcely interrupted triumphal progress.

It took Don a bare week to impress his extraordinary quality on the English scene; 236 below the Cathedral, followed by 185 not out before the rain came beside the gaunt cooling towers of the power station on the old Leicester ground at Aylestone Road; 421 runs for once out. He has always said he preferred English to Australian pitches, and I dare say it was the smooth Worcester turf, regularly fertilized in winter by the overflowing River Severn, on which the bowls players set up their jacks of an evening after stumps were drawn, that first appealed to him.

Of all English grounds Worcester and Headingley saw him at his most consistent and prolific. The felicitous, inevitable accumulation begun at Worcester reached its impossible climax on the close-shaven field of Headingley on 11 June 1930 when he followed innings of 4 and 131 in the First Test at Trent Bridge with the faultless 254 at Lord's and now 309 undefeated by the end of the first day – to be exact, after 352 minutes at the wicket. The cricket world had never known such phenomenal scoring. The critics had never seen such certainty of execution, such undeviating concentration on the matter in hand. The Bradman legend was born that day.

The impression that remains is of the smooth, unhurried rhythm of his play. Bat and man seemed one, the ball persuaded by a marvellous precision of timing. The wrists added speed to the stroke. Crude power did not come into it. One sees in memory an endless succession of delicate cuts and deflections, hooks (always downward and aimed generally *in front of* square leg), indeed, strokes all round the compass, as length and direction dictated. An attack comprising Larwood, Tate, Geary, Dick Tyldesley, Hammond and Leyland had been plundered on an easy-paced pitch and fast outfield at the rate of 52 runs an hour off his own bat. By the time he was out next morning for 334 he had played the highest innings in Test history.

I happened to be at the reception desk at the Queen's Hotel, Leeds, on his return that evening. He asked for a pot of tea to be sent to his room, and retired either to play the gramophone or dictate a chapter of *Don Bradman's Book*, or maybe both. The other Australians considered this unsociable, and so it was, though he might have pleaded the need to prepare for a further haul of runs next day. In his youth Don was shy, abstemious and – as he has since striven to remain despite non-stop publicity – a private person. It was not until after the war that another generation of players grew to admire as well as to respect him.

It was during MCC's tour of Australia in 1946–7 and his last English visit in 1948 that I really got to know Don and to appreciate the man behind the cricketer. He had been invalided out of the Army during the war – his health was always delicate – and at the Adelaide nets on a cool spring evening it seemed he would be hard-pressed to be ready for the First Test a month later.

At Brisbane how he struggled to find his touch in his first hour or so before there came the disputed slip catch that went in his favour! The ball from Voce was an uppish, wide half-volley. Don aimed to run it down to third man, and it was a matter of whether he trapped the ball or whether it came off the outside edge on the full as the bat struck the ground. We in the press box, far back over wide mid-on, could not possibly know. Through the glasses Ikin, the catcher, looked uncertain. So did the batsman, as one is when the bat's contact with ball and ground is almost simultaneous. At the end of the over Walter Hammond, as he walked across from first slip, said to his fellow captain, 'That's a fine way to start a Test series,' or words to that effect.

This pregnant moment fixed The Don's resolution, as for the rest of the day he *willed* himself into Test form. At close of play he was not out 162. After that close shave he never looked back.

The first function of the 1948 tour of England was a dinner given by the recently formed Cricket Writers' Club of which I had the honour to be chairman. (It was also the first cricket function for the newly wed Prince Philip.) Don caught the spirit of this nostalgic post-war return perfectly, so that the BBC held back the 9 o'clock news until he had finished. Here was the emergence of the boy from Bowral as a sporting statesman. And as such he has remained.

He has since been back to England only four times, each for a specific purpose. In 1953 he covered with exemplary judgement and writing style for the *Daily Mail* the tour of Lindsay Hassett's team which surrendered the Ashes that he had recaptured nineteen years before. He came again on a similar assignment for the *Daily Mail* in 1956. Responding to the crisis over throwing and its explicit threat to Anglo-Australian relations, he came as a Board

representative to the ICC meeting at Lord's in 1960 and was
largely instrumental, in collusion with that later knight of
cricket, Sir George Allen, in solving it.

In 1974 he accepted an invitation from the Lord's Taverners and
the Anglo-American Sporting Club to raise £10,000 for youth
cricket by speaking at a giant dinner. At the top of the menu was the
signature, Don Bradman, and when we inspected each other's cards
we saw that they were not facsimiles but the real thing. He had
spent the preceding weekend signing his name 900 times. Nothing
could better illustrate Sir Donald's perfectionism than this generous
gesture that went far indeed beyond the call of duty. When the
chairman conveyed his thanks it was the signal for the first of three
standing ovations during the evening. The second came when Don
rose to propose the toast to Cricket, the third when his admirable
speech ended.

It will be a pleasure indeed on his birthday on 27 August to
welcome such a lively, conscientious, intelligent recruit to the
Octogenarians' Club.

·THE CRICKETER
AUGUST 1988

——————————— *Voices from the Past* ———————————

*The launch happened today of an assorted collection of some forty BBC
radio cassettes, including just one on cricket in which I have introduced
many of the old heroes talking about great matches and other great men. It is
called 'The Golden Age', but the title stretches history quite a bit, for the
first voice describes Cobden's over in the University Match of 1870 and the
end of the last of the four half-hour tapes has Howard Marshall telling live
from The Oval in 1938 the story of Len Hutton beating Don Bradman's
record 334.*

*That first voice – and there is none clearer – is of the Mackinnon of
Mackinnon in his nineties, recollecting as one of the Cambridge side in the
field how Cobden, when Oxford needed 3 runs to win with three wickets in
hand, performed the most dramatic of all hat-tricks.*

*Thanks to the producing skills of Mark Jones I greatly enjoyed introduc-
ing the personalities and linking the BBC archive material together to make
a coherent whole. Thirty-eight voices come across, some several times, in a
wide diversity of accents: the northern tones of Hirst and Rhodes, Barnes,*

Larwood, Sutcliffe and Leyland; exciting and excitable narrative by Ben Travers, the playwright, who saw both Jessop's marvellous hundred at The Oval in 1902 and Hobbs and Sutcliffe at Melbourne on the 1928–9 sticky dog – 'concrete with great lumps and holes in it'; the Oxford inflections of C. B. Fry; the twang of the Aussies; the more melodious cadences of Constantine.

In my conceit I thought this must be a best-seller, but in the simultaneous release of so many cassettes cricket tended to be lost in the company of 'ITMA', 'The Goon Show', 'Fawlty Towers', 'Alice in Wonderland', 'Coward', 'Rumpole', yes, and not forgetting the Bard of Avon. As it was, 'The Golden Age' has done modestly well, and is still available for the trifling sum of £5.99. People tend to play it, they say, on car radios on their way to cricket.

DIARY
13 OCTOBER 1988

The Captaincy Dilemma

The consequences of Graham Gooch's appointment as England's captain in India are problematic, as I write, the only sure thing being, I suppose, that it has provided the militant anti-apartheidites with a propaganda opportunity which they will pursue ad nauseam. If the tour takes place at all only the most starry-eyed optimist can believe it will run its course as a purely cricketing exercise without political overtones. That ever increasing element of press coverage for whom the game itself is of completely secondary interest, if any at all, has been given a permanent story.

Gooch is England's most successful batsman on current form. Among those who have seen most of him as a captain I have found no one who regards him as a natural leader, either in terms of personality or tactics. It is not disputed that the selectors knew of his contractual obligation to Western Province when they first appointed him to lead England at The Oval or that they extended the availability deadline for India for his convenience.

The situation prompted John Woodcock to write on the day of his double act at Lord's and The Oval:

A good batsman, uneasy with the mysteries of captaincy, Gooch is being treated at the moment with the deference that might have attended a 'W.G.' in his heyday. It seems to me that our administrators must have gone mad. Either that or I have.

It says a lot when the cricket correspondent emeritus of The Times lets his feelings loose in such language as this.

I hold no special brief for the current selectors, watching or otherwise, and some of this summer's choices have been mystifying to the point of a widespread loss of confidence in their composite judgement. Taking one inexplicable example, to have named DeFreitas for the Fifth Test within a week or so of his having been suspended for seven days by Leicestershire for 'not trying' seemed, to me and to many, simply flying in the face of the chairman's pre-season declaration of an insistence on the highest standard of conduct in all respects. At twenty-two this talented young man, Dominica-born, Willesden-educated, may perhaps grow into an all-rounder of true Test quality, granted wise and firm guidance. He is, however, quite immature, and Leicestershire were certainly not pleased that their considered punishment was abruptly and so pointedly frustrated by his selection. County and player have since decided to part company – which can only be to the good of English cricket if a new employer puts DeFreitas under due discipline and he responds more sensibly to it than has been the case at Leicester.

Individual choices aside, in almost a year of unrelieved gloom surrounding the England team, criticism must surely, however, be balanced with sympathy for Peter May and his men, Philip Sharpe, Fred Titmus and the appointed manager (1987–90) Micky Stewart, in a job inherently difficult and made vastly worse by the long drawn-out Gatting saga.

It is part of Stewart's job to make the best of things, however bleak, and the endless postmortem press conferences when there is absolutely nothing to say which is not blindingly obvious must be a sore trial. After the Sri Lanka Test he touched the depth of under-statement when he said that having to call on thirty players during the summer 'had not helped'. The team manager must be thankful that he will be spared this particular ordeal for a month or two.

Selectors, after all, can only pick from the talent available to them, and the fact is that the batting of most of the leading England-qualified men has been shown once more by the West Indians as technically unsound. The bowling has lacked both a cutting edge and attacking spinners. There has not been an all-rounder of Test quality – that is to say, a man worthy of consideration in both departments – since the decline of Botham. Confronted by the currently strongest Test team, the selectors had been dealt, in fact, a singularly weak hand to play without the over-riding complication of Mike Gatting's accumulative peccadilloes, which led to his being removed from the captaincy after the First Test at Trent Bridge.

Nothing more disruptive to morale could be imagined that the happenings in Pakistan, followed by those surrounding the Trent Bridge Test. Though Gatting was found sadly wanting in so many respects, his personal popularity among the teams he had led must have been an adverse factor in the dressing room following his departure. It was surely reasonable first to promote the vice-captain, John Emburey, and equally to recognize after two Tests that his form did not justify his place. At that moment, in early July, Christopher Cowdrey was leading Kent from the front. His side stood at the head of the Championship with a 37 points lead; he topped the county's batting averages with 45, was in useful bowling form, and was, as usual, catching everything in sight. He was made Captain of the Month.

Accordingly, the selectors, who must have had Cowdrey in mind from early in the season as a likely touring captain, turned now to him, although he had no experience of playing in a home Test match.

It is history now how at Headingley Allan Lamb was injured when he and Robin Smith were boldly putting England in a good position in their first innings; how the lower order, Cowdrey included, collapsed, as they likewise did in the second innings; how Cowdrey had to withdraw from the Oval Test because of injury, being replaced by Gooch. For several weeks Cowdrey's county form likewise deserted him. Hence the retention of Gooch for the Sri Lankan Test even though it was still uncertain whether he proposed to spend the winter beside India's coral strand or under the shadow of Table Mountain.

It must be difficult for the average follower of cricket to appreciate that the leadership of a team on tour makes different and more exhausting demands on a man than the England captaincy at home. As I have written before, George Mann in South Africa in 1948–9 and Tony Lewis, in India and Pakistan in 1972–3, neither of whom had previously played in a Test match, are the most striking examples of men chosen to lead who made conspicuous successes of the job. Cowdrey might well have shown he was of the same kidney. (There are, of course, others, and notably Mike Brearley, who have equally got the best out of their sides at home and abroad.)

To my mind, the selectors might have deferred the choice of captain and team for India until the weekend of 17/18 September when the Championship season had ended and Cowdrey's test as captain of Kent, as well as his own form, had been finally explored. If there were over-riding reasons for making the decision when they did they could have given the job to David Gower, who made a notable success of it in India in 1984–5 and who had said how keen he was to go again. As it is, let us hope that Gooch, the reluctant tourist and captain, rises to the honour bestowed and develops with the responsibility placed upon him.

THE CRICKETER
OCTOBER 1988

─────────── *All Saints' Occasion* ───────────

The eve of All Saints' and Archbishop Runcie to All Saints' Church, Margaret Street. Before developing his major theme ('The Catholic faith is much more than sanctified sociology'), he began on a lighter note, telling how he was at the church on 15 August 1945, when Cyril Tomkinson was the vicar. It was VJ Day, the end of the greatest war in history. It was also the great Feast of the Assumption. Which of these events, he wondered, would claim the vicar's first attention. Father Tomkinson was a mildly eccentric little fellow, who enjoyed raising a rustle and a smile in the congregation. 'Today,' he began, paused, and added, 'is the birthday of Napoleon Bonaparte.'

DIARY
31 OCTOBER 1988

H. S. Altham's Centenary

Although the centenary of H. S. Altham's birth comes up on 30 November, St Andrew's Day, he will be widely remembered among *Cricketer* readers, for his active involvement in the game at several levels remained unabated until his death in 1965 at the age of seventy-six. He died, indeed, at the house of an old friend, David Wilson, only an hour or two after addressing the Sheffield Cricket Lovers' Society.

After his retirement from the staff at Winchester in 1949 he grasped with eagerness every opportunity to work for the game. For thirteen years from 1950 he was in the central position of authority at Lord's as Treasurer of MCC. In 1959–60 he was also President. In 1954 he was Chairman of Selectors. He chaired one of those all too periodic Committees of Enquiry. His list of presidencies reflects the scope of his interests: MCC, Hampshire (1947 until death), OU Authentics, Repton Pilgrims, Hampshire Hogs, Club Cricket Conference, Cricket Society and, from 1951 to 1957, the English Schools Cricket Association.

Harry's chief memorial, indeed, is his unceasing labour for the young, begun at Winchester in 1913 and continuing there, apart from the First World War (in which he was awarded the DSO and MC), for thirty years. With Gubby (now Sir George) Allen he wrote, and kept up to date, the *MCC Cricket Coaching Book*. He was chiefly instrumental in forming in 1952 the nationwide MCC Youth Cricket Association, later to be absorbed into the National Cricket Association. Within a few years thirty-five county or area Councils had been formed and were sending schoolmasters to the National Recreational Centre at Lilleshall in Shropshire, to qualify after instruction for one of the MCC Coaching Certificates. It is one of my regrets that I was never able to attend one of these courses and to see Harry at work. Group Coaching had its genesis here, and the most hard-bitten old cricketers used to come away starry-eyed, thanks to his inspiration. (What irony, incidentally, lies in the fact that the lovely Lilleshall estate was purchased and presented to the nation after the war by the South African government as a thanks offering for its sacrifice!)

The need to nurture teenage cricket was Harry's abiding interest, and it is appropriate that his last contribution for *The Cricketer*, entitled 'Bridging the Gap', was a plea to clubs to give a welcome and match practice to boys just leaving school. There are few clubs of consequence today who have not taken this advice to heart.

Harry's connection with this magazine was always close. His contributions – ninety-one of them from 1922 to 1925 – were gathered together and formed the standard work, *A History of Cricket*.

It was a proud day for me when a letter in that really terrible handwriting – rather like the wanderings of a fly with a hangover – invited me, in 1938, to collaborate with him in a second edition.

Shortly after his death his pupil, Hubert Doggart, edited *The Heart of Cricket*, a memoir of H. S. Altham, which was published by *The Cricketer* and is now a collector's piece. *The Heart of Cricket* comprised essays about him, and also some of his best writing and speeches on important occasions. His speeches, delivered with much charm and humour, reflected an encyclopedic knowledge of the game. Well did he deserve the title *The Compleat Cricketer*.

THE CRICKETER
NOVEMBER 1988

─────────── *'DT' Prizes for Boys* ───────────

A pleasing occasion at the Essex headquarters at Chelmsford. I present The Daily Telegraph *Schools Awards to three worthy young cricketers, after which Graham Gooch dishes out the cash to the schools which have produced them. Exams or no exams, boys who are sufficiently keen and of reasonable ability still contrive to play a great deal of cricket during the summer, thanks to the voluntary labours of the good men who run the county Schools Cricket Associations, in this case Essex. The two boys who won the senior prizes – Nicholas Knight of Felsted and Nadeem Shahid of Ipswich – both did the double, the latter (who has since made several auspicious appearances for Essex), glory be, with wrist-spin. The Under-15 winner, Darren Robinson, was an interesting case in that at Tabor High School there is scarcely any cricket. Therefore, the Telegraph's £1000 was divided equally between the school and Braintree Cricket Club, which had given the boy the essential coaching and encouragement. The only sadness for me was that but for a communications slip-up young Shahid might have come to Kent.*

DIARY
24 NOVEMBER 1988

Hayter: In the Old Tradition

The sporting fraternity gathered in London yesterday to honour Reg Hayter, proprietor of the agency that bears his name, who is seventy-five tomorrow and still going strong.

Henry Cooper, Basil D'Oliveira and Denis Compton were among the sportsmen who paid tribute, and it was announced that he had been made a life member of Surrey CCC.

Daily at his desk in Gough Square, Reg is the last active survivor of the Cricket Reporting Agency which, under the wing of the Press Association, did so much to shape the style and the standards of sports-writing in the early days of wide newspaper coverage.

I think of Sydney Pardon (to whom I was introduced as a youngster) and his successors as Editors of *Wisden* and partners in the CRA – Stewart Caine, Sydney Southerton and Hubert and Norman Preston, father and son.

Reg joined the agency in 1933, his first memory being – and who could forget it? – of taking down on the typewriter at his dictation for the 1934 *Wisden* Southerton's classic denunciation of 'Body-line' bowling. Reg was astonished that Southerton was so clear in his mind what he intended to say that he neither looked at the copy before it went to the printer nor even read the proof.

Southerton used to warn his young reporters, Reg recalls, against the trap of ascribing a team's low score automatically to bad batting. It might be, but what about the pitch, and should they not give credit to the bowlers?

Thus was trust and mutual respect built up between writers and players, a relationship maintained over the years by Reg but increasingly rare in today's world of superlatives, and odious personal blame and censure. It was a loss to the game when two of his protégés, Clive Taylor of *The Sun* and R. A. Roberts of the two *Telegraph*s died in their prime.

Before starting his own agency in 1955 Reg reported for PA and Reuter three major MCC tours, one each to South Africa (1948–9), Australia (1950–1) and West Indies (1953–4). It was during the first that Denis Compton, very much the golden boy, brought to him a suitcase full of letters and begged his help. Reg discovered business propositions – for instance, from the proprietors of a hair unguent that Compton subsequently made famous – among the autograph requests.

He would not himself take on the management of Compton's affairs, thinking it improper as an agency employee to establish business links with a player. On his return to England, however, he brought together Compton and a minor sporting publisher and businessman, Bagenal Harvey (recently deceased). Thus Harvey became the first of the sporting agents, who acted for more and more well-known sportsmen.

Like most of his fellow cricket writers, Hayter was a player – one could nearly write 'is' for last year he bowled one over, a maiden so he says.

Three years ago, for the Third XI of Stanmore CC, of which he is perpetual president, he and a detective inspector with combined ages of 122 bowled out a village called Botany Bay for 32: Hayter 6 for 14. One way and another he is quite a survivor.

THE DAILY TELEGRAPH
2 DECEMBER 1988

1989
AUSTRALIA TRIUMPHANT

—————————— *Spartan Carthusian* ——————————

'The trouble is, I'm afraid Jim Swanton is going to get in his obituary of me before they get in mine of him.' R. L. Arrowsmith made this crack to Andrew Barker, one of his old pupils, not many days before his death. Not everyone would have retained his sense of humour to the end after having been for half his life a martyr to arthritis. Bob Arrowsmith was a scholar-sportsman in the old tradition. Into Simon Raven, as to many generations of Carthusians, he instilled his love of Latin and Greek and the English poets. He wrote admirable histories of Kent cricket and (with B. J. W. Hill) of I Zingari. His indifference to normal standards of warmth and comfort was too much for some of the boys of his house, including Max Hastings, Editor of The Daily Telegraph, who added this pregnant sentence to my obituary in his paper: 'Those who endured five years in his house were well equipped for any subsequent hardships thrust upon them in war or peace.'

No doubt both may have considered that that more or less squared the account. I went to Bob's Memorial Service today in the bleak Charterhouse chapel. In this mildest of winters they were mowing the pitch.

DIARY
11 JANUARY 1989

Tragic Death of Wilf Slack

The death of a young sportsman can never be other than a poignant shock: all the more so when the victim is as popular as Wilfred Norris Slack, the Middlesex and England batsman.

Slack collapsed when batting in an exhibition match while touring with a team known as the Cavaliers. He was a West Indian, born in St Vincent, but learned his cricket at Wellesbourne Second-ary School, High Wycombe.

He made his name as a sound, dependable left-hand opening bat in 1981, and went on to score more than 1000 runs in eight seasons, 13,950 in all with an average of 38.96. He was tantalizingly close to the Test side often enough, but had only three chances – playing twice against West Indies in 1985–6 and once against India the following summer.

Though chosen for the tour to Australia in 1986–7, he was in perpetual reserve.

Slack suffered the buffets of fortune with an admirable cheerfulness which communicated itself to spectators everywhere. He will be greatly missed by Middlesex, both on the field and off.

THE DAILY TELEGRAPH
17 JANUARY 1989

South Africa and the ICC: Background to Isolation

The fateful meeting of the International Cricket Conference at Lord's next week is peppered with ironies concerning South Africa's marooned position in world cricket.

Not the least of them is that the moving spirit behind the foundation of the original ICC was a South African, Sir Abe Bailey, a leading figure in Anglo-South African affairs early this century. More poignantly, though, it was on South Africa's proposal in 1958 that the black members of the ICC – West Indies, India and Pakistan – were given equal voting rights, thereby, in effect, blocking South Africa's re-admission to the Conference after they had left the Commonwealth in 1961.

The subsequent history of the game in South Africa would surely have been different if their association had remained within the fellowship of the cricket-playing countries. Their administrators might then have stood up to their government with some spirit rather than taking, for several years, the supine attitude which was the despair of their friends.

But when Sir Abe, born at the Cape of a Yorkshire farmer, proposed a triangular series with England and Australia in England to advance the cause of South African cricket, the sporting world was quite a different place.

His proposal brought about the first meeting at Lord's in 1909 of the Imperial Cricket Conference and the Triangular Tournament of 1912 – and South Africa had a leading role on the cricketing stage.

The colour question had not been aired publicly in the formative years of South African cricket in the 1890s, but in view of the fraught situation today it is worth recording that the one and only meeting in South Africa between an English and a black or coloured team, over a span of eighty years, took place at the Cape in 1894. W. W. Read's team played against a Malay side and formed a high opinion of a fast bowler called J. K. Hendriks. He was named among the fifteen chosen to make the first tour of England the following summer by the newly formed South African Cricket Association, but was later omitted because of strong political pressure.

Organized tournaments among the black and coloured cricketers of the Cape Province were by that time regular events on the famous Newlands ground in Cape Town. In the Transvaal, though, less liberal influences prevailed. In the year that Bailey's ICC first met at Lord's, Lord Selborne, the British High Commissioner, was publicly denouncing the exclusion of black spectators from matches in Johannesburg.

From the outset, the Imperial Cricket Conference confined themselves to laying down the qualification rules for Test cricket and agreeing the dates of Test tours. They met infrequently until 1929 when Test status, already accorded the West Indies, was extended to New Zealand and India, all of whom were now represented.

The ICC sixty years ago were far from considering the implications of race on Test cricket. Yet a lone shadow was passing over the scene in that English summer of 1929.

K. S. Duleepsinhji, nephew of the great 'Ranji', Cheltenham- and Cambridge-educated and a batsman of wonderful potential, was chosen for the first Test against South Africa, and after making only a few runs was dropped for the rest of the series despite a highly successful season. There was evidence of political pressure from the South African end, a situation which caused much distress to the Anglophile Ranji, who had himself suffered some hostility early in his career.

A year later Ranji had solace aplenty when Duleep played his memorable innings of 173 against Australia at Lord's. I can see Ranji now behind the pavilion in full oriental rig, all smiles, jewels sparkling in the sun.

When the three junior countries were admitted to the ICC in 1929, they were allowed one vote rather than the two claimed by the foundation members, England, Australia and South Africa. But votes never needed to be taken. The Conference continued to be an executive body only in that they laid down Test qualifications and determined the dates of Test tours.

When the 'Bodyline' issue of 1932–3 shook the cricket world, the ICC contented themselves with echoing MCC's pious fiat that 'any form of bowling obviously a direct attack by the bowler upon the batsman would be an offence against the spirit of the game'.

In 1952, five years after Indian independence and partition, Pakistan, on the proposal of India, were admitted to membership of ICC and given Test status. Otherwise the ICC pursued their harmless way unchanged.

In 1956 it was proposed that the word International in the title should replace Imperial, which had long been an anachronism. Extraordinarily, the suggestion found no support – a critical decision, as things turned out.

Two years later came another, when South Africa proposed that all seven member countries should have equal votes, two apiece. This proposal was passed, with the consequent strengthening of the position of the West Indies, India and Pakistan.

At the 1961 Conference came the crux for South African cricket. As a result of increased criticism of their policies occasioned by the Sharpeville massacre and other events unacceptable to world opinion, South Africa withdrew from the Commonwealth so the ICC were obliged to apply their Rule 5, which stated that 'membership shall cease should a country concerned cease to be part of the British Commonwealth'.

I would make two points here. Firstly, if International had replaced Imperial in the title, the Conference might have amended Rule 5. Secondly, if South Africa had not initiated the voting change, the white members of the Conference would then have been able to re-admit South Africa by revising the rule, if necessary, on a majority vote. This would have been a logical step for them considering the English, Australian and New Zealand delegates all immediately announced that they would continue to play against South Africa both home and away.

Although anti-apartheid opinion in the coloured countries had not hardened to today's extent, West Indies, India and Pakistan might well have felt obliged to oppose re-admission, and on the equal voting system a deadlock would have resulted. In such circumstances no MCC President would have wished to exercise a casting vote.

The year in which South Africa paid what proved to be their last visit to England, 1965, was, coincidentally, the year the ICC were given their overdue face-lift. At last, while the South Africans were limbering up for the short series – which they won – the I of the title became International.

At the same meeting, on Pakistan's proposal, the door was opened to any country with a recognized governing cricket body. They were to be called Associate Members and the first group to be admitted comprised the United States – appropriately enough since the first of all tours had been by an English team to the USA and Canada 106 years before – Ceylon, as it then was, and Fiji.

An optimist as usual, I now thought and wrote that under a new image the ICC might come to fill the power vacuum at the summit of the game. There could be a permanent executive at Lord's and meetings in the other Test-playing countries.

Others, such as John Warr, also saw this revision as an opportunity. In *The Cricketer* he wrote in hope of the game being rescued from 'a bridge of groans across a stream of tears'. The phrase may seem to Mr Warr not inappropriate as he, being the 1988 chairman, sits as consultant with tomorrow's incumbent, Field Marshal Lord Bramall.

How vain were our hopes!

The complete rupture of cricket relations between England and South Africa was taken a stage nearer when in the autumn of 1968 the South African government refused to accept Basil D'Oliveira, the Cape coloured England Test cricketer, as a member of the MCC team due to visit there that winter, thereby effectively cancelling the tour.

It was a bitter moment for MCC that, having just made a voluntary transfer of their traditional authority to the Cricket Council and the TCCB, they should be the catalysts of the showdown.

This was not primarily an ICC matter since South Africa was no longer a member. Nevertheless, it was important to all countries in that it brought total exclusion nearer.

South Africa's cricketers, however, had one shot still in their locker, and a devastating one it was. In 1969–70 Bill Lawry's Australian side to South Africa suffered complete annihilation in all four Tests.

The sadness for cricket lovers not politically minded was that while the feats of Ali Bacher's team were indicating what an attraction their English visit could be in the following summer, their rugby-playing compatriots were facing perpetual harassment and disruption by anti-apartheid sympathizers all over Great Britain.

Although all evidence indicated that our Test centres would become battlegrounds, the Cricket Council persisted until the last minute in their determination to carry through a shortened programme. The arenas would be protected by barbed wire, with artificial pitches laid down in case the proper ones were dug up.

In early May there was a full-scale House of Commons debate on the matter, though no vote was taken, neither side wishing to make it a party issue with a General Election coming up. After hearing the debate I advocated the abandonment of the tour because in the prevailing atmosphere no one could possibly derive any pleasure from it, and the game would simply serve as a costly sacrifice to political demonstration.

Eventually, with the South Africans due in a few days, it needed a direct plea from the Home Secretary, James Callaghan, to the Cricket Council, who thereupon cancelled the tour.

One further effort was made to stage a Test series involving South Africa – this time in Australia. The SA Cricket Association at last plucked up courage to ask their government to include two non-whites in their team, while their cricketers at a trial match at the Cape staged a token walk-off in support, stating that 'merit alone must be the main criterion for selection'. This caused a sensation but, of course, failed to move the Vorster government, who turned down the proposal, and Australia accordingly cancelled the invitation.

The ICC's concern with racial issues has almost exclusively involved South Africa, but at the 1974 Conference there was an unprecedented flare-up on a proposal to admit Israel as an associate. When this was approved, A. H. Kardar, Pakistan's President, walked out of the meeting and announced, 'Pakistan will *never* exchange teams with the Israelis.'

However, one positive thing emerged from this meeting – the final approval for a World Cup to be contested under one-day limited-overs rules in England in June 1975 under the patronage of the Prudential Assurance.

Meanwhile, things were moving forward both in South Africa and at the Commonwealth Prime Ministers' Conference. In 1977 the white Board in South Africa dissolved themselves in favour of a multi-racial SA Cricket Union, with the Bombay-born South African, Mohammad Rachid Varachia, as their president.

This was progress indeed, but the timing was doubly unlucky. Firstly, the ICC were fully occupied with Kerry Packer's attempted take-over of world cricket and, secondly, the signing by the Prime Ministers of the Gleneagles Agreement bound Commonwealth countries to discourage all sporting contact with South Africa.

When the ICC and the TCCB unanimously decided to ban from Test and first-class cricket the players who had signed allegiance to Packer's rebel group, they lost the case on grounds of restraint of trade.

The future of Test cricket was in jeopardy for two years before settlement of a sort was reached. By this time adherence to Gleneagles frustrated any who might have wished to give practical encouragement to the Varachia régime.

The writing was plainly on the wall when even a proposal to send a fact-finding mission to South Africa was opposed by seven countries. On a majority vote the mission went under the ICC chairman, C. H. Palmer, their members representing England, Australia, New Zealand, the United States and Bermuda.

On the strength of their report, the ICC in 1980 invited South Africa to reapply for membership. Yet the following year the proposal, having obviously no possibility of acceptance, was quietly shelved. This was a crowning disappointment for Varachia, who, despite ill-health, had travelled the world pleading the case for his reformed Union, despite rebuffs, including being refused a visa by Australia. He died a heroic figure in December 1981, since when the SACU, under their chief executive, Dr Bacher, have been pursuing what Varachia stood for.

There followed the 'rebel' tours to South Africa by cricketers of several countries, attracted by rich sponsorship and high fees, and their consequent banning, either for three years or, in the case of the West Indies, for life.

It is certain that punitive sanctions against cricketers who in future visit South Africa, even if only to coach black youths, will be applied at next week's ICC meeting at Lord's, even though the exact formula remains to be decided.

We may know just what stance the England delegates may take after the TCCB meeting tomorrow – and, incidentally, may perhaps be told why the Board's executive committee compromised the negotiating position at last Friday's press conference.

The ICC countries, for the sake of order in world cricket and to attempt to satisfy the policies of their governments, are bound to agree one of the resolutions banning South African contact. But surely England, if no other country, should attempt to stir the ICC conscience by putting on permanent record how the cricketers of all races are being brought together in South Africa, their fellow ICC foundation member?

THE DAILY TELEGRAPH
18 JANUARY 1989

'Tuppy' Owen-Smith:
The Inimitable All-rounder

The name of H. G. Owen-Smith, known to the sporting world of the 1930s as 'Tuppy', will bring a smile of recollection to those in the sere and yellow, and I must hope that a brief pen-picture of a truly remarkable player of games may catch the imagination of generations unborn at the time.

Surely it is difficult not to be inspired by a man who, at the age of twenty, was smiting England bowlers hip and thigh at Headingley and later *for England*, at full-back, taking on the Welsh pack apparently single-handed at Twickenham?

He is, indeed, one of the select company who, in less regimented days, played both for and against England at either one sport or two. Owen-Smith came here with the South African cricket side of 1929 and returned two years later to Oxford as a Rhodes Scholar. Having qualified as a doctor at St Mary's Hospital, he returned to the Cape in time to serve in the Middle East with the South African Medical Corps.

After the war Tuppy resumed medical practice at Rondebosch, in Cape Town, and became president of the Cape branch of the Medical Association of South Africa. Now enjoying an active retirement, he will be eighty tomorrow.

Both as all-round cricketer and rugby player he concealed both a mental and physical toughness beneath a debonair, carefree exterior. He was medium-height at most, utterly unafraid, and had the instinctive, swift co-ordination of eye and muscle that marks out the born sportsman. His speed of foot was equally apparent when moving out to hit the spinners on the full-pitch or in clearing his line in the face of opposing forwards; or, for that matter, in the boxing ring, for he won the first of his three Blues as a welter-weight.

Cool and outwardly casual, he was spiritually akin, more than anyone I can think of, to Denis Compton, with whom, when he could spare time as a medical student, he played for Middlesex. Both would use the first bat that came to hand. Both were twice as formidable when their side were in trouble. With both, a joke and a laugh were never far away.

I see him now murdering the Cambridge bowling at Lord's and then spinning them to defeat in collaboration with E. M. Wellings (later the well-known cricket writer) at the other end; likewise, as captain, leading England on to Murrayfield in 1937 for their first win there, which brought with it the Triple Crown. He won ten caps and in his time England were only once beaten.

In Sir Neville Cardus's last book, *Full Score*, he refreshed memories of Owen-Smith's first impact on the sporting scene by reprinting his *Manchester Guardian* report of the innings he never saw. With South Africa only a handful ahead on the second evening, with three second-innings wickets left at Headingley in 1929, Cardus decided to return south to pursue a romantic attachment. He spent the third day of the match with the lady, only discovering with dismay from the evening papers how Owen-Smith, with the help of the tail-enders, had hit a brilliant 129. Set 184 to win, England were struggling at 110 for 5 before a characteristic innings by Woolley brought victory after all. Hurrying to the National Liberal Club, Cardus, never one to allow facts to clutter his style, set his imagination to work and dashed into the paper's Fleet Street office as though hot-foot from the Leeds express. The prose was purple indeed – and no one would have enjoyed the funny side of the story more than the prime hero.

In a *Daily Telegraph* article of twenty years ago on famous all-rounders, I instanced men who had represented their countries at two games. There were a dozen who combined cricket and soccer caps, from Alfred Lyttelton in the 1880s to Willie Watson, of Yorkshire, Huddersfield Town and Sunderland, and Arthur Milton, of Gloucestershire and Arsenal. C. B. Fry adorned that list and also equalled the world long-jump record.

Among several England cricket and rugger doubles, the most recent was M. J. K. Smith, twenty-five times cricket captain and chosen at outside-half against Wales on the strength of a brilliant Oxford partnership with D. O. Brace.

Another England cricket captain, Ted Dexter, by every estimation would also have played golf for Great Britain if he had given more time to the game.

On a wider front, Hubert Doggart, now Treasurer of MCC, won five Cambridge Blues as well as a Test cap for England.

The subject is wide ranging, but I still give the palm to that supreme exemplar of ball-game skill and a modesty to match, Dr H. G. Owen-Smith.

THE DAILY TELEGRAPH
17 FEBRUARY 1989

The Beleaguered Umpire

There can scarcely be a thoughtful cricket-lover, let alone any cricket administrator, who does not today recognize that the authority of the umpire, at the top level of the game, is in urgent need of support.

Consider the position of the Test umpire today. The time has long passed when captains in all cricket regarded the behaviour of their teams to be an accepted part of their responsibilities. Indeed, the captains themselves have been at the centre of disputed decisions.

What is even worse is that team managers, far from attempting to restore discipline in their ranks, have issued statements criticizing the umpiring. Things have come to a desperate pass when famous ex-player managers such as Clive Lloyd and Intikhab Alam forget the responsibility they owe to the boards which have appointed them and act this way. Who, we may be thinking, would be an umpire today?

At Kensington Oval, Bridgetown, last weekend, while Barbados and Jamaica were contesting the championship of the West Indies – the Red Stripe Shield – I sought the views of the man who has probably done more than any other to lift the status of umpires and improve their standards.

Not many years following his retirement from Test cricket, Gerry Gomez managed the most successful of all tours, that of Frank Worrell's West Indian team to Australia in 1960–1. It was the one that began with the tied Test match and ended in the motorcade tribute to the West Indian team through the streets of Melbourne. Half a million people brought that city to a halt. Manager and captain had announced at the outset that their side would accept all decisions without demur, and throughout the series Australia under Richie Benaud responded in the same spirit.

When Mr Gomez came home he devoted himself to organizing the umpires, first in his own island of Trinidad and then by forming the West Indian Umpires Association. The first convention was held in 1962 and these affairs have since become biennial, to the clear benefit of all.

It was as long ago as 1972 that the West Indies, at the instigation of their Umpires Association, proposed to the International Cricket Conference that a world umpires' convention should be called, with a view to forming an international body. If this initiative had been followed up it would no doubt have provided the machinery from which would have come the international panel of umpires which is now surely overdue. 'I blame the ICC for their inaction,' says Mr Gomez.

He believes it is not the umpires who have got worse but the behaviour of the players. He dates the decline in respect for umpires' decisions to Kerry Packer's Roman Circus, a gladiatorial version of cricket, with the players encouraged to express themselves, with no holds barred.

Since it is the players who have tended to run the show, they have made the umpires' job infinitely more difficult by appealing for everything and, in some cases, attempting to intimidate when decisions go against them.

Mr Gomez mentions blatant cases of defiance of recent years: Lillee holding up the game for 10 minutes or more when prevented from using an aluminium bat; Lloyd and Botham refusing to start a Test match in Trinidad until ordered to do so by the president of the West Indies Board; Lloyd again, with the support of a weak manager, actually preparing to abandon a tour of New Zealand and bring his team home; Gatting's never-to-be-forgotten display in Pakistan.

He recognizes, of course, that it is normally only when the financial stakes are highest (chiefly in Test cricket) that the worst excesses occur. Regional cricket in the West Indies and the County Championship in England, on the whole, are still reasonably well conducted. Ultimately, however, those lower down will reflect the standards at the top.

The ICC, to do them justice, have not been wholly inactive, cumbrously slow though the machinery is. At the 1988 meeting they appointed a sub-committee to examine and report back on the subject of neutral Test umpires. They were due to meet at Lord's in January but the South African business took up all the available time, so they will now meet immediately before the full Conference in mid-July. In other words, the very best to be hoped for immediately would be a decision in principle in favour of an international panel.

A system of neutral umpires for all Tests, favoured by Pakistan, will certainly be unacceptable. The TCCB would never agree to a home Test series from which English umpires were excluded. Neither would Australia, or perhaps any other country. An exchange procedure whereby from a panel of the best, one or two stood in other countries alongside home men could, however, be practicable, granted the will to act.

There are obvious snags, not least being that only English umpires are professional. Elsewhere umpires are released from other employment. Again, who selects the Test Panel? Clyde Walcott, president of the West Indies Board, and Mr Camacho, the secretary, while recognizing how great the difficulties are, believe that they should be faced.

A combination of home and neutral umpires would at least greatly dilute suspicions of favouritism. This will be another test of ICC's will and purpose.

THE DAILY TELEGRAPH
I MARCH 1989

Dexter's Task

The appointment or otherwise of Ted Dexter as Chairman of Selectors when the Test and County Cricket Board meet at Lord's tomorrow has evoked stronger feelings and created wider press coverage than any similar decision in one's memory. The personality of the chief contender, who today faces a question and answer session before the main committee of the TCCB, is one reason and, obviously, the thirst for a change in England's fortunes is another.

No cricket topic excites a higher degree of fascination at any time than the picking of the England team. We all think we can do a better job than the selectors. Of recent years those with close experience have, however, had good grounds for criticism. Events both on and off the field have brought cricket authority in general and some individuals in particular into deplorably low esteem. The unforgivable choice of Graham Gooch for India was the nadir. Such being the case, the responsibility faced by any new chairman speaks for itself.

The popular image of Ted Dexter should encourage hope. To all those old enough to remember, he has symbolized courage and a spirit of challenge ever since he confronted the speed and fire of Wes

Hall and Charlie Griffith in the Lord's Test of 1963 by driving of classic purity and awesome power.

His 70 was the best innings of its kind I ever saw. One associates Dexter with Lord's in the same way as his great contemporaries with memorable innings on other grounds: Peter May at Sydney and Edgbaston; Colin Cowdrey at Melbourne and Kingston; Tom Graveney at Port of Spain.

For all his evident talent his Test career had a chequered start for which selectorial folly was surely responsible. He was first chosen, aged twenty-three, against New Zealand at Old Trafford, where the assembled selectors were about to choose the 1958-9 side to Australia. Rain so held up the game that Dexter had not batted when the selectors sat down to the job. Instead of delaying the final choice they picked and announced their team without him, whereupon on a decidedly awkward pitch he fulfilled all reasonable hopes with an admirable innings of 52. Called to Australia several months later in a mid-tour emergency to join a hard-pressed team, he failed, not surprisingly, to find form.

The following winter in West Indies he underlined the selectors' Old Trafford mistake by heading the England averages. Let us hope that, come the Dexter régime, today's promising young cricketers may profit from the moral of this tale. If they merit attention in the first place they are entitled to decent consideration.

In what can only be a highly demanding job, the measure of Dexter's success (supposing that his appointment is agreed by the Board) must substantially depend on who his fellow selectors are to be. I believe the Board would be badly misjudging the popular mood and doing English cricket poor service if they failed to provide their chairman with three or four good men and true to cover the country.

Of course, selectors can only pick from the talent available, and top quality in recent years has been thin on the ground. Yet even the most seasoned cricketers can gain from judicious encouragement, and a happy relationship between selectors and players has a clear reflection in team morale.

County committees like to feel they are in contact with the fount of honour. No single manager (as has been suggested) could fill the bill nationally. Indeed, the evidence of counties is that in general the most successful sides – Essex and Middlesex, for instance – have no team manager with a say in the cricket. England's recent exploits have suggested likewise. Playing authority should surely belong to the captain.

I trust Dexter can be persuaded to modify his reported preference for a duo comprising himself and a manager, reinforced by a corps of scouts.

Chairmen have always taken advantage of outside information supplementary to that of those with the status of the job. Finding fresh selectors may not be easy but it should not be impossible to discover men with good credentials acceptable to the chairman.

If Ossie Wheatley could find time to add selection to his chairmanship of the TCCB cricket sub-committee might he not cover the West and Wales? Here are a few tentatively put forward whose availability might be worth determining: Ray Illingworth; Geoff Pullar; Keith Fletcher; and two reputedly unwilling to take on the chairmanship, Donald Carr and M. J. K. Smith. To appoint a broadcaster would be a departure, but no one knows the modern game better than Illingworth.

A more surprising name, that of Colin Ingleby-Mackenzie, has gone the rounds, and when mentioned at a couple of recent dinners as a possible chairman, before Mr Dexter's hat entered the ring, the suggestion drew spontaneous applause.

The impact that Dexter might make on the scene is intriguing. It is a gain that, unlike Mr May, who had to conduct his honorary chairmanship from the City, he would be a salaried appointee of the Board on a full-time basis, free to travel as necessary. One wonders, by the way, how he will do so. The man who once flew his family single-handed to Australia is apt nowadays to arrive at Lord's on a fearsome-looking motorbike.

His unorthodoxy might surprise people. There is, for instance, the paradox that the most natural striker of a ball in the approved manner, whether at cricket or golf, amuses himself with unorthodox theory. I happened recently to hear from Sunningdale that though he was striking the ball marvellous distances, he had taken to putting one-handed, and not with any great success.

I trust that Dexter will guide England's batsmen into more orthodox ways rather than the reverse, and let us hope that if he signs on the dotted line he will have better luck than his predecessor.

THE DAILY TELEGRAPH
6 MARCH 1989

——————— *Leader in Peace and War* ———————

Peter Foster moved all present at the Kent AGM telling us of the discovery of the body of F. G. H. Chalk, his brother-in-law, forty-six years after his death in the cockpit of his fighter plane, shot down into the depths of a French copse behind Calais. There is, it seems, an organization whose object is the locating of crashed aircraft in both world wars. Gerry was leading a squadron of Spitfires, having transferred from Bomber Command after flying more than thirty sorties as a tail-gunner and winning a DFC. The RAF now saw to his burial with due honours in an Allied cemetery near Boulogne, the service attended by Leslie Ames, 'Hopper' Levett, Godfrey Evans and Peter (last cricketing descendant of the seven Worcestershire brothers), all of whom had played under Gerry Chalk's captaincy of Kent in the last two summers of peace.

Here was a leader who epitomized all that was best in the amateur contribution to cricket between the wars – friendly, ever cheerful and no fool as a tactician. Brought up at Uppingham under the careful tutelage of Frank Gilligan, he developed his batting and his captaincy experience at Oxford. He played some innings for Kent (carrying his bat for 115 at Dover against Yorkshire in a total of 215, for instance), which suggested that in the 1940s Test honours might not have been out of reach.

DIARY
21 MARCH 1989

——————— *As Host at Vincent's* ———————

At Oxford I give a drinks party at Vincent's Club to the committee and a few friends in token of having been made an honorary member. Since I had never been up at the university this came as one of the biggest and most pleasing surprises of my life. The great point about Vincent's is that it has always been a social club requiring some sporting qualifications as distinct from a Bluetocracy. Having known the club as a guest for the best part of sixty years I would say that its distinct ethos seems to have been faithfully maintained. Needless to say, I am greatly honoured to have received such a rare accolade.

I wrote long ago in The Sunday Telegraph *that the Vincent's tie of dark blue with small silver crowns was the earliest of all ties with crests or other motifs. It dates from 1926, since when we have seen many imitators.*

DIARY
23 MAY 1989

C. L. R. James

C. L. R. James had three passions in life: cricket, English literature and West Indian independence. The last of the three led him to political extremes, but the others produced a writer on the game of unique depth and lucidity.

He was concerned to show West Indian cricketers in context, and in his *Beyond a Boundary* traced the game's influence in the cultural evolution of the Caribbean from the time of George Challenor, the white founder of their batting tradition, through George Headley to Gary Sobers.

At one stage he went distinctly beyond the boundary in a long-running polemic as Editor of the *Trinidad Nation*, advocating Frank Worrell as Test captain in place of the lighter-skinned Gerry Alexander. He later admitted that 'for the first and I hope the last time in reporting cricket I was unfair'.

In general, his appreciation of cricketers with style and beauty of execution transcended nationality and race.

His first book, written in collaboration with his great friend Learie Constantine, was *Cricket and I* in 1933; and he lived on to see the recent republication of an anthology of his work simply called *Cricket*.

THE DAILY TELEGRAPH
2 JUNE 1989

Memorable Days at Headingley

The Test ground at Headingley on the outskirts of Leeds, where England meet Australia on Thursday, may surprise on first acquaintance: nothing of the dark Satanic mills about it as at dear, departed Bradford and Bramall Lane.

Surrounded by modest suburban houses and with the spire of St Michael's Church on the skyline, the sporting complex contains Rugby League ground and cricket field divided by a stand facing both ways and looking, as Tim Heald has written, like a beached aircraft carrier. There is also a bowling green. It is all owned not by Yorkshire CCC but by Leeds Cricket, Football and Athletic Club, still so called although the athletes have long since moved out and the bowlers moved in.

All Test grounds of their nature spell drama and heroics, but few within my memory more so than Headingley. Yorkshire crowds react sharply to the play, whether in appreciation or the opposite. The men in the middle are rather more conscious than on most grounds that they are under critical inspection.

If the verdict is favourable the roar is uniquely powerful, a fact that was first borne in on me on the morning of 11 July 1930. Don Bradman walked in in the second over of the match, with the board showing 2 for 1, to face the bowling of Larwood and Tate. At lunch he returned not out 105, the score 136 for 1. The pitch was easy-paced, the light good, the outfield fast, and The Don tireless. By the close it was 309 undefeated out of 458 for 3 with broken records galore, the spectators sated with clapping and shouting.

From that day on there was an unshakeable empathy between Bradman and the Headingley crowd, culminating in the 173 not out eighteen years later which against all the odds brought Australia to 404 for 3 and the victory that settled the rubber. In four Tests there he had made four hundreds, two of them trebles, average 192.60. After forty years the thought of England's dismal performance on the last day of the 1948 Test still has the power to sting.

Naturally enough, a special warmth embraces Yorkshiremen playing for England on their own midden. Len Hutton made three Test hundreds here, Geoffrey Boycott four, each commanding the stage in turn. And it was here that F. S. Trueman, the miner's son from the Doncaster coalfields, made such an explosive impact on the Test scene. He was fiery Fred all right, careering down the hill from the Kirkstall End on that Saturday afternoon in 1952 as India lost the first four wickets of their second innings without a run on the board.

Like the late lamented J. M. Sims, the batsmen seemed, as Jim admitted to his partner on another occasion, 'not exactly frightened, Patsy, just a trifle apprehensive'. Ever since the war England had sighed for a fast bowler. Now here he was, one of Yorkshire's own, who year after year thereafter brought forth his best in Headingley Tests. The star performance was his 11 for 88 against Australia on a peculiar piebald pitch in 1961, the last 5 of them, on Peter May's advice, with medium-pace off-breaks.

In relatively modern times the crowds have mostly had to make do with Yorkshire contributions from Boycott and Illingworth, the latter with both bat and ball when England's captain and as an expatriate with Leicestershire. Boycott's highest Test innings, 246 not out against New Zealand in 1967, occupied 9½ hours, as a result of which he was dropped for slow play. An infinitely happier occasion, indeed his proudest moment, came when against Australia, after a self-imposed exile from Test cricket for three years, he made his 100th hundred (151 in all) and in so doing helped England to retain the Ashes. Then the welkin rang.

The roar of a Headingley crowd is deafening. However, equally eloquent can be the silences. I will mention two moments of dreadful disappointment. In 1948 (when there were spinners around) England went into the field against Australia with only one, Jim Laker. Norman Yardley, captain of Yorkshire and England, at the end of his tether, eventually decided to give Hutton a bowl, the eighth man tried. Len could turn the wrist in a useful leg-break on a less demanding occasion, but not here, not now, against these. After a flattering maiden his full-pitches were smacked casually away for 30 runs in 3 overs.

It was a painful hush, but no more so than when Australia came again five years later. As the first over was being bowled I was still climbing up to the commentary point out of sight of the play. There had been not a sound. Yet when I reached the box Hutton was making his slow way to the pavilion. Lindwall's second ball had been a yorker which had sent his middle stump flying. The atmosphere was charged with a sickening, wordless grief.

So many moments stick in the mind's eye: the rain pelting down in 1934 to save England from wholesale defeat; George Mann hitting a prodigious six on to the football ground via the roof of the stand; Cyril Washbrook, aged forty-one and on a reluctant return to Test cricket at the urging of his fellow selectors, coming in at close of play having made a priceless not out 90 ('One does not decline to play for England, but it will not be easy.'); John Edrich in a golden patch making 310 not out, alternately missing altogether and hitting fours; Gary Sobers at his incomparable peak putting England to the sword, and making 103 between lunch and tea.

I have written only of what I saw in my time as a reporter; but with many, of course, Headingley is synonymous with Botham's phenomenal 149 not out against Australia in 1981 which, followed by Willis's inspired bowling, swung the game from almost certain defeat to incredible victory. This was almost but not quite the last of English successes at Headingley because Australia were beaten again in 1985.

Otherwise the story is gloomy indeed, with five heavy defeats in the last six years, twice by West Indies, once each by New Zealand, India and Pakistan, the last two by an innings. It is doubly significant, surely, that since 1982 the only Yorkshireman to be seen in the England side (and he on the last three occasions) has been Bill Athey, who had by then migrated to Gloucestershire. Perhaps with luck Paul Jarvis may be given the chance to start a new chapter.

THE DAILY TELEGRAPH
3 JUNE 1989

—— *With Norman Yardley at Headingley* ——

It has been arranged with David Welch, Daily Telegraph *sports editor, that I should contribute commentaries on the Mondays of all Test matches, which naturally involves revisiting the old haunts. I shall not have seen Headingley, Edgbaston, Old Trafford and Trent Bridge since my last summer's reporting in 1974. I enjoyed the reunions and meeting some of the new generation of cricket writers more than much of the cricket – certainly the England part of it.*

Bobby Simpson came to dine on the evening of the first day of the First Test. With the scoreboard showing Australia 207 for 3 the world was a happy place for him. The Australian coach – not manager, he insisted – had a clear philosophy of the modern game and evidently an easy rapport with his players. Equally, it seemed clear that he would crack the whip firmly enough if he needed to. A delightful evening, but George Plumptre and I left it with distinct English forebodings.

I watched awhile with Norman Yardley, captain of England against Australia back in 1948. He had quite gone in the legs but was wholly alert mentally. He spoke of his war with the Green Howards, that famous Yorkshire regiment whose forthcoming tercentenary celebrations were to include a cricket match at Hovingham, home of the Worsleys, who were traditionally Green Howards. Herbert Sutcliffe was commissioned into them in the First World War and served also in the Second, as later did his son Billy. And Captain Hedley Verity, taken prisoner in Sicily before dying of his wounds in an Italian POW camp, was also a Green Howard.

Norman followed up with a letter giving the names of other cricketers with whom he served. He hoped to get to Hovingham in July, but he was stricken shortly afterwards with a stroke from the effects of which he died a few months later. A nicer fellow there never was.

DIARY
8 JUNE 1989

Easy-paced Headingley Pitch
Exposes Lack of Bowling Variety

A fast outfield and easy-paced wicket; green caps and runs galore. In many ways Headingley recalled old times; in some, such as the lunatic Mexican wave, it did not.

The euphoria which has built up around English cricket since the name of Ted Dexter first commanded the headlines several months ago was always due for dilution once the serious fight for the Ashes took shape. Nevertheless, the extent of disillusionment as Australia eased and sometimes raced along to their vast score came as a nasty shock, only partly relieved by the spirit of England's reply.

The plain truth is, of course, that the England XI can only reflect the strengths and weaknesses of county cricket. The type of fast-medium bowling which has for so long ruled the day on poor pitches was cut down to size by some admirable batting in more favourable conditions than Headingley has produced for several years.

Australia's 601 for 7 declared stirred the memory. That was their score, with one more wicket lost, when Len Hutton, with less justification than Gower, put them in in the First Test of 1954–5. Gower omitted Emburey while at Brisbane two admirable spinners, Appleyard and Wardle, watched from the pavilion the massacre of Bedser (scarcely fit), Statham, Tyson, Bailey and Edrich.

I hope all the remaining Test pitches are good and true. Then, at the end of the summer, irrespective of the result of the series, we shall have been reminded how necessary is a much larger variety of the arts of bowling – necessary, that is, unless a country possess four awesome fast bowlers who pose a constant physical as well as technical threat, such as those of the West Indies. In 300 Tests, give or take a few, I never saw the bowling of both sides so utterly uniform in pace.

Australia can rejoice in the flowering of three batsmen of the quality of Dean Jones, Steve Waugh and Mark Taylor. All stand still until the ball is bowled, and all wield bats of around 2 lb 7 oz rather than those clumsy 3 lb weapons. Their method is generally orthodox, and their speed and judgement between the wickets was a constant joy. About Waugh, in style and physique, and wearing a cap rather than the anonymous helmet, there was more than a hint of Stan McCabe – a tenser edition.

The influence of Bobby Simpson was plain to see. The man who, after ten years' retirement from the Australian leadership came back, aged forty-one, to hold the fort as captain once more against Packer's attempted take-over, and at fifty-three still adding to a record number of runs in grade cricket, holds the players' respect.

The Australian bowling, with the class of Alderman standing out as did that of Foster for England, has likewise suffered inevitably from the surfeit of one-day cricket. When Alderman took Gooch's wicket he was mobbed by his fellows in the modern manner which the old timers observe wryly. It is said that when the son of Arthur Mitchell, that toughest of archetypal tykes, was asked what his father would have thought of all the hugging and kissing, he laughed and said, 'Why, I don't think he ever kissed moother.'

The chief event of Saturday, apart from Lamb's flawless hundred, was Barnett's innings. His antics as the bowler nears the crease defy every canon, but, that said, a good eye and a determination to play his natural attacking game saw him through. If the supremo can modify that stance and drop the strongest hint to exercise his wrist-spin regularly for Derbyshire he could serve England well.

The press quarters are now wonderfully plush following more than 'an element of refurbishment'. Apart from a temporary edifice like an ocean liner buckled in the middle and comprised solely of hospitality boxes, Headingley has changed as little as its pundits' forthright talk.

I found much after my own heart. Cricket will not be right, they say, until they uncover the pitches (and the run-ups). An indoor school opposite the ground as good as MCC's, and a youthful academy of cricket at Park Avenue, Bradford, reflect the yearning to regain old standards.

The Bradford League prospers; likewise the York and District in which Hovingham play. A pilgrimage to that loveliest of country-house grounds on which the village have played for upwards of 150 years was, for me, a must. In 1858 All-England defeated 22 of Hovingham by two wickets. But did they all field? The scorebook does not relate. W. G. Grace is said to have described his 400 not out against 22 of Grimsby as the innings he enjoyed most 'because they all fielded and they hadn't cut the outfield'.

THE DAILY TELEGRAPH
12 JUNE 1989

FIRST TEST – PLAYED AT HEADINGLEY ON
8, 9, 10, 12, 18 JUNE

AUSTRALIA: 601 for 7 declared (Taylor 136, Border 66, Jones 79, Waugh 177*, Hughes 71) and 230 for 3 declared (Taylor 60, Border 60*)
ENGLAND: 430 (Barnett 80, Lamb 125, Smith 66, Alderman 5 for 107) and 191 (Gooch 68, Alderman 5 for 44)
Australia won by 210 runs

Australia Extend Their Superiority at Lord's

The eight days' play of this Ashes series so far have, of course, been miserably disappointing to English eyes. Equally, Australia's performance has been meritorious beyond all reasonable expectation. Surely, therefore, the critics' first duty is to give credit where it is manifestly due, to Border and his team for playing the better cricket at all points – the sounder cricket, both technically and tactically.

Waugh has emerged as a player of very high class while Taylor at Lord's built on the reputation which had its foundation at Headingley, No one has disappointed, while Border's leadership, having gone through a long and testing period of adversity, is now mature and assured. He clearly used to advantage the knowledge of English idiosyncrasies he has picked up playing for Essex. His only indiscretion, ironically, was the mis-hit sweep, that unsound and grossly over-used 'English stroke' which raised home spirits on Friday afternoon.

Another congratulatory note goes to the Lord's crowd. They never failed to accord honour where it was due, and one could take pride in the impartial generosity with which they applauded fine cricket, sad though they were that mostly it came from one side.

Not all, though. The English fielding could scarcely be faulted, while Emburey bowled better, surely, than he can have done since his palmy days in the early 1980s. The folly of his exclusion at Headingley was fully exposed, and if there were no other conclusion to be drawn from his performance it is that never, never, never must England play without at least one slow bowler.

If Emburey had not been at hand to curb and restrict and at times worry, we could almost have seen the Lord's scoreboard showing a seven in the hundreds column as it did when Australia ran riot here back in 1930.

As to the English tactics, one would have liked to have seen Jarvis bowled more at the pavilion end and the medium pace of Gooch used earlier. Dilley looked eager in his opening spells, but he has never had the spirit to keep going in adversity.

It was obvious all through Australia's innings that the excellence of the pitch was too much for bowlers accustomed to surfaces which do their work for them. It is also true that from start to finish the luck persistently ran against them.

Every cricketer knows of perverse days when absolutely all goes wrong. That it should happen on the otherwise blissful Saturday of the Lord's Test must have been heartbreaking, and for the England captain to be obliged, according to modern custom, to face a press grilling proved the last straw. That David Gower, of all people, and for the first time, unfortunately lost his cool was a reflection of the seemingly intolerable tensions that today exist between players and a large section of the media.

If Mr Dexter ever doubted the difficulties of his task he can have no illusions now. He is an unconventional fellow in some ways, but he is thoroughly orthodox regarding cricket technique, and he has been disappointed, I know, by the evidence of his eyes these last two months. I would not put out of court some sort of winter seminar where technical faults might be rectified. As a golfer he well knows the necessity of the practice ground, however eminent the player.

He is only too well aware how English cricket has been undermined by the proliferation of one-day matches, by the indifference of so many county pitches and, most recently, by the high-seam ball. I am delighted that he is strongly against the covering of pitches in county cricket, as also is Sir Leonard Hutton and other wise men I saw again in Yorkshire a fortnight ago.

Although nothing is yet arranged, the TCCB are certainly sympathetic to the idea of a 'B' team touring overseas for the blooding of a younger generation, the likes of Keith Medlycott and Michael Atherton, to name two of a promising young crop. Personally, I would far rather see the TCCB spend money in these directions than in locking up into two-year contracts a bunch of seasoned top-liners already well rewarded with rich individual sponsorships and handsome tax-free benefits.

The executive committee of the TCCB is meeting shortly to consider contract ideas suggested by the England committee. I hope they do not put their credibility at risk, as they did earlier this year, by publishing proposals which the full board subsequently fail to endorse.

The Lord's Test is the scene of a thousand reunions, interspersed with some fresh acquaintance. My neighbour, in one of the seats considerately reserved by MCC for members of twenty-five years' standing who are also over seventy, suddenly asked me how the game was progressing in Philadelphia. There is a league there, I told him, but the Gentlemen of Philadelphia had not come to England since 1908. 'I remember them well,' he said, and got up (between overs, of course) to demonstrate the rather peculiar action of the Philadelphian, Bart King, said to have been one of the best bowlers in the world. As a Nottingham boy he had secured the autograph of the great Tom Wass when Nottinghamshire won the Championship in 1907.

He was the famous baritone and teacher of Kathleen Ferrier, Roy Henderson, so I discovered from his friend alongside, another distinguished singer, Sir Keith Falkner. Mr Henderson will be ninety next month, Sir Keith a mere eighty-nine. Those late Victorians were a tough breed all right.

THE DAILY TELEGRAPH
26 JUNE 1989

SECOND TEST – PLAYED AT LORD'S ON
22, 23, 24, 26, 27 JUNE

ENGLAND: 286 (Gooch 60, Gower 57, Russell 64) and 359 (Gower 106, Smith 96, Alderman 6 for 128)
AUSTRALIA: 528 (Taylor 62, Boon 94, Waugh 152, Lawson 74) and 119 for 4 (Boon 58*)
Australia won by 6 wickets

Nostalgic View from the Playing Fields of Oxbridge

When Michael Atherton and Mark Crawley go out to toss in the 144th University Match at Lord's on Wednesday, it will be the first time in eighty-four years that Oxford and Cambridge will be captained by undergraduates from the same school.

Manchester Grammar School can indeed be proud of its distinction: proud, surely, rather than completely surprised, seeing that the exceptional all-round achievements of this pair enabled the school, in 1984–6, to win thirty-one matches and lose only one (to Shrewsbury).

There cannot be a master in charge of cricket at any school who does not envy the record of David Moss, not least in that his First XI managed to get in fifty-six matches in the three summers, without apparently prejudicing A-level results.

The last school to supply both universities' captains at Lord's was Harrow (K. M. Carlisle and E. W. Mann) in 1905; before that it was Eton in 1875.

These facts derive from the ample appendix to the second MCC Cricket Library publication, *Oxford and Cambridge Cricket*, by George Chesterton and Hubert Doggart (MCC/Collins Willow, £14.95). With university cricket generally in the public eye, this book has come out at a timely moment. It brings together for the first time in a comprehensive history of the two clubs, the salient facts and personalities of the oldest first-class fixture. A total of 1569 Blues have taken part in it; 121 have played Test cricket, and the great majority for counties. No nursery in the past century can

begin to compare with Fenner's and The Parks. Cambridge has
given England twenty Test captains, Oxford ten. Seven overseas
Test captains have emerged from Oxford, five from Cambridge.

The authors have researched widely and wisely, painting the
picture of their respective universities' fortunes decade by decade
and, on the first-hand evidence of many old Blues, producing brief
reports to accompany the 143 scorecards. All are set in the broad
social context of the times.

Most of the great English amateurs march through these pages,
from Lord Harris, the three Studds, Fry, Warner and Jackson of the
last century, to Chapman, the three Ashtons, Sheppard, May,
Dexter, Cowdrey and M. J. K. Smith. Likewise, among the post-
amateur generation, come Brearley, Lewis, Edmonds and Pringle.

The nub of the matter is whether the tradition can be sustained.
Of the fourteen in the Combined Universities team which has
made history by reaching the Benson and Hedges Cup quarter-final
only five were from Oxbridge. Granted, several of the others had
attempted entry into one or other of the older universities.

The rejection of one, Martin Speight, promptly recruited by
Durham, was in spite of three A-grade A-levels, a decision which
the head of an Oxford college described to me as a positive disgrace.

Peter Roebuck has mentioned that only one Oxford Blue in the
past fifteen years has failed his final exams. It needs only a few
colleges to give a higher priority to the scholar-sportsman, and the
immediate future of The Parks and Fenner's would be secure.

As the book makes clear, if on the other hand the TCCB ever
took away first-class status from the Universities' matches against
the counties, the two clubs with their lovely grounds would fade
into oblivion.

THE DAILY TELEGRAPH
1 JULY 1989

Cloudburst at Edgbaston

In mid-afternoon on Thursday all was for the best in the Third Test
at Edgbaston – some combative cricket, blissful weather and a good

crowd. The contrast thereafter was complete: downpour, drizzle, dim light and the dowsing of all hope of an English victory. Likewise, with 9½ hours' cricket lost, Australia's prospect of turning their cast-iron position into a winning one is much reduced though not entirely eliminated.

Edgbaston is scarcely an ancient citadel of the game compared with the other England Test grounds, but it is now as well equipped as any – a far cry, indeed, from the suburban field of 1902 when the redoubtable secretary, R. V. Ryder, is said to have managed the first Test here without the benefit of a telephone.

The support for the present match has been thoroughly satisfactory – £600,000 taken as against £500,000 at Headingley – and the crowds have borne their disappointment like sportsmen.

Dean Jones has exemplified the aggressive spirit of Australia's batting with a polished innings, orthodox in method, and when he reached his hundred he earned further good marks by a lengthy acknowledgement of the crowd's reception, taking off his helmet to do so. Would all batsmen everywhere kindly note.

At Headingley England went into the field without a spinner. Here it was evident from Emburey's first over that he should have had a slow left-armer at the other end. On the Australians' last visit here in 1985, when they lost 3–1, England played two spinners in all six Tests.

It could have been a different story here with Cook included or Medlycott given his baptism. At least, though, we can rejoice at the arrival of Fraser, who was very much more effective than Dilley and young Jarvis, and twice as economical.

The tropical violence at Edgbaston recalled all too vividly the Brisbane storms of 1946 and 1950 which, for England, made survival impossible in the first case and any prospect of victory highly improbable in the second. Hailstones like golf balls (which pierced the roofs of cars) descended on the galvanized iron roof of the press box.

The deluge of 1946 was my first experience of the extremities of Australian weather, the occasion made even more memorable by the comment of my neighbour, cupping his hands together and shouting in my ear to be heard: 'We often get it worse than this.' Australians, as I learned, are rarely given to understatement.

Whatever the next two days may hold at Edgbaston, the more important cricket news in the long term must surely come later in the week from the International Cricket Conference at Lord's. I put it in this way because all too often in history the elephant has given birth to a mouse. To their credit, however, the ICC were able to agree unanimously in January a pragmatic course of action in respect of South Africa, a solution which the West Indian Prime Ministers in session have just accepted, clearing the way officially for England's winter tour.

The ICC are due to debate revisions in their constitution including the length of duty of the chairman, who has always been the current President of MCC. If the ICC are to fulfil the more forceful role that the modern situation demands, a chairman's term of, say, three years is clearly desirable.

Field Marshal Lord Bramall earned the respect of all by his handling of the South African meeting, but it is a question whether he would feel able to continue with the ICC when his Presidency of MCC ends in October. He is Lord Lieutenant of Greater London and has other public duties in addition.

My impression is that a majority of the seven Test countries want the chairmanship to remain with MCC, if only because it is thus by tradition neutral and apolitical. Failing Lord Bramall, one hopes another acceptable MCC figure may be forthcoming.

I trust the major countries will agree a second annual meeting in winter during a Test series in one of them, an idea first advocated in these pages twenty-odd years ago. 'Jaw, jaw is better than war, war.'

THE DAILY TELEGRAPH
10 JULY 1989

THIRD TEST – PLAYED AT EDGBASTON ON
6, 7, 8, 10, 11 JULY

AUSTRALIA: 424 (Jones 157, Fraser 4 for 63 on début) and 158 (Taylor 51)
ENGLAND: 242
Match drawn

———— *Return to Old Trafford* ————

After fifteen years a nostalgic return to Old Trafford. After a long hiatus all is well with Lancashire under a chairman in Bob Bennett who, as captain of Bacup, played for the county with credit in the 1960s: cricketer/businessman is an ideal administrative combination not always easy to come by. Cyril

Washbrook goes about his presidential duties with the dignity which characterized all he did on the field. Alick Leggat, treasurer emeritus, dispenses hospitality with traditional Lancashire liberality.

I recalled my first visit to an England–Australia Test at Old Trafford in 1930: Church of Scotland minister Peebles giving his boy Ian a pat on the back as he passed through the Long Room on his way out to bat; and Ian's last meeting with Aubrey Faulkner.

Ian's youthful promise as a leg-break and googly bowler had been brought to full fruition by Faulkner at his famous indoor school (the first of its kind). The great South African cricketer could be a difficult fellow, subject to depression, and their friendship had dissolved in disagreement. Now, returning from the ground by taxi, the pupil spotted his mentor waiting at a bus stop. A lift into Manchester was followed by a happy evening of reminiscence for which Ian was grateful ever after. The rift was healed.

Within a month or two Faulkner was found at his school, dead by his own hand.

DIARY
28 JULY 1989

Life Vice-President

A letter from John Stephenson informs me that I have been elected an Honorary Life Vice-President of MCC. There could have been no greater surprise, nor could I possibly have visualized so great a distinction.

The office was created in 1961 as a final salute to Sir Pelham Warner on his retiring as a trustee and has been accorded since to men who have been thought to render special service to MCC. There have now been twelve Vice-Presidents in all, ten of whom have served as President, and seven of whom are still alive. The only other to be honoured from outside that august Presidential circle is Sir Donald Bradman, elected last year to mark his eightieth birthday. Prestige apart, I now enjoy the freedom of the Committee Room by right, rather than by courtesy, likewise the Committee Dining Room and Car Park. Nor can I be ejected for non-payment of my subscription!

DIARY
29 JULY 1989

England on the Ropes

The Fourth Test so far follows completely the sad one-way pattern of the first three. England started climbing uphill on 8 June at Head-ingley, and they were still doing so eighteen playing days later without so much as a spell of level going to break the monotony and cheer the spirit.

Success has made Australia's corporate strength greater than the sum of its parts, as is apt to happen with a touring side who are well led, managed and coached.

Man for man, England, by contrast, have done themselves far less than justice. Ted Dexter, while continuing to lament English techniques, characteristically offers no excuses, though he does mention, fairly enough, that in the thirty-six selections for the first three Tests, eleven enforced changes had to be made.

If this match, and with it the rubber, is not saved, as it still could be, David Gower's team are sure to be amended – though where alternative bowlers are to come from goodness knows. Meanwhile, one can only be thankful for the efforts of the three youngest England players on view – Robin Smith, Russell and Fraser.

Discounting miracles, a belligerent defensive must be England's tactical formula henceforward, just as it was when that loveable Lancastrian, George Duckworth, was sent in as night-watchman – after Don Bradman had completed his 334 at Headingley and received a wire from an anonymous admirer, duly publicized, which ended, 'Please receive £1000.'

Aided by a good many hours of rain, George was still in posses-sion on the last morning – 4 hours' batting all told for 33. The match was saved, and England's wicket-keeper was also delighted to get a wire saying simply, 'Please receive a thousand thanks.' A dose of Duckworth do-or-die now would earn the deep gratitude of us all.

Talking of Bradman and Duckworth, bear with me if I recall that in the next Test of 1930 at Old Trafford I saw, from the Stretford End press box, Ian Peebles on a slow, turning pitch, reduce The Don, for the one and only time that summer, to ordinary stature: c. Duleepsinhji at slip, b. Peebles 14.

Now we watch more comfortably from the Warwick Road End, in what the ragged boy who climbed the wall to see Trumper in

1902 – or was it Ranji in 1896? – and lived to become president of the ever friendly Lancashire CCC, would have been amused as well as proud to see named after him as the Neville Cardus Suite.

What would not have amused either Cardus or any subsequent cricket writer of repute is the grossly offensive personal abuse now emanating from elements therein, to the deep embarrassment of responsible journalists. In these circumstances I think the England captain was abundantly justified in declining to trust himself on Saturday evening to another face-to-face press conference with the worst of the tabloids.

In contrast to much that debases cricket journalism, the TV commentators interpret what viewers are seeing on their screens with moderation and with the understanding that comes from playing experience.

Occasionally, one old Test player lets another off too lightly, as, for instance, Tom Graveney (who could never have perpetrated anything remotely like it) describing on Thursday Ian Botham's as 'a fairly poor stroke'. As he showed at Edgbaston, Botham's talent as a batsman is based on a sounder method than anyone in the side. What is missing is self-discipline. Taking all the circumstances into account – Gower just out, himself just in, tea at the end of the over, Smith going strong and, with four wickets down, the innings, and with it the Ashes in the melting pot – I don't know when I saw a more deplorable stroke by an experienced batsman than his attempt to pull Hohns for six.

With the ball Botham has played the unfamiliar part of the steady stock bowler tolerably well. The failure lay in the false philosophy behind the spin attack of Emburey and Cook.

On the first day Hohns turned the ball; yet both bowled over after over in the flat, defensive one-day style, with Gower himself perched close at silly mid-off, inhibiting by his presence the slower, flighted ball truly spun, such as we would have seen from a Titmus or a Tattersall. Almost the only time Gower moved back Emburey lured Taylor down the pitch in just this way and had him stumped, whereupon Gower returned to his perch and the dull routine was resumed. In his last eighteen Tests, including this one, Emburey has taken 22 wickets at 64 runs each, and at an inordinate strike rate.

This nice old dog has had ample time to relearn the tricks he once knew, but, like so many modern cricketers, he sticks to his chosen ways regardless. In this case, he and the disappointing Cook made easier the survival and quiet accumulation of Border, Waugh and Co., which was their prime objective.

THE DAILY TELEGRAPH
31 JULY 1989

FOURTH TEST – PLAYED AT OLD TRAFFORD ON
27, 28, 29, 31 JULY AND 1 AUGUST

ENGLAND: 260 (Smith 143, Lawson 6 for 72) and 264 (Russell 128, Emburey 64, Alderman 5 for 66)
AUSTRALIA: 447 (Taylor 85, Border 80, Jones 69, Waugh 92) and 81 for 1
Australia won by 9 wickets

South Africa Entices . . .

The recruitment of some sort of English team to tour South Africa in the winter was the inevitable result of the International Cricket Conference's pragmatic resolution last January to ban players for a defined period who in future contracted sporting links with South Africa.

Nevertheless, the speed of the South African Cricket Union's clandestine operation and the quality of the team which they have been able to persuade to take part, will come as an unwelcome surprise to all concerned with the control and management of English cricket, from Ted Dexter's committee to the ten county clubs affected.

Of the ten, Nottinghamshire and Middlesex are supplying three men each, Kent and Gloucestershire two each, and Worcestershire, Essex, Lancashire, Yorkshire, Derbyshire and Glamorgan one apiece.

The sixteen men have signed themselves out of international cricket effectively for seven years, since they are each contracted for two winter tours and the resolution passed unanimously by the ICC specifies a minimum ban of five years for involvement in a team, the suspension dating from the termination of the engagement.

In most cases – all, perhaps, except those of the youngest, Maynard (23), DeFreitas (23) and Jarvis (24) – these men have effectually said goodbye to their hopes of playing again for England.

The chances of some, no doubt, were slim, but as many as nine have taken part in the present series. Indeed, three – Emburey, Foster and Robinson – played in the Old Trafford Test.

All except Graveney have played Test cricket and only one, Roland Butcher, at thirty-five, can be said to be coming to the end of his career. His presence, like that of a fellow West Indian, DeFreitas, is no doubt considered important by the SACU from a propaganda point of view.

Graveney's name as player-manager is significant in that he has done effective work as an officer of the Cricketers' Association, the players' union, who tried in vain last winter to agree a minimum wage structure with the TCCB.

Mr Dexter has naturally deplored the situation and spoken of the defections from international cricket as extremely damaging. His immediate concern must chiefly be the loss of young bowlers, but in a wider context is the limitation of his future field of choice, since sixteen more cricketers ineligible for England will be occupying places in county teams. They will be 'overseas players' in effect if not in name.

It is particularly disturbing that the captains of no fewer than five counties, Gatting of Middlesex, Robinson of Nottinghamshire, Athey of Gloucestershire, Cowdrey of Kent and Barnett of Derbyshire, must accept divided loyalties. A county captain has winter as well as summer obligations to his club, especially, it may be thought, if as in Gatting's case he has just enjoyed a £200,000 benefit. Cowdrey's benefit is now proceeding.

Opinion, of course, will continue to be sharply divided in the cricket world on the moral argument of sporting contact with South Africa. My personal feeling is of disappointment at their decision in some individual cases, but not of blame or censure.

The players have made their case in a clear and dignified way. They draw attention to the efforts of the SACU to bring the game to all colours and classes, and they assert their right to capitalize on their skill and to assist in the process. SACU correspondingly affirm their need for overseas visits to motivate their players and to attract revenue in order to aid their development scheme. Those who disagree with the players' rationale must at least respect it.

The team, incidentally, looks roughly equal in potential to that designated the South African Breweries' English XI which slipped out of England in great secrecy under Gooch's leadership in

February 1982 immediately on the return home from India of the England team.

None of the seven matches was won, *Wisden* describing the whole operation as leaving much to be desired. A three-year ban from international cricket was applied by the TCCB to all fifteen 'rebel' players on their return. The penalty is longer now, but the sobriquet 'rebel' is arguably less appropriate.

When all is said and done there is a distinctly brighter side to the picture from the point of view of England's immediate commitments – the West Indian tour preceded by another one-day fiesta in India.

The decks have been cleared and in certain cases some may murmur 'good riddance'. It happens, by the way, that about half of this party to tour South Africa have been involved in disciplinary cases of varying gravity. There should be no more misguided talk about 'persuading' men (for example, Gatting) to go to the West Indies. There need now be no reluctant tourists looking over their shoulders towards home.

The Ashes are lost, and Mr Dexter and his advisers have two Tests against Australia and the rest of the county programme in which to assess talent and to give trials to fresh blood. The test to come is the most severe of all, and courage and orthodoxy of method are the ingredients necessary.

THE DAILY TELEGRAPH
2 AUGUST 1989

Australia's Deserved Supremacy

When I last wrote here Australia appeared likely to regain the Ashes but they had not quite done so. Let me first, therefore, salute them on a mission diligently accomplished by making the most of their talents, individually and, in particular, as a team.

Allan Border, having been through the fires, has emerged as a mature leader, forming with Bobby Simpson a partnership to which England have no parallel. An ex-Test captain doing duty as travelling coach is a new thing.

The modern player, for the most part, does not take kindly to advice and correction and it says much both for Simpson and for the new Australian generation that he has established such an easy and comfortable rapport with his team, backed wholeheartedly, of course, by the Australian manager, Lawrie Sawle.

In theory, the Australian attack looks limited, but it has operated with a mountain of runs at its back and Alderman has never failed to make early penetrations. In a nutshell that is the story.

The most important of all the top six batting successes has been that of Mark Taylor, correct in method, tenacious, tireless, and with a full quiver of strokes when set. If he continues as he has begun we shall indeed be able to mention him in the same breath as Arthur Morris.

Never was the value of a left- and right-hand partnership better exemplified. For 13 solid hours in the field England had to cope with either Taylor or Border. With so many records broken, including even the 323 of Hobbs and Rhodes at Melbourne, I am relieved that Stan McCabe's 232 remains the highest Test score in the series at Trent Bridge. That was a magical innings, in quality unsurpassable.

When I first took an adolescent interest in cricket in 1921 our colonial cousins were completing a sequence of eight victories in succession, a unique state of affairs then and never exactly repeated since, though both England and Australia have enjoyed lengthy spells of success and endured similar periods of failure. In other words, the sadly unequal struggle at Trent Bridge is not quite the end of the world, a sentiment that seemed to predominate in the crowd at this ancient home of cricket. The mood was rather one of sympathy for English misfortunes.

Robin Smith, I hope and expect, will make many more hundreds for England but never one more fervently acclaimed. Moral opprobrium does not necessarily attach to defeat, however severe, and the composers of screaming headlines and the authors of the purple prose underneath reflect no opinions but their own.

The prince of all games-writers, Bernard Darwin, put the matter into civilized perspective when he wrote, of his own sport, that a man may miss a 3 ft putt for the Championship and still be a good husband and father. England have missed too many 3-footers these last two months and have not had the luck to hole any long ones. In fact, they have not had any luck, full stop.

I must say I found the belittling of this Test match in advance as an event of little significance because the Ashes had already been lost and won both strange and irritating. Every contest in an Anglo-Australian series has its own significance, and it is ungenerous to our oldest adversaries to harp introspectively on our domestic weaknesses and thus minimize the Australian effort.

When the present situation has happened in reverse in Australia I recall that the sporting pages were apt suddenly to reflect an unusually keen pre-season interest in Australian Rules football or some other manly exertion. Nevertheless, they gave the Poms a fair hand. And, as I say, Border and his men richly deserve our congratulations and, for rubbing in a few basic truths, our sincere gratitude.

Their cricket was horribly mauled by the Packer business, and there are areas (such as spin-bowling) in which their resources are slender. Their success, however, will undoubtedly re-enthuse Australian followers and heighten interest – which in the long run will also be to English benefit.

Reverting to post-Ashes attitudes, one can point to several excellent games when the chief prize had already been decided, headed by perhaps the most famous of all the classics, the Oval Test of 1902. On a spiteful pitch England, needing 263 to win, were 48 for 5 when Jessop set about the bowling: 104 he made by brilliant scientific hitting in 85 minutes. In the end Hirst (58) and Rhodes (6), coming together for the last wicket, safely scored the 15 runs needed.

The odds, no doubt, are enormous against England lasting out two days and emerging with a draw. Reputations and self-respect are, however, very much at stake.

THE DAILY TELEGRAPH
14 AUGUST 1989

FIFTH TEST – PLAYED AT TRENT BRIDGE ON
10, 11, 12, 14, 15 AUGUST

AUSTRALIA: 602 for 6 declared (Marsh 138, Taylor 219, Boon 73, Border 65*)
ENGLAND: 255 (Smith 101, Alderman 5 for 69) and 167
Australia won by an innings and 180 runs

Frindall's Who's Who Extraordinary

Would you believe it? Bill Frindall, with all his resources, has failed to find the photograph of an England Test cricketer. Well, well. We shall have to accept his regretful explanation that Reginald Wood was not a member of Arthur Shrewsbury's team to Australia in 1886–7 and as an expatriate Old Carthusian from Lancashire playing as a professional for Victoria was roped in for the one Test at Melbourne because, we read, Billy Barnes had injured his hand aiming a blow at P. S. McDonnell and hitting a wall instead. Presumably the author's enquiries drew blank both at Charterhouse and Old Trafford.

However, all frivolity aside, Mr Frindall has produced at least one photograph of the other 535 men who have represented England from the shadowy beginnings of Test cricket in 1877 to the end of last summer. They illustrate *England Test Cricketers*, published by Collins at – thanks to the patronage of The Carphone Group – £19.95.

Within the decade cricket's reference library has been enriched immeasurably by Christopher Martin-Jenkins's *Complete Who's Who of Test Cricketers*, brought out in 1980 and twice since updated, the *Who's Who of Cricketers* by Philip Bailey, Philip Thorn and Peter Wynne-Thomas, published in 1984, and the *Collins Who's Who of English First-Class Cricket, 1945–1984*, by Robert Brooke in 1985. And now this.

With proper respect to the authors of these admirable works within their chosen parameters, the statistical maestro of the 'Test Match Special' team has surely produced the ultimate in this line of country. He gives for each England cricketer dates of birth, and death where appropriate; teams played for and tours undertaken; biographical sketch; a selection of his notable feats; his individual score, mode of dismissal, bowling analysis and number of victims if a wicket-keeper, in every Test played in; topped off, of course, with full career figures. Where a photograph does not accompany the text there is a cross-reference to the page on which it may be found in a team or action group. So much detail might have looked an unsightly jumble had the designer been less expert than Humphrey Stone, whose overall hallmark is plain to see.

I took Ken Taylor of Yorkshire as the first specimen, and noted how Mr Frindall had worked into his potted biography the several humanizing things about him aside from his cricket: talents as painter and footballer, brother and son as sportsmen of equal versatility. For illustration the reader is referred to page 329, where we see the Yorkshire Championship-winning team of 1962 led by Vic Wilson, nine of whom were or became Test cricketers. This group decorated the entry of Doug Padgett, that admirably orthodox batsman who has served the county over many years as coach and mentor to the Second XI.

Talking of coaches, how does Don Wilson emerge? The answer is with full credit for the skill of his teaching and the 'marvellous atmosphere' he has created at the MCC Indoor School. The first Indoor School chairman recalls with satisfaction how we engaged him from under Yorkshire's noses prior to the opening in 1977 when there was no other comparable candidate in sight.

On either side of Don are two other Wilsons, the inimitable Winchester don, Rockley, who went to Australia with MCC in 1920–1 and got into Lord Harris's bad books by sending home some press cables which read mildly enough today, and his elder brother, the Rev. C. E. M. Both captained Cambridge and they are the only brothers who have made hundreds in the University Match. How amused Clem was in later years when he was suddenly glorified into a Test cricketer. For it was only a decent scratch side which Lord Hawke took to South Africa in 1888–9, most of the matches being against odds. There they all are, uniformly straw-hatted, moustached and in His Lordship's blue blazer with thin yellow and white stripes, colours which are now perpetuated as the Yorkshire committee tie. The author has dug up many fascinating photographs new to me.

So one could go on, one esoteric item leading to another. In 528 pages there must be a few venial slips. For instance, it was Duleep not Ranji, who was known at Cambridge as 'Smith'. To the obituarist the book is, naturally, a gold-mine. I found it riveting.

Salute to the Australians

The thirtieth Australian team to visit the old country, the last match of whose tour starts today at The Oval, has been under scrutiny, as always, not only for the quality of its play but because of its attitude to the game, to its opponents and also to the paying public. The Australians, of course, have been to English eyes distressingly successful on the field, both in the Tests and county matches. They also seem to have made a popular impression all round.

On the whole this has been a series fairly fought, with the umpires held in due respect by both sides (apart from one Australian fall from grace at Trent Bridge), and in this respect a welcome example to the young and, indeed, cricketers everywhere. After the brawls and bitterness of the last few years in overseas Tests – on the field, in the press, and over the air – this is indeed something to be thankful for.

There are things at which the traditional follower wrinkles his nose, not least the ecstatic embraces which nowadays accompany the fall of a wicket. I don't think the old players were any less pleased even if, as Harold Larwood observed when questioned on this, 'We just sat down and waited for the next bloke.' One thing the spectator certainly resents is the ugly, anonymous helmet. Cricket and hero-worship have always gone together and one can often not tell one helmeted batsman from another, let alone see their faces. The Australians at least mostly remove the disguise when they acknowledge the applause for fifties and hundreds, and when they return to the pavilion. Their comrades then reflect team spirit by crowding the dressing-room balcony and joining in the tribute.

Australian sides are largely remembered by their captains. In times within memory the Australians were for long typified in English minds by their enormous Warwick Armstrong, who lay down on The Oval outfield and read a newspaper. When asked why by the horrified Anglophile Arthur Mailey, he said he wanted to know whom they were 'plying'. Invited down to their room by the MCC Committee (chiefly peers and retired cricketers) to iron out a few points, he stood in the doorway, baggy green cap on head, and answered all their requests with a laconic 'naow'.

Billy Woodfall, the schoolmaster, courteous and charming,

altered the Armstrong image, while Sir Donald Bradman on his last tour came across as a likeable personality, aside from the vast admiration he had always commanded as a batsman. Continuing the role of captains, Lindsay Hassett had a charisma all his own. It was he who, at Old Trafford, after missing a second catch at long leg, picked off a policeman's helmet and held it out for another. Ian Johnson, Richie Benaud, Bobby Simpson and Bill Lawry all led tours well received and leaving many friends behind.

Ian Chappell introduced a new and unwelcome sort of aggression on the field, partly inherited by his brother Greg, whose era exploded into that of the attempted Packer take-over of international cricket and his subsequent contract to 'promote' the game in Australia. Under Packer the old courtesies were buried, sportsmanship was irrelevant. Confrontation and controversy were the aims.

Kim Hughes, immediate predecessor to Allan Border in the captaincy, tried vainly to introduce a more civilized philosophy. May Australia under the manager-Sawle, coach-Simpson régime continue to show an acceptable face to the cricket world in the more critical times that surely lie ahead.

THE DAILY TELEGRAPH
24 AUGUST 1989

SIXTH TEST – PLAYED AT THE OVAL ON
24, 25, 26, 28, 29 AUGUST

AUSTRALIA: 468 (Border 76, Jones 122) and 219 for 4 declared (Border 51*, Jones 50)
ENGLAND: 285 (Gower 79, Small 59, Alderman 5 for 66) and 143 for 5 (Smith 77*)
Match drawn

Tour Captaincy Candidates

It says almost everything about the state of mind of all present who are concerned with and for English cricket, that the break in the weather at The Oval on Saturday was greeted with relief. No doubt the Australians at the end of their tour were not sorry, for they have nothing more to prove, while England must have been grateful for the respite.

The disappointed ones, naturally, were the crowd, as sadly deprived as those had been on the Saturday at Edgbaston. As has happened everywhere this summer, they gave England generous support at the slightest excuse.

The talk, of course, revolved around the team for the West Indies, and in particular about the captaincy. There may be as many as seven or eight candidates for the honour – in alphabetical order, Gooch, Gower, Greig, Lamb, Neale, Nicholas, Parker and Roebuck.

Until recently there was another prime candidate in Marks, who, however, is going to wrap his spinning finger round the pen rather than the ball, a gain for responsible cricket journalism, a loss to Somerset and maybe England. As an all-rounder, with admirable leadership credentials and the only alternative off-spinner to Eddie Hemmings, my vote might well have gone to Vic Marks.

The qualities needed for a touring captain differ distinctly from those charged with the job at home. A tour throws men together for several months with the strains and stresses as well as the cheerful camaraderie of close contact.

It follows that the leader has to be an unselfish fellow of sense and sensibility, of tact and resilience, a man with a cricket brain who can come close to justifying his place as a player: something of a paragon, you may be thinking, to which I would say I could name several who have approached the ideal.

David Gower was a leading figure when, with Tony Brown as manager, he led what by all accounts was a model tour to India five years ago. In contrast, neither Tony Lewis nor George Mann had played in a Test when they captained with great personal success sides to India and Pakistan and South Africa respectively. Mike Brearley, never *quite* worth his place as a batsman, emerged as a model touring captain in Australia.

As to the candidates for West Indies, has not the time come to put a fresh man at the wheel if Gower opts out, or is superseded? England will look chiefly to Gower, Gooch and Lamb, initially at least, to cope with the most formidable attack in cricket. That is burden enough. So much for the old guard, except to say that on every ground, of form, reputation and record as a captain, Botham disqualifies himself.

There remain in the ring Greig, Neale, Nicholas and Parker, captains of Surrey, Worcestershire, Hampshire and Sussex respectively, and Somerset's former captain, Peter Roebuck.

Ian Greig, by force of personality, and with the strong backing of the Surrey committee, has transformed The Oval dressing room. And Paul Parker has done much the same thing at Hove. Likewise no one on the county circuit is better respected than Phillip Neale, a man who has welded together a good side and is a gritty bat in the middle order. Hampshire have also tasted success under Mark Nicholas, an attractive attacking batsman at his best and, not least, a real enthusiast who thinks cricket. Roebuck's moral courage during Somerset's days of crisis is remembered with gratitude in the West Country. Having been chosen to lead the brief flag-flying visit to Holland, he presumably has a place in the selectors' thoughts.

In short, there seem to be several men who would tackle a formidable job with determination and dedication. But whoever is chosen, the fortunes of the tour must depend greatly on the nature of the support given to the captain by the officers of the TCCB.

Peter Lush is the appointed tour manager and as such responsible for general administration and relations with the overseas authorities concerned, also, along with the team manager, Micky Stewart, with discipline within the English party.

It is this aspect which chiefly worries me. Rather than two managers, what is needed, surely, is a manager and a coach after the Australian manner. Mr Stewart is reputedly a good coach, who could, no doubt, be a useful help and adviser to a captain behind the scenes. Where he is miscast is as a TCCB spokesman, happy to comment for publication on anything at the drop of a hat.

In announcing that he was trying to persuade named cricketers to make themselves available for West Indies, he was surely going beyond what should be his brief. To have said before the present Test that Igglesden was the umpteenth opening bowler on the list was hardly likely to raise the morale of a young cricketer called to the colours for the first time.

To satisfy the greed of the press for quotes, the TCCB have their own recently appointed media manager, the highly experienced Peter Smith, himself until last year a respected cricket writer. Mr Stewart is also too close to the players to be an effective disciplinarian, as we have seen, at home as well as in Pakistan. In short, his role should surely be adapted in the light of experience.

The best news on the directional front regarding the West Indies tour is that Ted Dexter is planning to see a good deal of the cricket. As the man ultimately responsible to the board for English cricket at top level, events must have convinced him that he needs to spend more time and effort than he envisaged on his appointment. He is the supremo in a dark hour and, as with American Presidents, the buck stops with him.

A postscript: I wonder if the critic is still around who once wrote that the distinctive sound of a Monday morning was EWS barking up the wrong tree. If so, I hope he is relieved by the fact that these summer contributions have been much fewer than of old, and, believe it or not, shorter!

THE DAILY TELEGRAPH
28 AUGUST 1989

Jeffrey Stollmeyer

Jeffrey Stollmeyer, who has died at Melbourne, Florida, aged sixty-eight, was a leading figure in the world of West Indian cricket for half a century. He had been flown to a Florida hospital after suffering multiple gun wounds from an attack by bandits last month in his home at Port of Spain, Trinidad.

Aside from his cricket, Stollmeyer was a devoted son of Trinidad, active in public life as landowner and employer, parliamentarian and newspaper executive. He served as senator in the Trinidad parliament after independence and at his death was chairman of the *Trinidad Guardian*.

Jeffrey Baxter Stollmeyer was born on 11 April 1921, the youngest of six sons of Albert Victor Stollmeyer. Most of his brothers migrated to America, while Rex spent much of his life in Canada, becoming trade commissioner there for Trinidad and also for the West Indian Federation.

He inherited the family coffee, cocoa and citrus estates at Santa Cruz outside Port of Spain and ran them for many years. He sold out and moved into the city largely on grounds of security.

Stollmeyer was an opening batsman of style and polish. He came first to England with the 1939 West Indian team at the age of eighteen, along with his nearest brother, Victor. Jeff made 59 at Lord's in his first Test innings and 59 also at The Oval where Victor, on his only Test appearance, scored 94.

After the war he and John Goddard were the captains who first brought West Indian cricket to the front. He toured India and Australia in addition to coming again to England – along with the celebrated trinity of Walcott, Weekes and Worrell, and the spin partnership of Ramadhin and Valentine – in the victorious team of 1950, the first to succeed here against England's full strength.

He played in thirty-two Tests, finishing in 1955 with an average of 43, and an aggregate of 2159 runs, including four hundreds.

Stollmeyer was the last white captain whose appointment went unquestioned in the West Indies. He advocated the promotion of Worrell (afterwards Sir Frank) five years before it happened; and in his memoirs, *Everything Under the Sun*, described Worrell being overlooked in 1954–5 when he himself was injured as 'a preposterous decision' by the white selectors.

Stollmeyer's first important work for the West Indies Board was as manager of the 1966 team to England which marked the start of Gary (afterwards Sir Garfield) Sobers's reign as captain. The tour was a great success, the turning point being a vast sixth-wicket stand of 274 at Lord's between Sobers and his cousin David Holford when it seemed England had the game in their hands.

That was the time when, on the fourth morning, the MCC Secretary was inclined to ring Buckingham Palace with the idea of bringing forward the Queen's visit that afternoon. Jeff suggested waiting for an hour to see how the game developed. The pair were still together next day when Sobers declared, the match being drawn.

Stollmeyer became president of the West Indies Board in 1974, and so was in office when the Australian Kerry Packer recruited many of the best cricketers, including most of the West Indies team, to his so-called 'World Series Cricket'.

When the International Cricket Conference passed a resolution barring Packer's players from Test cricket, the West Indies, disliking the retroactive principle implied, was the only ruling body to vote against the resolution, which was afterwards over-ruled in the High Court.

He leaves a widow, Sara, now nearing recovery from the wounds suffered in the attack, a month ago.

THE DAILY TELEGRAPH
11 SEPTEMBER 1989

Season's-end Thoughts from Lord's

There are worse places from which to see the passing season in perspective than the Nursery ground at Lord's where the Cross Arrows, comprising the MCC groundstaff with a sprinkling of members, disport themselves in club matches through the mellow month of September.

Next door, the great battleground with that massive Victorian pavilion both enshrines the past and beckons to the future. Beyond it, in the offices of the Test and County Cricket Board, various functionaries and committees begin their annual wrestle with the complicated problems of the modern game.

Here in the Nursery (on what was once a market garden) the young choices are parading their skills under the sharp eye of the MCC head coach, Don Wilson. This straight-speaking Yorkshireman, who has had thousands of young cricketers through his hands since the building of the Indoor School brought him to Lord's twelve years ago, is critical of modern techniques: 'We want more batters who bat straight and bowlers who bowl straight.'

He endeavours to instil the basic orthodox skills into all who come into his ken, boys and young men and, not least, his assistant coaches. Incidentally, he is properly proud of the fact that as many as fourteen members of the Warwickshire and Middlesex teams in the Nat West Final graduated through the MCC staff.

No space here to go into theoretical detail, except to offer one illustrious quote: 'Watching the recent Tests on TV I've been appalled at the awful technique of the English batsmen . . . their stances are hopeless and destroy all rhythm.' So wrote the greatest of modern batsmen to me from Adelaide recently, condemning the preparatory bat-in-air fashion. The Australians stand still. So do the West Indians. So have almost all the greats in history. 'Nuff said.

It is an antidote to the pessimism pervading English cricket to talk to the likes of Wilson and the NCA's Keith Andrews, and the schoolmasters who serve ESCA as well as their own schools, and also to meet some of the most successful schoolboy cricketers.

I have little doubt that there is plenty of talent and enthusiasm awaiting recruitment by counties and universities, examination demands notwithstanding. It is up to the cricket authorities to provide a system and a fixture structure which will develop skill and bring merit to the top: back, therefore, to the TCCB.

When Ted Dexter was appointed chairman of an England committee of which Test selection was the chief, though not its only, function, I welcomed the positive, inventive mind he might bring to the job, but added that he would need fellow selectors to help to cover the broad county scene, to see and to be seen. I mentioned several retired cricketers held in good esteem, who might be worthy successors to those selectors who have functioned four at a time since the beginning of the century.

This has not happened. Mr Dexter named certain unofficial scouts but has depended for topical form assessments largely on Micky Stewart, now nearing the end of a three-year appointment as England team manager.

They have been unlucky in the number of injuries. Nor have they had abundant talent to choose from, especially in bowling. Even allowing for this, the feeling in the county clubs and among the faithful public at the end of another summer of abject defeat is highly critical.

The prevailing mood has been far from helped by the exclusion of David Gower from the touring side to the West Indies. To have relieved our best batsman from the captaincy in favour of a different style is understandable; to have discarded a man with more than 7000 Test runs to his name – and a left-hander to boot – in the present state of England's resources can be explained only by a conflict of personality, as between Gower and Mr Stewart.

In Gower's dignified, albeit revealing, interview with Michael Calvin in *The Daily Telegraph* last Saturday he queried the scope of Stewart's managerial role and went on to name Keith Fletcher as the sort of respected manager-coach he thought to be required – a significant suggestion in the light of the Test series just past.

As to the forthcoming West Indies tour, while it would be unrealistic to think in terms of success, we must hope for cricket of courage and character from Graham Gooch's team while two younger parties are picking up experience, the England 'A' team in Zimbabwe (and possibly also in East Africa) and an Under-19 team in Australia. The more of such tours the better.

While the new generation are being put through their winter paces the TCCB face deep-rooted problems. Pitches and some lesser penalty in addition to the swingeing 25 points; whether to continue to cover; the weight of bats and the height of the seam; another revision of the pattern of fixtures, first-class and one-day; Test selection; a fair minimum wage for players – this adds up to a weighty programme.

THE DAILY TELEGRAPH
20 SEPTEMBER 1989

The Bradman Museum

Sir Denys Roberts, QC, the new President of MCC, and Colin Cowdrey, the new chairman of the International Cricket Council, set off yesterday to take part in a unique occasion – the opening of the Bradman Museum in the great cricketer's home town of Bowral, New South Wales.

The President has taken on a testing appointment: unlike all his predecessors, he has spent so much time in Hong Kong and other places that he has come in without any close experience of the workings of MCC. However, in a highly active and successful year, Field Marshal Lord Bramall has rolled the wicket nicely for him, and as an accomplished speaker Sir Denys, on his first public appearance since he took office on 1 October, is sure to get off to a good start at Friday's celebratory dinner, given in Sydney by the Prime Minister, Mr Bob Hawke.

Moreover, he bears gifts for the Museum from MCC, in the shape of two appropriate pictures hanging at Lord's. These are, of necessity, reproductions, but imperceptibly so. One is Charles Cundall's much admired panorama painted during the Lord's Test of 1938 in which Sir Donald captained Australia and, as usual, made a hundred. The other shows him in later life in city clothes, an oil by R. Hannaford, sponsored by the Commercial Bank of Australia, the subject indeed looking as though a client seeking an overdraft might have to face a pretty thorough scrutiny.

For Mr Cowdrey the occasion gives the happy chance, as ICC chairman, to meet the Australian Cricket Board, as well as the new chairman of the New Zealand Cricket Board, Mr Barry Patterson, who is flying in for the occasion.

Next month at the Nehru Cup Final in Calcutta he will see the chiefs of the three Asian Test countries, while in December he will be visiting the president of the West Indies Board, Mr Clyde Walcott in Barbados.

Thus, by Christmas, Mr Cowdrey will have been in personal touch with all seven Test-playing countries. He is keen to lead ICC towards addressing the problems of international cricket in a more positive way than in the past. I dare say that in certain directions and on certain issues, such as intimidation and international umpires, to name only two, the chairman may need all his diplomatic skills.

He has the advantage of a term of office, renewable annually, of up to four years, rather than the one year of previous Presidents of MCC (and ipso facto ICC chairmen) in what has always been, and will continue to be, a dispassionate, neutral chairmanship.

THE DAILY TELEGRAPH
11 OCTOBER 1989

Gubby Allen's Last Meeting

Brian Johnston and I go to see Gubby Allen, just brought home to St John's Wood from the London Clinic after nearly four months there following an operation for cancer of the stomach. We three had been deputed by the Forty Club to choose the best World team of the last forty years to play a Test at Lord's – five days, starting in good weather. It was for a fund-raising competition within the Club.

We had met first in June before Gubby had been taken ill. Now we had just to agree the last places. We found our old friend alert and interested, giving as always a firm and balanced judgement. The side we picked (assuming all to have been at their best) was: Hutton, Gavaskar, Vivian Richards, G. S. Chappell, Sobers (captain), Botham, Benaud, Hadlee, Lindwall, Evans, Laker; twelfth man, Miller.

Compton or May or Harvey or Pollock for one of the batsmen? Lillee, Marshall or Holding for opening bowler? Gibbs or Bedi for Laker? Tallon for Evans? Obviously. Not surprisingly, no one got it 100 per cent right.

We left Grove End Road thinking Gubby just might be going to pull through. But he grew weaker rather than stronger and the end came quite peacefully a few weeks later. Of all the thousands of cricket meetings he must have attended in a long life this little confab round a sick-bed was assuredly his last.

DIARY
17 OCTOBER 1989

False Prospectus for County Cricket

Sir – Inured to shock as they are, English cricket followers may not all be sufficiently aware of how crucial to the game's future will be next week's debate on the future shape of the county season as from 1991.

The recently formed England Committee of the Test and County Cricket Board is making a presentation advocating abolition of the three-day game which has been the focus of national interest and the training ground for England XIs for more than a century.

Now, although it is generally agreed that a surfeit of one-day cricket is a major cause of the decline in playing standards, the ironic plan is to cut first-class cricket and leave the one-day competitions untouched. It proposes a reduction in the first-class programme from twenty-two matches to sixteen of four days each as a panacea for the unprecedented run of ill-success in Test matches. I suggest the seventeen counties and MCC should consider that:

• Limiting county batsmen to an average of about twenty-five innings a year as against the 1989 figure of thirty-six is drastically to restrict their experience. The bowlers would suffer proportionately.

• The reduction of matches by more than a quarter would specially limit opportunities to young cricketers.

• Although the current programme of seventy days of county cricket (eighteen three-day matches and four of four days) would only be decreased by six days in the event of sixteen four-day matches, the loss to cricket would be considerably greater because many matches would finish within three days, some even in two.

• With so much time available and yet fewer innings per season the batting would tend to be more careful and the cricket therefore less attractive.

There are other cricket arguments, but what now of the effects on county members who in most cases provide the second largest source of clubs' income and whose support is crucial?

They would get only eight home county matches instead of the present eleven. Unless these are to be pushed to either end of the season, rather than played in the heart of it, they must clash with Tests and one-day Internationals. Members would see their full team including stars in only about five county matches each summer.

The seventeen counties at present use fifty-four grounds for first-class play plus twelve more for one-day games. Seven of them spread their major cricket over four grounds or more, running traditional weeks which have aroused local interest for generations. The clubs would be forced to utilize their main grounds and strike lesser ones off their lists, thereby depriving members and denying crowds.

There are positive remedies for cricket's malaise which I have suggested already. I am concerned here to throw light on what I see as a false prospectus.

LETTER TO THE DAILY TELEGRAPH
29 NOVEMBER 1989

Sir George Allen

Sir George Allen, universally known as 'Gubby', who has died aged eighty-seven, had a stronger influence on the world of cricket and for a longer span of years than anyone since the 4th Lord Harris.

Allen played the first of his twenty-five Tests in 1930. He captained England both at home and in Australia; was elected to the Committee of MCC in his early thirties; and served the Club as both Treasurer and President, as well as on successive committees for more than fifty years.

Harris, who led England in the first Test in this country in 1880 and was a dominating influence in the game until his death in 1932, had trodden all these paths, and when it came to mastery of argument on important issues, those who sat in committee with both probably accorded them equal attention and respect.

George Oswald Browning Allen was born in Sydney on 31 July 1902, of a family with deep roots in Australia. His great-grandfather emigrated in 1816, was the first man in Australia to serve his articles as a solicitor there, and founded what today is the oldest legal firm in Sydney.

Gubby's father, Walter, brought his family to England in 1909, and at the outbreak of the First World War joined the Metropolitan Special Constabulary, eventually becoming Commissioner and earning a knighthood.

From his private schooldays at Summerfields, Oxford, young Allen showed that he had cricket in the blood. An uncle had played for Australia and it was said his father might have played for Cambridge in the era of Ranji and Stanley Jackson if he had exerted himself rather more. That was a charge which could never have been made against his son.

When Eton and Harrow resumed their rivalry at Lord's in 1919, Allen was run out in the first over on the first morning without receiving a ball. However, things turned out well for him – as they generally did – in the second innings, his 69 not out helping Eton to an easy victory.

He was lucky in having for a housemaster C. M. Wells, formerly of Cambridge and Middlesex, who ran the cricket, and for a coach the celebrated George Hirst.

By the time their mettlesome protégé left Eton, his promise as a fast bowler, with a beautiful action and late out-swing, was clearly recognizable, whereas he was correct and determined as a batsman.

Allen walked into Hubert Ashton's powerful Cambridge side of 1922 and his nine wickets in the University Match for 78 runs sped Oxford to an innings defeat.

After two years he left Cambridge for the City, where he became a successful stockbroker, and thereafter became his own brand of amateur, playing never even half a season for Middlesex and, despite this, reaching the top of the tree as an all-round cricketer. Commuting, so to speak, between the Stock Exchange and Lord's, he rarely failed to make an impact for Middlesex whenever he turned out, either as batsman or fast bowler, or both. His performances generally spoke for themselves, but the Allens and the Warners were close friends and Gubby was lucky to have a powerful friend at court in Sir Pelham, who was either a Test selection chairman or cricket correspondent or even both.

The first of his twenty-five appearances for England was against Australia in the famous Lord's Test of 1930 when, substituting for Harold Larwood, he bowled expensively but, with A. P. F. Chapman, made 125 for the sixth wicket in the second innings.

The following year he and L. E. G. Ames against New Zealand at Lord's combined in a stand of 246 which is still a world record for the eighth wicket in Tests, both making hundreds.

His choice for D. R. Jardine's MCC team in Australia in 1932–3 was strongly criticized. Yet he was one of the successes of the tour, taking 21 wickets in the Tests and averaging 23 with the bat.

It is a matter of history that although entreated by his captain to do so he declined to bowl 'Bodyline', and was always frank in his disapproval of it.

Allen first led England in the 1936 series against India, in obvious preparation for the captaincy in Australia the following winter. After winning the first two Tests there, England were defeated in the following three – thanks chiefly to some phenomenal scoring by Bradman.

In 1938 Allen was commissioned into the Territorial Army and after serving in the City of London Yeomanry ('the Rough Riders') he joined an anti-aircraft battery which defended RAF Fighter Command HQ at Stanmore and Canvey Island.

He was invited into Dowding's celebrated 'ops' room and developed a close relationship with the RAF which led to a posting as flak liaison officer at Bomber Command's No. 5 group. Determined to assess enemy anti-aircraft fire in action, Allen flew over the Ruhr in the air gunner's seat of a Handley Page Hampden in the autumn of 1940. His increasing flak expertise was then used, first as GSO2 of MI 14E and then as GSO1, in the rank of lieutenant colonel, with MI 15 (as the War Office centre for collating intelligence on German air defences became known). He was awarded the American Legion of Merit.

Just as Allen's leadership in Australia before the war had come in for the highest praise on all counts, so it did again in 1947–8 in the West Indies, even though Allen was now forty-five and, with a weak side, MCC could not match the emergent brilliance of the 'three Ws', Worrell, Weekes and Walcott.

He was a model touring captain in that he took infinite trouble over every member of his side. At his best Allen was a valuable Test all-rounder, a fast bowler whose speed stemmed from a perfect action, a sound bat, and excellent close fielder.

He took eighty-one wickets in Tests at an average cost per wicket of 29.37, and made 750 runs, averaging 24.19. His first-class record was: 784 wickets at 22.24; 8866 runs, average 28.05, including ten hundreds.

Allen's most notable feat was in 1929 at Lord's when he took all ten Lancashire wickets for 40 runs, this after arriving late on the field (by arrangement, naturally) and so missing the new ball. In county cricket at Lord's it was a unique feat, and so it remains.

The Lord's Committee Room was the scene of his work for cricket from 1932 to 1985 – an unprecedented span interrupted only by the Second World War. In 1963–4 he was President, and from 1964 to 1976 held the Club's key post of Treasurer.

An amateur in the most complete sense on the field, Allen was very much a professional in committee. No one had a wider knowledge of every facet of cricket politics and administration. No one was better briefed, nor, it should be added, more tenacious in his opinions. He had more time than most, and he could show infinite patience in order to win his point. It was sometimes whispered that the easiest way to get a thing through was to persuade the *éminence grise* that it had been his own idea. There is no doubt he could be difficult. Likewise it generally had to be admitted in the end that 'Gubby is probably right'.

Allen was the chief instigator of the national post-war movement in cricket for the involvement and teaching of the young. This was hitherto an uncharted field, but now there are associations covering every area. It led to Allen's authorship with H. S. Altham of *The MCC Cricket Coaching Book*, a best-seller for many generations.

When England and Australia were very much at odds over the perilous issue of throwing after the MCC tour of 1958–9 it was Allen who, with Sir Donald Bradman's eventual strong co-operation, devised a successful formula for eliminating the 'chucker'. He performed no more vital service than this. Not the least of his labours was his seven seasons' chairmanship of the Test Selectors from 1955 to 1961.

Allen was not only a shrewd judge of a cricketer but he was also, on the testimony of all who served with him, an admirably fair and thorough chairman with a flair for finding the man for the occasion. In all he did there shone his great devotion to the game and helpful, unfailing friendliness to all cricketers.

He was awarded the Territorial Decoration in 1945, appointed CBE in 1962 and knighted in 1986.

Gubby Allen never married. His family said he was always wedded to cricket.

THE DAILY TELEGRAPH
1 DECEMBER 1989

Wise Men Split
on Four-day Game

It grieves me to correct my friend Tony Lewis, but he must not tell us to listen to 'the three wise men' (*The Sunday Telegraph*, 10 December) since the senior of the three Chairmen of Selectors referred to as advocating 100 per cent four-day Championship cricket is and always has been strongly against it.

Alec Bedser, whose record of service as chairman lasted from 1969 to 1982, favours three-day county cricket and also, emphatically, a return to uncovered pitches. This is precisely my position.

I feel sure that the three letters you published last Sunday in support of Simon Heffer's article in defence of three-day county cricket reflected the views of most county club members and lovers of Championship cricket.

Everyone agrees that a major reason for the serious decline in English playing standards is too much one-day cricket. Yet the England Committee propose to leave the one-day programme untouched, while asking the seventeen counties, who with MCC form the TCCB, to agree an exclusively four-day Championship as from 1991, thus reducing each county's matches from twenty-two to sixteen.

In the light of this it is a bit rich to disparage the 'county self-interest' of those unwilling to see the loyalty of members and public put under strain and many grounds inevitably closed by a severe cutting-down on Championship cricket for reasons which in any case they do not accept.

LETTER TO THE SUNDAY TELEGRAPH
17 DECEMBER 1989

Hopes and Fears for Cricket in the 1990s

An optimist all my life, my natural instincts are more anxious than sanguine as I survey the immediate future of English first-class cricket. I do not say that current trends in respect of standards of administration, play and conduct are irreversible, only that in several crucial directions attitudes need to change and some new men given a chance. This, as we know, is due to happen next year in the case of the chairmanship of the TCCB, which is to pass from Raman Subba Row of Surrey to W. R. F. Chamberlain of Northamptonshire.

Let me first salute the latter's fortitude in picking up a singularly hot potato. The incoming chairman's background differs from his immediate forerunner's, for after the old Hampshire captain, C. G. A. Paris, had steered the Board skilfully through the seven years from its formation in 1968, the four chairmen following him since 1975 have all worn the England touring cap. Frank Chamberlain was a good club cricketer from his days at Uppingham and in the Navy until the age of fifty, is a successful businessman, and has digested a wide knowledge of county affairs since he assumed the Northamptonshire chairmanship four years ago.

While appreciative of Mr Subba Row's unsparing efforts for the game, most of the counties favour a less executive style of chairman and his successor's attitude will certainly reflect this feeling. With the advent of an England Committee who have made a proposal which, if accepted by the counties, would amount to the most revolutionary change since the Championship assumed something akin to its present form nearly a century ago, Mr Chamberlain is certainly about to put his pads on at a crucial time.

Cricket has been called 'that beautiful, complicated game', and as such needs to be cherished by those who play it. In a message to the Forty Club at its Jubilee a few years ago its Patron, the Duke of Edinburgh, expressed the philosophy of it in these daunting words: 'Cricket can only flourish if it is played by civilized people with the highest standards of sportsmanship and good humour.'

The corollary is that if winning becomes so important that defeat is accompanied by surly excuses and reflections on the umpires, if their verdicts are queried on the field, if batsmen are assailed by taunts and foul language, if intimidation by fast bowlers leads to batsmen dressing up like American footballers, the game is not flourishing in the true sense, however large the takings from advertisers and hospitality boxes filled by men mostly with their backs to the cricket.

I do not say that this catalogue of misbehaviour is general, but it has been far too prevalent, especially in Test matches, and so seen and heard by the imitative young. In this respect the recent four defensive Pakistan–India draws at least had the merit that they were amiably contested, according to Imran Khan, because there were two 'third country umpires', John Hampshire and John Holder. Here is evidence in support of the formation of an international panel of umpires under the authority of the ICC – a flexible system, it would need to be, certainly not one which would debar a man standing in his own country.

The character of the England team management and the consequent dressing-room atmosphere as attested by several players and suggested further by the departure of so many good cricketers to South Africa must be a major concern of the TCCB on the international front.

The chief immediate problems of the Board, however, concern the implementation or otherwise of the new England Committee's remedy for England's abysmal Test record of one win (against Sri Lanka) in the last twenty-five Tests. They think that a severely restricted diet of sixteen four-day matches will better fit aspiring men to the disciplines of five-day Test cricket. Although all agree that too much one-day cricket is the principal cause of declining standards, that will remain unchanged for financial reasons. (In the twenty-three weeks over which the 1990 season will be stretched no fewer than sixty-one days are set aside for limited-over cricket.) For many years Surrey and Warwickshire have been pushing for four-day cricket, both owners of city grounds patronized by very small county gates but with Test matches to boost the revenue. Back in 1969 the Editor of *Wisden*, commenting on the idea, remarked, 'I can imagine nothing more dreary than a four-day county match,' and adding significantly, 'The basis of county cricket and club finance is membership subscriptions.' Within the last twenty years membership revenue is apt to take second place to a share of Test receipts and sponsorship. The loyalty of members, however, remains a county's prime responsibility.

Figures here are significant. In 1985 when members had privileges at twenty-four matches (half, of course, at home) the aggregate membership among the seventeen counties was 106,982. When the present formula of six four-day and sixteen three-day matches, twenty-two in all, came into force in 1988 this figure dropped to 93,353, a decline in three years of almost 13 per cent. The membership loss in the nine years up to 1988 works out at 25 per cent. What the loss would be with sixteen fixtures – a drop of 50 per cent as against the twenty-four of a few years ago – is anyone's guess. With the estimated reduction of the present figure of fifty-four first-class grounds to thirty or so as counties are forced to concentrate on their major ones, it scarcely bears thinking about. Traditional county weeks of long standing would have to go. Is not this the time to nourish and expand county interest? And is it not hypocritical to a degree to retain all one-day cricket for commercial reasons against cricket commonsense and then to accuse counties hostile to the proposed revolution of self-interest?

The counties have usually lived on the edge of crises, and cricket committees have come up with some rum, not to say ridiculous remedies, briefly tried and discarded. A new ball after 55 overs, stepped up by stages through the years to 65, 75, 85 and (now) 100; suspension of the follow-on; maximum 75-yard boundaries to encourage six-hitters; and constant changes in the bonus points system were a few of the nostrums.

Ted Dexter's England Committee are to be congratulated on instigating systematic coaching for a few of the top young cricketers and one hopes the idea will be pursued and extended; also for backing 'A' team and Under-19 tours; also for emphasizing the need to bring back variety by encouraging spin-bowling.

They say more four-day cricket would have this effect. Maybe, but so would the provision of hard, *dry* pitches in fine weather and the uncovering of pitches to allow rain and sun to do their work in the course of nature. So it has been in England from the beginning of time until 1981. That was the evil year when county cricket was made more uniform and dully formalized by rugging up the pitches and so, too often, retaining the moisture for the benefit of 'the quicks' or the nearly quicks who manipulate the seam.

Most of the county captains are calling for sixteen games rather than twenty-two, and one can sympathize with their travel-weariness in certain cases. They have against them, however, the big majority of the old players. As for the captains' views, it is not out of disrespect that I say they are surely too closely involved to see the issue in perspective. I always remember how when the lbw Law was about to be extended to the off-side the change was approved by every captain except R. E. S. Wyatt, who was dead against it. Sooner or later they would all have agreed he was the only one right.

The current Championship structure has run for only two years. The sensible thing, surely, is to let it continue on trial and to hope that the 1990s will bring a return to batting orthodoxy, a renaissance of the bowling arts, and, not least, more 'civilized' leaders of flair and principle.

THE DAILY TELEGRAPH
28 DECEMBER 1989

INDEX